TEACH US TO SIT STILL

Born in Manchester in 1954, Tim Parks moved permanently to Italy in 1980. Author of novels, non-fiction and essays, he has won the Somerset Maugham, Betty Trask and Llewellyn Rhys awards, and has been shortlisted for the Man Booker Prize. His works include *Destiny*, *Europa*, *Dreams of Rivers and Seas*, *Italian Neighbours*, *An Italian Education* and *A Season with Verona*.

ALSO BY TIM PARKS

Tongues of Flame

Loving Roger

Home Thoughts

Family Planning

Goodness

Cara Massimina

Mimi's Ghost

Shear

Europa

Destiny

Judge Savage

Rapids

Cleaver

Dreams of Rivers and Seas

Non-fiction

Italian Neighbours

An Italian Education

Adultery & Other Diversions

Translating Style

Hell and Back

A Season with Verona

The Fighter

TIM PARKS

Teach Us To Sit Still

A Sceptic's Search for Health and Healing

VINTAGE BOOKS
London

Published by Vintage 2011

2 4 6 8 10 9 7 5 3 1

First published in Great Britain in 2010 by Harvill Secker

Vintage
Random House, 20 Vauxhall Bridge Road,
London SW1V 2SA

www.vintage-books.co.uk

Addresses for companies within The Random House Group Limited can be found at: www.randomhouse.co.uk/offices.htm

The Random House Group Limited Reg. No. 954009

A CIP catalogue record for this book is available from the British Library

ISBN 9780099548881

The Random House Group Limited supports The Forest Stewardship Council® (FSC®), the leading international forest certification organisation. All our titles that are printed on Greenpeace approved FSC® certified paper carry the FSC® logo. Our paper procurement policy can be found at: www.randomhouse.co.uk/environment

Printed and bound in Great Britain by
CPI Cox & Wyman, Reading RG1 8EX

To those who got me out of gaol:
David Wise and Rodney Anderson;
Ruggero Scolari, Edoardo Parisi, John Coleman.

Author's Note

Over the period when I wasn't well, and again when I was writing this book, I found myself spending more and more time looking at images. It began with a need for clarity, the desire to see my physical problem represented, but more and more the contemplation of images of any kind – illustrations, photos, paintings – seemed to offer relief from the language-driven anxieties inside my head. Eventually I decided to include some of these pictures in the book; not all of them are beautiful, not all of them are of the highest quality; they had simply become part of the tale.

Foreword

I never expected to write a book about the body. Least of all *my* body. How indiscreet. But then I never expected to be ill in the mysterious, infuriating way I have. Above all it never occurred to me that an illness might challenge my deepest assumptions, oblige me to rethink the primacy I have always given to language and the life of the mind. Texting, mailing, chatting, blogging, our modern minds devour our flesh. That is the conclusion long illness brought me to. We have become cerebral vampires preying on our own life-blood. Even in the gym, or out running, our lives are all in the head, at the expense of our bodies.

I had no desire to tell anyone about my malady, let alone write about it. These were precisely the pains and humiliations one learns early on not to mention. You need only look at the words medicine uses – intestine, faeces, urethra, bladder, sphincter, prostate – to appreciate that this vocabulary was never meant to be spoken in company. We just don't want to go there. My plan, like anyone else's, was to confide in the doctors and pretend it wasn't happening.

On the other hand, this is *reality*, and in my case there was the happy truth that just when the medical profession had given up on me and I on it, just when I seemed to be walled up in a life sentence of chronic pain, someone proposed a bizarre way out: sit still, they said, and breathe. I sat still. I breathed. It seemed a tedious exercise at first, rather painful, not immediately effective. Eventually it proved so exciting, so transforming, physically and mentally, that I began to think my illness had been a stroke of luck. If I wasn't the greatest of sceptics, I'd be saying it had been sent from above to invite me to change my ways. In any event, by now the story had become too inviting a conundrum to be left unwritten.

What it boils down to, I suppose, is an extraordinary mismatch between the creatures we are and the way we live. I grew up in a family of evangelical Anglicans. They were also solid middle-class Brits. What they most instilled in us, as children, was purposefulness, urgency. Everything about the world had long been understood, so the right moves were obvious. We must save our souls, we must save other souls, we must perform well at school, we must go to university and get good jobs. And we must marry and have children who would share our same goals and live as we did. Even singing was purposeful. It was to praise God. Playing, we were soldiers bent on killing each other, in a good cause. When we did sports, of course, we had to win.

Meantime our bodies were the 'vessels' which allowed us to get on with all these pressing tasks. Confusingly, a vessel was a ship or a jug for storing liquids. Either way it was *useful* only in so far as it contained something else: the Christian soul, the middle-class self. In any event, the body had no purpose or identity *as such*. When we were dead we would be better off without it, though for reasons not explained God wanted us to hang on with bodily grief for as long as we could. Perhaps it was to *purify* the soul, to *ennoble* the self, the way some people find a sort of virtue in hanging on to an old car. The body was a necessary hassle on the way to success and paradise.

This will sound like a caricature. But it was entirely in line with school biology where they merely told us how complicated and alien that fleshly vessel was, a matter best left to the experts. Even today I meet few people who accept a substantial identity between self and flesh. At most, they have a more attractive vision of what pleasures and enjoyments life affords: sex, food, music, booze. Otherwise, everyone seems equally busy asserting their points of view, furthering their careers, saving against the day when the decaying vessel will start to leak. In the main, *doing* cancels out *being* as noise swamps silence.

To date I have written twenty books, with this twenty-one. I may have shaken off my parents' faith, then, but not the unrelenting purposefulness they taught me, that heady mix of piety and ambition. And like my father I have lived under a spell of words. He read the Bible and wrote his sermons. He told you what was true and how you must behave. Rhythmically, persuasively, the way politicians do, and the pundits of opinion columns; the people who know everything and are sure of themselves. My novels have tended the other way, suggested how mysterious it all is, how partial anyone's point of view, how comically lost we are. But even this is preaching of a kind. The fact is, as soon as you start with words you're locked into a debate, forced to take a position with respect to others, confirming or rebutting what has been said before. Nothing you say stands alone or is complete in the present: it has its roots in the past and pushes feelers into the future. And as we grow heated, marking out our corner, staking our claim, we stop noticing the breath on the lips, the tension in our fingers, the pressure of the ground under our toes, the tick of time in the blood. None of my father's admirers noticed how tense his jaw was, how much his hand shook when he raised a glass or microphone, what an effort it was for him to assert assert assert, to keep the 2000-year-old faith, giving encouragement to the doubters, finding clever arguments to confound the devil's advocates. When I think back on Dad's cancer and death – he was sixty and I twenty-five – there is a certain inevitability about it. Forever ignored, the carnal vessel cracked under strain. Sometimes I think it was the invention of language that started this queer battle between mind and flesh.

Shortly after Dad's funeral I left England for Italy and have lived here ever since. The illusion of escape was reassuring. Another language plunged me into other debates. I worked and worked. I wrote and translated and taught. But in retrospect I see I never really deviated from the initial project, never looked to right or left, was always true to my parents' obsession with vocation. 'Your handwriting,' I remember my brother observing, in those last years when one wrote letters by hand, 'has never changed.' He was right. It's still the same: ferociously slanted to somewhere off the page, some distant goal.

Then at an undetermined moment in my forties, the symptoms began, the pains, embarrassments, anxiety, anger. Was I going my father's way? But I mustn't get ahead of my story. Suffice it to say that in choosing to write this book I have decided to set down, often in disagreeable detail, all the things I scrupulously avoided mentioning for years. Had what happened been merely a problem of diagnosis, one bunch of doctors getting it wrong – in their eagerness to cut me up – and then another finally suggesting just the drug that would fix me in a jiffy, I would never have bothered to write about it. Likewise, had the whole problem turned out to be in my skull, something to sort out with a psycho-drug and a few sessions on the analyst's sofa.

No, it was infinitely more complicated and interesting; to me, I don't exaggerate, *amazing*. I was amazed, when someone showed me a way back to health, to realise that I knew nothing of my body at all, nothing of its resources, nothing of its oneness with my mind, nothing of myself. And if the reader is surprised to find, in a book that might sound like a health manual or a self-help spiel, reflections on D.H. Lawrence and Thomas Hardy, Velázquez and Magritte, on Gandhi and Mussolini, Italy as opposed to England, Jesus and the Buddha, faith-healing and white-water kayaking, that is because illness is not a separate thing circumscribed in symptoms, diagnosis and cure, but part of a whole that has no separate parts.

'All very well, but how do you want us to categorise it?' the publisher asks. 'Health, Psychology, New Age, Biography, Criticism?' My immediate response is indignation: this is *exactly* the problem I have been writing about! Reductionism, labels. On second thoughts, though, I have to accept that if we didn't slot things into categories we'd never find what we were looking for. I'm uncertain. I can't decide. Until it occurs to me that, with books at least, the best experiences are not when you find what you were looking for, but when something quite different finds you, takes you by surprise, shifts your taste to new territory. 'Put it where the true stories go,' I tell him. It's only stories that gather the world up in unexpected ways.

PART ONE

TURP

Shortly before my fifty-first birthday, in December of 2005, my friend Carlo sketched a tangle of tubes and balloons on a corner of newspaper.

We were in a café in the southern suburbs of Milan.

'The prostate is like a small apple, right? Here. But it's getting bigger and more fibrous with age, it's pressing on this tube going through it, the urethra. It's choking it, see? So, what do we do? We sort of *core* the thing, from the inside. With a laser. Going up your penis. Make it wider.'

I could see that Carlo had made this sketch many times before. Chewing a doughnut, his voice had a believer's enthusiasm.

'Then we just burn away a bit of this valve, or sphincter, here, to make sure it opens properly. That's the base of the bladder.'

My bladder.

I asked: 'Why?'

'So it empties better, then you go less often.'

'What about sex?'

Now he needed a proper sheet of paper. He opened his briefcase. There was a complication. Expertly, his surgeon's wrist traced out the same diagram a couple of times larger. 'When you pee, there are two sphincters have to open, right? The one we've burned away a bit at the base of the bladder and another lower down. Well, when you climax, the sperm shoots in here, *between* the upper and lower sphincters. Got it? From the prostate into the urethra obviously. The lower sphincter opens and the upper one shuts tight. But, after the op, since we'll have opened the upper one permanently, you can get a situation where the sperm whooshes off up into your bladder instead of down through your penis. So you get a dry orgasm. Same feeling, but no stains on the sheets. An advantage really.' He smiled and took another bite of his doughnut.

I examined the smudgy tangle of tubes and cisterns. It was a question of dodgy plumbing. My sink was blocked. The loo tank needed looking at.

'What about the pain?'

'Not that painful. You'll be in bed for a few days, then a couple of months before you can start sex again.'

'I meant the pains I'm getting *now*.'

'Ah.'

Carlo is a big man with an open, honest face.

'We can't actually guarantee they'll go.'

I had quite a repertoire of pains at this point: a general smouldering tension throughout the abdomen, a sharp jab in the perineum, an electric shock darting down the inside of the thighs, an ache in the small of the back, a shivery twinge in the penis itself. If the operation didn't solve these problems, why do it?

'Your bladder will empty better. You'll pee less at night. The pains will probably recede, it's just I can't *guarantee* they will.'

I said OK.

In the meantime I should try a variety of pills.

'These problems tend to be hit and miss,' he said. He would put me in touch with a colleague who was up to date with the most recent drugs; for the moment I could start with alpha blockers. 'They inhibit the reaction to adrenalin which is connected to the impulse to pee.' He thought I might wake up only once or twice a night instead of five or six times.

I tried the alpha blockers. After a couple of weeks I was still getting up six times a night and now I was constipated too. I stopped taking the pills and after another week things were back to normal. Normal bowel movements, normal pains. It seemed like progress.

Then shortly before Christmas, the 'up-to-date colleague' Carlo had sent me to, a small tawny haired woman with a strong southern accent, handed me a sample of something absolutely new. 'Christmas present,' she smiled wrily. 'Different approach. Let's see what happens.'

For a while I didn't notice any change. Then I was happy to find I wasn't peeing so often. Then I was concerned that I wasn't peeing enough. Come New Year's Eve I was in serious trouble. I hadn't peed for ten hours. I had the impulse. I stood over the loo. Nothing but pain. I stopped taking the pills. I called Carlo, but his mobile didn't respond. I didn't have his home number. In the end he was only one of a circle of friends at the university where I teach in Milan, while I actually live in Verona, two hours away.

Should I go to hospital? The casualty wards would be packed on New Year's Eve. There was also the consideration that I knew people in the local hospital. My next-door neighbour worked there. If I had gone to someone in Milan, it was precisely out of a childish desire for secrecy close to home. Who wants to admit to prostate problems?

I cried off our small party and went upstairs to bed well before midnight. I lay there rigid and angry. I was angry with the doctor who had given me these pills. I was furious with life for dealing me this card. My body seemed alien and malignant. We couldn't get comfortable together. Perhaps I am a parasite in my own flesh, I thought; and now the landlord has had enough.

In the past I'd always imagined I owned the place.

From downstairs, I could hear my wife and youngest daughter chatting and laughing with the neighbours and their kids who were getting ready to let off fireworks in the garden. Their voices sounded distant. I was locked up in this stupid health problem. The space between us, between myself and my family, suddenly presented itself to me as part of a story, a scene in a film. It was the story of my decline into a pissy, grumpy old man.

When the New Year's fireworks began, I didn't get up and go out to the balcony to watch. All over town people were celebrating. I was in a dark cell, trying to figure how to get out, how to shake off this unhappy story that had started telling itself inside my head. Self-pity is a great teller of boring tales. I was at a turning point, with nowhere to turn.

Towards three a.m. I managed a trickle of pee. It took a while, but afterwards I felt better. To celebrate I found what was left of the champagne and drank it. A good half bottle. Then I went down to the basement, turned on the computer, brought up Google and typed in 'TURP'.

> ***T**rans-**U**rethral **R**esection of the **P**rostate is the gold standard to which other surgeries for Benign Prostatic Hyperplasia are compared. This procedure is performed under general ...*

Gold standard seemed an odd term to use. But what if my prostatic hyper-whatever wasn't benign?

> *Following surgery, a catheter is used to remove blood or blood clots in the bladder.*

I read through the same information on a dozen sites, then, without thinking, clicked on images. Immediately there was a photo of the grotesquely dilated opening of a penis suckering like a fish's mouth around a metal tube. I quickly moved the cursor and clicked on a more reassuring pencil sketch. A man in a doctor's coat and strangely old-fashioned hat was staring into something that looked like a cross between a telescope, a syringe and a gun. About eight inches long, the instrument had little pistol triggers and flexible tubes entering and leaving from above and below. The man had his fingers on the triggers and an eye pressed to an eyepiece; at the other end of the tube was the tip of a penis, lodged in a conical opening. A rigid tube protruded from the instrument, travelled down through the penis, which was unnaturally straight as a result, and penetrated into a shaded area about the size of a squash ball just beyond the scrotum.

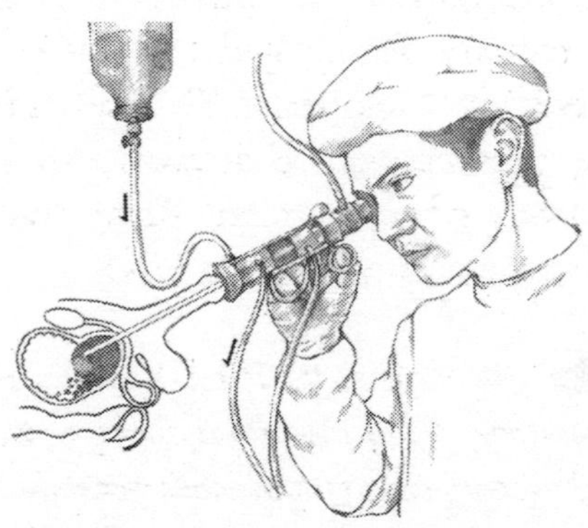

Beneath the image, a caption announced: *In TURP, a wire loop is used to cut away pieces of the prostate.*

I remember gazing at this sketch for some time. What struck me about it was the hubris of its clarity. This handsome, clean-shaven young doctor with his curious hat was Renaissance Man exploring the heavens with his telescopes, Enlightenment Man discovering the power of surgical instruments. He saw clearly right inside the body, *my* body, right into the quick of life, and he made neat, clinical cuts there with the most sophisticated equipment.

I switched to the *Guardian*'s football page and read about a game settled by two goals in injury time. I need not decide about this operation just yet, I thought.

Stupid Pains

After all, nothing had been proved. This enlarged-prostate diagnosis was mere conjecture on Carlo's part. True he was a urologist but we had only spoken as friends. There was a battery of tests I must do. They were complicated and would take time. In a month the problem might be gone, the pains would disappear whence they had come. I had done the right thing to talk to him, but precisely because I had talked to him I could now stop dwelling on it and get on with my life. I would do the tests without thinking about them or what they were for, as if they were the merest annoyance.

Such was my resolution on New Year's Day, 2006.

The pains had different plans. The pains had no intention of returning whence they'd come, wherever that might be. It wasn't something I had ever thought about. I wasn't even sure *when* they'd put in their first appearance. For months I had gone around muttering things like, 'God, you feel uncomfortable today, Tim,' or, 'Oh dear what a bore waiting for this pee to come!' But without ever telling myself that what I was looking at was an array of interrelated and intensifying symptoms.

'I feel a bit uncomfortable today,' I would say to my wife to explain why I didn't want to dig over the garden.

'OK,' Rita would smile, 'next week maybe.'

The word 'uncomfortable', I discovered, had something safe about it, something rather comfortable.

Discomfort is not pain.

'So, how long has this been going on?' had been Carlo's first question when finally I found myself talking to him.

'Well, let's see …'

I frowned. Now I thought about it, I realised that I had been 'uncomfortable' for a long time. It might even be a matter of years. Being uncomfortable had become part of being me.

'It's got worse over the last few months,' I said.

I would have to do regular blood and urine tests, he told me. Plus, a urine flow test, a scan of the whole area, a urogram, a three-day urine test, and maybe a cystoscopy. Assuming the results were as he expected, I could look forward to being operated on in April or May. He made a point of never operating on his friends, Carlo said, but he would refer me to a colleague here in Milan, an excellent surgeon.

Look forward to it? Quite the contrary. In four months the pains would be gone, I hoped.

The pains intensified. I now found myself having to loosen my trousers when I sat down. Everything was stiff and sore. Waking in the early morning, at five, or five thirty, I couldn't get back to sleep. There was a lump of hot lava in my belly. I got out of bed, wandered round the house, brewed up a pot of tea and ate some cereal. I knew this would send me running to the bathroom. The pain would then melt away a while and I could go back to sleep.

Could it be, I phoned Carlo to ask, that the real problem was with the intestine? I had bowel cancer.

He laughed. 'No.'

I felt chastened. I was becoming a hypochondriac, spending all my time thinking about my bodily functions. How absurd to bother people with the details of my bathroom routines! I mustn't speak to him again, I decided, until all the tests were done. What's the point of speaking when you've arranged to do proper clinical tests? The tests will speak for you. All the same, it was a relief to know that if I went down to eat breakfast at five, I could rely on an immediate trip to the bathroom followed by a release from pain and an hour's sleep.

It seemed odd for a prostate condition.

But is it really true to say that I was thinking too much about these pains? I was often anxious. I did wonder about possible solutions. But on the whole I did everything I could *not* to dwell on the matter, not to 'wallow', as my mother would have put it. And if Carlo or any of the other doctors I would see had ever asked me to describe these various pains carefully, I doubt I would have been able to do so. The fact is that my body was not ordinarily present to me. I was only aware of it when it caught me by surprise, when it interrupted me. Pain was an intrusion into a busy schedule. I didn't examine it. I didn't give it time. 'How can I finish all the stuff I've got to do,' I would fume, 'if I have to keep dealing with these stupid interruptions?'

I always referred to the pains as stupid pains, in much the same way as I referred to the noise of roadworks outside my office as a stupid noise. You wouldn't catch me trying to find out exactly what it was they were doing to the road. No, I shut the window, sat down at the computer and inserted a fresh pair of earplugs. I had recently bought a five-year supply of the best quality earplugs from a mail-order company in the USA. To block out life's noise.

All this was automatic, the only sensible reaction, I imagined, to anything that got in the way of a day's work. So when, finally, I did acknowledge a feeling as pain, real pain, rather than discomfort, it was because it now constituted an interruption of such ferocity it could no longer be ignored.

You couldn't work through it. Even then, the imperative was not to explore the pain, to find out about it, but simply to return to normality as rapidly as possible. A good hot bath, I thought, might be a solution to a deep throb in the perineum. I could read in the bath. I could do some research.

The pain did not dissolve. Hot water was not a solution. I only remember flying into a fury when Calvino sank in the suds.

It reached a point where I could no longer sit down at the computer. I needed to stand.

I set my laptop on top of a bookshelf at chest height and, shifting my weight regularly from one foot to the other, continued with my work.

After all, Victor Hugo wrote standing up. And Günter Grass, I've heard.

Physical exercise, I decided, might help. We live in the countryside and it's easy to run. Not that I really *liked* running. The point of physical exercise, I had always imagined, was to keep your body in shape so it would leave you alone, leave you free to get on with the stuff you have to do, without stupid interruptions. I timed myself over six miles.

And I went canoeing. The Adige in Verona is not a bad river for paddling up and down. I had a couple of kayaks stored in the canoe club and there was no reason why I shouldn't take them out more often. I actually liked canoeing far more than running, but it eats deeper into your schedule. You have to drive into town, you have to change in and out of your kit, you have to hang the kit out to dry afterwards. The advantage is that since canoeing requires more attention than running you don't worry about the lost time while you're losing it.

For a couple of months, then, in the autumn of 2004, I had run and canoed as many as four or five times a week and, so long as I was on the move, exerting myself, the pains did retreat into the background. But only to flare up again as soon as I had taken a shower, often more viciously than before. Considering which, it occurred to me that perhaps all this pounding up and down steep hills and straining my abs to paddle my kayak up the Adige might feasibly be making things worse rather than better. Perhaps the best thing was not to exercise more, but to cut out exercise *altogether*.

The thought was attractive. Acting on it, or ceasing to act, I confirmed that physical exercise was neither the problem nor the solution. These pains didn't care whether I went running or not.

Diet, my wife insisted. I should look into diet. And I did. Again and again I tried to establish some relationship between the various items of food and drink I customarily consume (I'm a creature of routine) and the various pains that were plaguing me.

Coffee was an obvious suspect. Cut it out! For a month I went without my ten a.m. cappuccino and two p.m. espresso.

To no avail.

Next came alcohol. It's always the pleasures that have to go. I cut out my evening Scotch. I was surprised how difficult that was. Around ten thirty, I would be overwhelmed by a craving for whisky. Apparently, this modest habit, pursued over many years, had become an addiction. Making myself, on my wife's advice, a cup of camomile tea, to fill the gap as it were, I was half hoping that my body would rebel and take matters into its own hands; yes, my body, I thought, would start trembling and grow extremely itchy, until, brushing aside my noble resistance, it would walk resolutely to the drinks cabinet and splash out a Scotch.

I couldn't wait.

My body did nothing of the kind. On the contrary, as the days passed, it seemed happier and happier with the camomile. Irritated, I took encouragement from the thought that if the whisky hadn't agreed with my body as much as I had supposed, there might soon be some improvement in the pain.

Not so. The pains stayed exactly where they were, or rather moved around exactly as they had previously, and when, after a month or so, I terminated the experiment and poured myself a very ample tumbler of Laphroaig, I actually slept better than I had for some weeks. I had a pain-free night, *with the Scotch.* Naturally, I repeated the performance the following evening, only to find that everything had returned to normal. Normal discomfort, normal pain, excellent Laphroaig.

After the whisky I cut out early-evening beer.

After the early-evening beer, I cut out weekend wine.

At one point it occurred to me that red meat was the problem.

It wasn't.

By the time I spoke to Carlo, such experiments had become a constant in my life. My diet was a speculative shuffling and reshuffling of a fairly limited pack in the hope of hitting the winning combination that would allow me to get on with my life without pain, without these stupid interruptions.

Not that I was scientific about it, I didn't keep records, and more often than not at some official lunch or dinner, or maybe just out with friends, I would forget that I wasn't supposed to be eating this or drinking that. I'd happily indulge. Afterwards I'd start the experiment again from scratch. Or just drop it altogether.

Waking to acute pain in the early hours, swinging my legs out of bed to escape the fiery rock in my belly, these dietary experiments seemed extremely important. I must find a solution. But in the evening, relaxing in company, I really didn't know anything about the old guy who dragged his ball and chain back and forth from the bathroom half a dozen times every night. Or, yes, I did know him, but as a distant acquaintance, an elderly relative. Best forgotten.

The Waterseller

Holding a test tube between my legs and waiting for the pee to come, some words crossed my mind, something I had read about the nineteenth-century Italian poet, Giacomo Leopardi: 'Reflecting on the subtleties of urination he would be unable to pass water.' He had to wait until he could 'steal a moment's inattention from himself'.

What a crazy idea this was! All the same, the story stuck. Years after reading the poet's biography I still remembered the phrase 'steal a moment's inattention from himself'.

It was mid-January, middle of the night; the following morning I had the first clinical tests. Blood and urine. True to form, I had contrived to put them off for two weeks in the hope that the pains would subside: first for a visit to London to see my brother, then for a few days' skiing and walking in the mountains with my wife and daughters.

My brother lives in America and I in Italy, but we sometimes get together for a few days in London after the New Year. John is a painter and likes to take me to whatever art shows are on in town. He enjoys expressing provocative opinions in a highly audible voice and I enjoy listening to someone who sees and knows so much more than I do.

On the second day, between one museum and another, we stopped at Apsley House, the Duke of Wellington's home, to look, among other things, at Velázquez's *Waterseller of Seville*.

In exactly the kind of chiaroscuro you get under a portico in summer, an old man in a tattered cloak, the waterseller, passes a brimming glass with a black fig in the bottom to a smartly dressed young boy. It's a painting I've seen half a dozen times and always felt drawn to, but today I was almost shocked by its impact. Those two faces, staring so intently, but neither at each other nor at the water, their two hands, one old, one young, meeting on the stem of the glass, the light in the transparent liquid above the dark fullness of the near invisible fig, they seemed to hold some obscure message for me.

I asked my brother if there was a story behind the painting. Who was the third guy in the shadow behind the seller and the boy? 'Just a street scene,' John said, 'just a moment in Seville.' He drew my attention to the water dribbling down the jug in the foreground and began to talk about the kind of paints Velázquez used. There were two other versions of the *Waterseller*, he said, one in the Uffizi and one in the States somewhere. Gazing at the painting as he spoke, the precious fullness of the glass and its precarious passage between those two hands made me excited and anxious; leaving the museum, it was as if I had had an important dream and needed someone to tell me what it meant.

On the last day we took a long bus ride out to Finchley where our father had been a clergyman through the 1960s and '70s. The grand old vicarage we lived in has long since been demolished and replaced with nondescript flats, but the ugly neo-Gothic church is still there. John was enthusiastic, talking a great deal about the past. He seemed at once nostalgic and scandalised. When he was four he had had polio, been close to dying. He has always walked with a heavy limp. Mum and Dad, he said, had never wanted to face up to the enormity of this. They went on singing 'count your blessings' as if nothing had happened.

It was raining and I needed a bathroom. Finding the recreation hall behind the church open, we went in and saw, in the corridor, a black-and-white photograph of Dad in his robes together with a plaque commemorating his many years of service. Harold James Parks, 1920–1980. He had his arms raised to give the blessing. The place smelt of damp. Peeing in a bathroom that hadn't changed in thirty years, I wondered if maybe my problem had its origin in those childhood days. Had it been passed on to me in a brimming glass? But I wasn't interested in exploring the past. When I got back to Italy I'd get the tests done, find out what my problem was, have it fixed, then forget it and get on with my life. I've always felt critical of my brother for his fixation with the past.

'Remember how Dad used to peel oranges?' John asked. We were walking into the wind on Finchley High Road.

Violently, was the answer, tearing into the peel with bitten fingernails.

'He used to take something called Sanatogen, for his nerves.'

'I believe they still sell it.'

'Remember when he confiscated "Let's Spend the Night Together"?'

Over drinks in the Tally Ho, we laughed about this. During the night, back in the flat we were in, I peed into a plastic bottle so as not to have to walk through my brother's room to get to the loo. John is three years older than me but he sleeps the night through. I had no intention of letting him know what state I was in.

There were the same night-time problems the following week in the flat my wife and I had rented in the mountains of the South Tyrol. I couldn't help feeling a sense of shame as I slipped in and out of the bathroom trying not to wake Stefi and Lucy, my daughters. How much easier everything would be, it occurred to me, if I lived on my own.

That was a new thought.

During the day, while the girls skied, Rita and I walked through the woods on the lower slopes, wrapped up in scarves and hats. We were mostly silent. In my head I was trying to solve a problem with something I was writing; I couldn't make the plot come out. It was one of those situations where you think and think and nothing budges, not unlike the silent winter streams, choked with ice. Rita complained that I was withdrawn. 'You're more and more driven,' she said. 'It's boring.' The air under the dripping pines was raw. Every time we stopped at a Stube for coffee or lunch, I was aware, sitting on my pains, that things were not getting better.

For the urine test I had been told to bring a sample of the morning's first pee, presumably because it's chemically different from what you pee later; it has had a good few hours to stew in the bladder. But since I was going to the bathroom any number of times during the night and usually took a gulp of water before going back to sleep, in my case a pee at seven a.m. would hardly be like anyone else's. It would be more diluted.

If that was so, and if this circumstance made a significant difference, perhaps I should give them my first performance of the night. Or maybe, so as not to offer something too close to the digestion process, I should give them the second. Or, even better, I could pee all the night's pee into a single container – a bowl, say, or a jug – and then pour out a tube's worth in the morning; after giving it a good swirl, of course. That way they would get the full minestrone.

I couldn't decide. The whole thing was irritating. It seemed extraordinary that there weren't specific guidelines for people in my predicament. Before going to bed, I phoned Carlo for advice.

'Pee any time,' he said drily.

I decided on the night's second, which turned out to be around two, and stood there, over the loo, holding the test tube, thinking about Leopardi who used to think so hard he couldn't go. In his case the problem could hardly have been an enlarged prostate because the description of him struggling to perform refers to the adolescent Giacomo. The source of the info, as I recalled, was the poet's competitive father, Monaldo, who explained that to help his son to urinate he had to keep him company with the chamber pot and distract him. Imagining my wife waking six times a night to help me distract myself into passing water raised a chuckle and I began to pee, taking care to steer the thin thread of liquid into the tube. But the smile must have caused my hand to shake, or a moment's inattention, because a few drops trickled over the rim and wetted my fingers. Quickly adjusting the position of the tube, I inadvertently touched it against my foreskin.

Damn! The instructions on the green box the tube had come in specifically said that you weren't to touch the rim of the tube with your 'genitalia' because superficial bacteria would then get into the urine and alter the results.

What to do? The sensible thing would be to delay the tests for a day or so while I procured another tube.

But hadn't I already delayed for too long?

The hell with it. I lifted the tube to check if it was full enough. The urine was a pale lemon colour, not exactly the waterseller's brimming glass, but not unattractive, in its way. I pushed in the stopper and washed my hands.

But if I didn't care about the bacteria and consequently misleading test results, why had I spent so much time worrying about when was the best time to pee?

I've no idea.

Going back up to bed – we sleep in a room under the roof and have to go down a flight of stairs to the loo – it occurred to me that Carlo had been offhand about the timing of the sample because the readings that mattered wouldn't be affected by the relation between the urine and my food intake. Right. What they were testing for was something ominously simple, like blood in my pee, or cancer cells.

But hadn't I promised myself, I reflected, that I wouldn't think about any of this until the tests were over and I could make a pondered decision?

I thought about Leopardi instead. Not only did the poet have problems in the bathroom but having spent his childhood bent over books he soon developed severe scoliosis. At twenty he looked like a hunchback. He also suffered from stomach pains, was lazy with personal hygiene and, later on in life, rarely washed his clothes. When asked why she hadn't been to bed with him, a certain lady remarked, 'My dear, he stank.'

Nevertheless, Leopardi wrote sublime poems. Just a few evenings earlier I had been helping Stefi to learn one for school. It tells how the poet takes pleasure in sitting behind a hedge high on a hillside. The fact that the hedge blocks the view allows him to imagine the vastness of eternity beyond it. His 'thoughts drown in this immensity', and in the last line he tells us that it's 'Sweet to be shipwrecked in this sea'.

How interesting, it occurred to me, pulling up the bed covers in the shadowy room while my wife snored softly, that Leopardi found it positive when 'thoughts drown'. And how interesting, too, that he associated such happy moments with high water. Does water dissolve thoughts? In Velázquez's painting, both the boy and the old man seem to have been placed under some kind of spell by that full glass of water with its fragrant fig.

I lay quietly. If anyone is dismayed at the idea of having to get up six times a night, let me assure them that I always loved the business of returning to my bed and going back to sleep. Sometimes I actually thought I was lucky to get the chance to drift into dreams so many times in a single night.

Worrisome Dissatisfied Individuals

The 'work' I insisted on doing day by day, whatever state I might be in, was no more and no less than telling stories. Surely an innocuous occupation. But over the following weeks, I suddenly found myself wrestling with a disturbing and decidedly noxious story, something that came back to me from twenty years before with the dry clunk of a lock turning in a heavy door.

The morning of the blood and urine tests I had gone to the clinic, as was my wont, with the intention of not really *being* there. I had taken a book so that my mind would remain focused on my mental world, not my bodily fluids, nor the people around me. I had been asked to write an essay on the Austrian writer Thomas Bernhard. Certainly Bernhard, I thought – I was reading his autobiography *Breath: A Decision* – had a far worse deal health-wise than I ever did. Hospitalised for pleurisy at seventeen, then diagnosed with tuberculosis, he spent a year at death's door, followed by a lifetime of debilitating lung disease, until in 1989, he finally succumbed, aged fifty-eight, two years younger than my father had been when he also died of lung problems, cancer in his case. One thing you must put in your essay, I told myself, was that Bernhard's lungs were his destiny. Like D.H. Lawrence, he never breathed easy. It must have affected his writing.

Already I was aware of a small presentiment fluttering against the fogged window of my early-morning consciousness. I ignored it, concentrating on Bernhard and keeping half an eye on the illuminated number that showed where the staff were up to. Each ping was another patient dealt with.

My number eventually flashed up and I went to a window where, without any exchange of words, a young woman at a keyboard transformed my prescriptions into barcodes on adhesives to be attached to various test tubes. How reassuringly efficient and impersonal this was, I thought, compared to the old days when they would make you stand in line for hours.

Then I remembered.

The marvel is that I should have contrived *not to remember* for so long. Still, my first response was self-congratulation. Thank God, I told myself, you haven't been asked to do the sperm test this time! The awful sperm test. But now it was only a question of seconds before my whirring mind settled on the words: '*after decades of pain and frustration such patients will inevitably leave their problems on the operating table in their fifties or sixties.*'

The lock turned. Waiting outside the room where they take your blood, I could no longer concentrate on Thomas Bernhard. All this had been foretold.

More than twenty years previously, suddenly finding I had to go to the bathroom literally every ten minutes, I had been diagnosed with acute prostatitis. I must do a sperm test to find out what bug had got in there, what antibiotic could treat it. On my arrival at the front of a long queue in this same clinic, the nurse, seeing my foreign name on the prescription, had announced with the kind of clarity and booming volume some people imagine all foreigners appreciate: 'SPERM! MAKE SURE THE FIRST DROPS GO IN

THE CONTAINER. IT'S *THE FIRST DROPS THAT COUNT WITH SPERM.*'

This was the funny side of the story, something I had told at parties a hundred times, mimicking the surprise on the faces of the others in the queue as the nurse yelled 'Sperm!' and then my embarrassment, minutes later, trying to produce that sperm in one of only three cubicles available while others queued outside to provide urine samples, coughing and shuffling and complaining that I was keeping the loo too long. I distinctly remember how relieved, pleased, even *proud* I was when the crucial first drops were safely steered into the little plastic container.

Olé!

But that wasn't the end of the story. Vital as it is for the continuation of the species, the prostate is particularly well protected by layer after layer of near impermeable membrane. It is not easily infected. Once infected, it isn't easily treated. Once treated, it rarely returns to its pristine state. You get over the acute phase to find you're looking at the chronic. About three months after these troubles began, I came across a young doctor who, in his eagerness to be candid, gave me a publication that was meant only for people like himself, doctors specialising in urology. The last paragraph of this booklet read as follows (I quote from bitter memory):

> It has to be born in mind that the chances of a complete recovery from prostatitis are minimal, almost non-existent in fact. Prostatitis sufferers tend to be restless, worrisome, dissatisfied individuals who drag their miseries around from one doctor to the next in search of a cure they never find. The urologist must be careful not to let himself be demoralised by these people and their intractable pathologies. In the end, after years, perhaps decades of pain and frustration,

> the vast majority of such patients will inevitably leave their problems on the operating table in their fifties or sixties.

The urologist must be careful! Poor fellow. Nobody wants to be demoralised. But I was a young man of thirty being told I would be sick in my intimate parts for the whole of my virile life. My soul rebelled. I flew to London, paid a man in Harley Street who put me on more or less permanent antibiotics and after something like a year I was cured.

'I am cured! *Completely cured!* The booklet was *wrong*!'

I remember yelling those words to myself in delight and rage, time and again. 'Wrong, wrong, *wrong*! The book was wrong!' I wanted to find the author and stick his miserable prophesy right up where his prostate was. 'What a hateful story, *and not even true*. He got it wrong. I'm cured! **CURED!**'

But was I?

Had I ever been?

'Urine sample over there,' the nurse said.

I turned and slotted my test tube into a rack with a community of other test tubes, thirty or forty of them, in orderly rows, cosy and indistinguishable as crosses in a war cemetery.

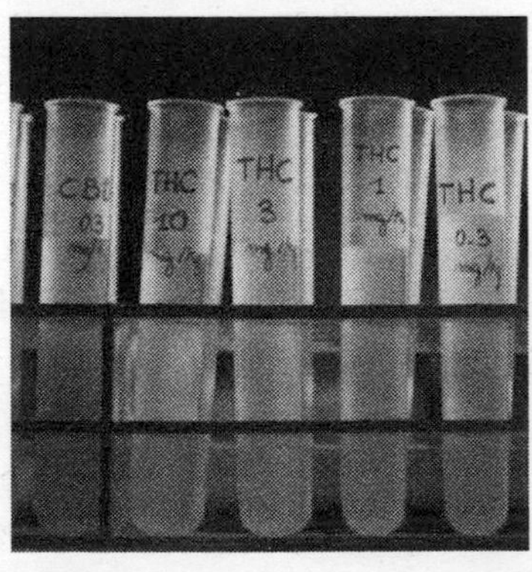

Perhaps my condition had simply been dormant. Or I was lying to myself. I had *always* been uncomfortable. Just that I was used to it, to a certain level of it. I had told myself the tale of being cured because it made me feel better. I so much wanted the booklet to be wrong. Wasn't it strange, for example, that I had been unable to tell Carlo when these pains actually began?

'Clench your fist,' the nurse said. She smiled. 'No need to look so worried.'

In the past I have sometimes had trouble watching blood flow from my arm. Now I barely noticed. The dark liquid bubbling into the syringe had nothing to do with me. What mattered was this ugly story: 'inevitably ... on the operating table … in their fifties or sixties'.

For the following days and weeks I was in thrall to this version of my life, 'the official medical version', I kept saying to myself. That's what you're up against, the version you chose twenty years ago to deny and which now is taking its revenge. Here I was, barely past my fifty-first birthday, and a doctor, entirely innocent of my medical record, was prospecting *exactly* the operation that had been foretold when I was thirty.

What was the point of struggling?

Or was it rather a question of *suggestion*? The medical publication of so long ago, written in a style and from a point of view that were no longer acceptable, probably out of print for over a decade and read by absolutely no one, was nevertheless acting as a powerful spell, a hex, a curse. My primitive mind was unable to wriggle free from the words of a witchdoctor who had told me I would wither and die.

But he didn't tell you you'd *die*! I protested out loud. I was in my office no doubt, pacing up and down by my laptop.

Just that you'd need a simple, routine operation. Nothing more ordinary. Prostatitis and enlarged prostates are neither of them life-threatening conditions. Why get so upset?

Then I recalled that there were cancers of the prostate that were indeed life-threatening. I stopped. But no, this didn't frighten me. What was mortifying wasn't the prognosis; it was this loss of confidence in my version of the past, my sudden uncertainty as to what the last twenty years had really been.

So how long has this been going on?

Well ... I don't know.

Do I try to write stories, I wondered now, because in general I have such a weak grip on the story of my own life? I remembered having once thought something of the like about my father. Every Sunday, matins and evensong, the man's sermons repeated the same story: sin, despair, redemption, paradise. At fourteen, fidgeting on my pew, it came to me that the person he most needed to convince was *himself*. That was the day I stopped believing. And what had I just written? What was the plot of my latest novel? The story of a man whose son has written a defamatory biography of him, undermining his sense of who he is, forcing him to revisit the past and reaffirm his version of events. But the reader knows from page one it's a lost cause. The guy is finished.

Your stories and your illness are pathetically mixed up, I told myself.

These unhappy reflections didn't help with my famous pains, which were all at once more insistent than ever. Not for the first time, then, I had to ask myself whether there wasn't a psychosomatic element to all this. 'Prostatitis sufferers tend to be restless, worrisome, dissatisfied individuals,' the booklet said. The doctor didn't declare in so many words that the problem was psychosomatic, but he did imply that *personality and pathology were related.* If that was the case, how should I react? Had my cry of 'cured' so many years ago been an attempt to respond to the booklet's predictions by refusing to be the worrisome, dissatisfied individual it described? Every illness is a narrative. What matters is the version you tell yourself.

Could I try that ruse again? Simply deny it?

I was in a hall of mirrors. And the problem for the person who spends all day on his own writing stories is that the only resistance he has to such reflections are the stories he's trying to tell. There is no phone ringing, no business to be done that might force the mind elsewhere. D. H. Lawrence, I recalled, denied his illness right to the end. He refused to accept that he had tuberculosis. He went on regardless. And the characters in his books are notoriously people who set their wills against the world, who thrive on opposition, even hopeless opposition. Full of vitality and wilfulness, the books themselves are part of Lawrence's denying he is ill, they are barriers thrown up against sickness. Whereas Bernhard's genius was to *take on* his disease by telling it. Bernhard constantly denounced the scandal of illness. He got his energy from the scandal. He scolded his illness. So both men did more than any ordinary human being usually can because they feared illness would stop them doing anything at all.

But I was paralysed. Nothing would flow. I couldn't get on with the novel I was writing because with the sudden flaring of this health problem, and in particular the return of an unhappy story I thought I'd shrugged off twenty years ago, what I was writing seemed pointless. It made no sense to me. This is the worst thing that can happen when writing. The words and stories seem pointless, mere constructions to sell a book or two. Every word you write you cross out.

It's mere invention. Even if the book were successful, which it won't be, who cares? Who *needs* it? You change from the novel to non-fiction because it suddenly seems absolutely essential to write straightforwardly about something that matters. Otherwise you can't write. But then realising that you will never be able to say exactly what has happened, exactly what life is – it's too complicated, it's too cruel to the people around you – you go back to fiction, hoping to construct some story that at least offers a fair analogy. Only it doesn't. You can't find the formula that will make the words seem necessary. You go back and forth between novel and non-fiction, unable to be or become anything at all, the story won't settle. And meantime a hateful paragraph in a second-rate medical publication of twenty years ago is dragging you towards the operating table.

So just go and get it done now! Get yourself cut and start living again!

In a dream, a dark patch on the floor flew up in my face, closing its wings around my nose, mouth, eyes. A bird. A bat. Choking me. The floor was the floor of my father's church as visited a month before by myself and my brother.

Would it help to know, I wondered, that my nervous father had suffered from the same condition? Had he? Were prostate problems hereditary? I remembered Mum making fun of him because, when she called him to meals, he always had to 'slip away and spend a penny' before coming to table. He wanted to be comfortable. So perhaps Dad had had to go to the bathroom a lot at night too and I had known nothing about it. I should phone my mother, I decided, and get the story from her. As soon as I had confirmation that the condition was congenital, I would accept the situation, do the operation, and get it over with; though of course my father had never had such an operation, at least as far as I knew.

Could it be that it was precisely his worrying about a possible operation that brought on his cancer?

Certainly my father had been a worrisome, dissatisfied individual.

I resolved to call my mother. For some weeks I was on the point of calling her. But I didn't. I realised that if she said, 'No, Dad didn't have that problem,' then things would be worse: it wasn't the gene pool; I couldn't blame it on Dad. On the other hand, if she said, 'Yes, Dad had that problem too, poor soul, oh dear, and you too now, Timothy,' again things would be worse. At that point it would be quite impossible to deny it. It would be written in stone. Better not to know, I thought. If there was one thing I didn't want it was to be like my father, though I wasn't so blind as not to see that I was, in fact, very like him. I shared his nerves, for one thing. If I haven't yet started tearing oranges apart, I will certainly never hold a glass of water with the same beautiful stillness of Velázquez's waterseller.

In His Image

My parents had two overriding concerns in their children's regard: our spiritual welfare and social position. To have brought into existence souls destined for eternal damnation would be a catastrophe. We must be steeped in the Christian story. We would sin, naturally enough, but we would always be wise enough to repent and stay on course for paradise. At school our achievements would guarantee us a position among the diligent middle classes, or with any luck the free professions. As far as our bodies were concerned, what mattered was that they be respectable. We must be tidily dressed, our hair tidily cut, our hands, necks, mouths and fingernails tolerably clean. As long as one scraped the mud off one's shoes afterwards, sport was an acceptable way of letting off steam, but not important in itself. The fact that I was captain of the school football team was not important. If I scored a winning goal it was not a cause for congratulation. That my brother would never be able to participate in sports, never be able to run or jump, was thus no great loss. A well-knotted tie was important. And clean shoes. Keeping your shirt tucked in, your hair combed. We must not use obscenities or blasphemies. We must not masturbate. Not that the word 'masturbate' was ever uttered. There was a fear of words like that and of the shared knowledge implied when two people used them. We must not 'touch ourselves'. We knew where. I remember my embarrassed amusement when the Harley Street urologist (he who 'cured' my prostatitis) told me, 'You must climax, every day, Mr Parks. If not with your wife,' he coughed, 'then alone.' Primates, he explained, climaxed many times every day. In evolutionary terms, we were programmed to keep the prostate busy and its sperm on the move. 'To avoid congestion in the prostatic ducts,' he assured me.

'You little monkeys!' had been my mother's indulgent protest when we did something mildly improper. She did not believe in evolution. To be seen slipping one's hands in one's pants elicited a more flustered and aggressive response; to the point that I sometimes wonder whether the anxiety and repression that surrounded adolescent stirrings was not responsible for putting the first strains on my prostate. Was the little organ supposed to shoot its load or not? I would start to indulge, begin to enjoy, hear my mother's anxious voice, stop. But all this is the merest speculation and I've no desire to blame my parents. They cared for us as much as parents can. The fact is that the whole society was, still is, unsure as to what our relation with our bodies should be.

The human body was the temple of God, my father explained, and made in His image. But this did not mean we should worship the beautiful bodies on show in magazines and cinema (actually, there were no magazines in the vicarage and I went to the cinema only once before age eleven, to see *Sink the Bismarck*). What it meant was that the body must be kept pure otherwise we would be offending God; being made in His image was a cause for caution, not celebration. Ugly, ungainly people were also made in God's image; if they washed and dressed properly and stood up straight, they were as respectable as anyone else.

At school the body featured in biology lessons. It was made up of bones, organs, muscles and tendons that could be shown in diagrams. A list of names must be inserted in the right places below the diagrams. Trapezius. Biceps brachii. Deltoids, flexors, abdominal transversals. These basic anatomical elements were nourished by a network of arteries and veins which likewise lent itself to two-dimensional representation and simple, quiz-like challenges. A day's swotting guaranteed you eighty out of a hundred in the end-of-term biology exam.

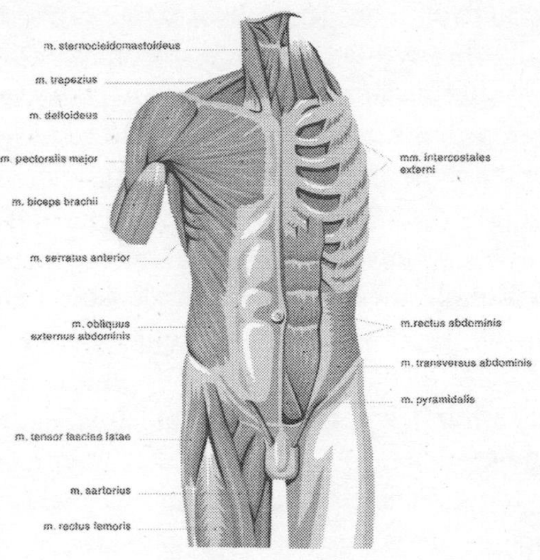

But as the years passed and the diagrams grew more coloured and intricate, accompanied by chemical formulas and names that were hard to spell, it became clear that only the most assiduous and determined among us had any chance of understanding this prodigious machine with its lymph nodes and cell structures, its proteins and mucous membranes. At no point were we invited to compare our own bodies with the diagrams we studied. Phenomenally complex it might be, but the body was still only a mechanism, an object of study. The body wasn't *us*. Which was why it was fine, once you'd grasped the basics, to leave deeper understanding to the experts, the same way you do with cars and computers and central heating systems. Only a handful of us would pursue biology beyond O level. If ever something were to go wrong with the body that you personally happened to be in, these were the people who would fix it for you.

My wife phoned me at the office to say the blood and urine results had arrived in the mail and I went out on the river in my kayak. I refused to be anxious. In winter I use a light slalom kayak. Sometimes I paddle three bridges up the river and surf on a wave in the rapid by Ponte Pietra, the old Roman Bridge. This inevitably becomes a form of exhibitionism. Tourists standing at the parapet take photos of the city. They point their cameras down at the surfing canoeist, no doubt wondering if you will hit a rock or capsize. They want a memorable snap. If you make the effort to force the boat up the rapid and under the bridge to the other side, they applaud when you climb the last rush. They aren't discerning enough to appreciate that you are only a moderately competent paddler. Certainly they won't be thinking you have a prostate problem.

Or I practise threading the slalom gates at the bridge near the club. There was a canoeing move which obsessed me, had obsessed me for a long time, because although I knew perfectly well in my head how it worked, I could only rarely do it. One of the slalom gates is placed just inside the eddy that forms downstream of a bridge pillar. You have to pass from the main flow to the milling eddy and turn the canoe so that it heads upstream through the gate. To do this efficiently you must drop the downstream thigh as you cross from stream to eddy while swivelling your trunk round and digging the paddle deep on the upstream side. If you get the coordination right, the tail of the canoe slides down into the water of the eddy, the nose rears up, and the boat rotates on the spot. Well performed, it is an elegant, effortless move.

I never got the coordination right. Not true. I got it right sometimes; let's say, just often enough to keep trying. But I never really learned it. My body got it, or didn't get it, at random, as if it were a question of throwing six on a dice.

Why? I can ride a bicycle. I can ski. It seemed to be a problem with right–left coordination. I am very left-footed and though I write with my right hand, I catch a ball with my left. Could I have been, in society's general eagerness for conformity, a suppressed left-hander? Does the sort of tension generated by such suppression produce restless, worrisome, dissatisfied individuals who pester urologists? Why is the body such a mystery and why is the mind so frustrated in its dealings with it, as if faced with an equation that won't come out? A situation not unlike the mind's perplexity before some works of art. These are futile trains of thought. Yet I seem condemned to entertain them.

For example, when I set out from my office for a coffee of a morning I often pass a moustachioed man in his seventies who walks with a stick, dresses in a double-breasted suit and invariably sports a white cowboy hat, this in a drab, working-class district of Verona. One day, as we drew close to each other in the street, this debonair pensioner stopped and rather peremptorily announced: 'For God's sake, young man, stand up straight!'

I raised my head to look at him. We had never spoken before. He was comically erect, chest puffed out, chin held high, white moustache waxed, a veteran on parade. The stick was a rifle, the tropical suit a uniform, neatly creased; the hat brim was absolutely horizontal.

'Stand up *straight*,' he repeated, as if genuinely irritated by my bowed shoulders. Then, swinging his stick, he strode on.

I was disturbed, but not angry. He had called me 'young' after all, and it was true that my shoulders were bowed. This goes with the writer's profession. Other people had commented on it. At least I don't have Leopardi's scoliosis, I told myself. I wondered if the poet's scoliosis and his urinary problems were linked. And for many weeks I continued to imagine that if by some miracle I could stand up straight, naturally, without forcing myself, and not only stand but *walk* upright, at ease, my neck free from tension, my head high, then I would be entirely healthy. My problems would dissolve. And the same would be true, I told myself, if I could do that elegant turn in my canoe; to do that turn every time, with nonchalance, moving from the fast-flowing water to the still and out again, would be to be *healed*.

Illness, I realised then, like love, or hate, draws everything to itself, turns everything into itself. Whatever I thought about came back to that: my condition.

At home, the envelope was the official kind with a transparent window and the address beneath. I sat on the sofa. It was not unlike, I thought, receiving a formal communication from a lawyer clarifying something as personal and intimate as one's relationship with one's wife. For better or worse, richer or poorer, I was about to get some hard information about that enigma, my body.

It was a biology test too far.

P-Colesterolo totale
P-Trigliceridi
P-urea
P-creatinina
P-bilirubina totale

I had no real idea what these words signified. Or what that P was about. Even the units of measure were alien to me. Mmol/L. μmol/L.

There were fifty or so entries, forty of them for the blood, the others for urine: *Linfociti, monociti, eosinofili, basofili. Urobilinogeno, corpi chetonici.*

What did I know about these things, my body parts? Nothing. The only thing a layman could understand on the printout was that my pee was officially 'straw yellow'.

Fortunately, beside each entry, in parentheses, there was a range of values considered within the norm. My eye went directly to *Sr-PSA totale.* Again, I have no idea what PSA stands for, but I do know that a high PSA is associated with prostate cancer. It was the last entry but one and the acceptable range was 0-4.00 μg/L. Mine was 0.31.

'Heavens, you're healthy!' Carlo laughed when I read him the results on the phone. 'No blood in the urine, incredibly low PSA, no infections; all as expected.'

As I put the receiver down Rita was anxious to know what the verdict was.

'It seems I'm fine.'

Our friend Larry, she kindly reminded me, had died exactly forty-eight hours after a battery of tests had told him he was in perfect health.

Urodynamics

In *Breath: A Decision*, the book that talks about Bernhard's pleurisy and tuberculosis, the 'decision' is his resolve to leave the hospital without permission and consider himself cured. He would have nothing more to do with the medical profession. Thus he declared his control over his own destiny.

On the other hand he could only do that because he was feeling well enough.

I too was planning to make a decision, but only after I had the results of all the medical tests. Then my decision, most likely, would be acquiescence to necessity, to that 'official version' of my condition I had read about so long ago. At the same time, I still hoped the pains would evaporate. I was still playing with my diet.

The blood and urine tests had excluded two possible explanations: prostate cancer and stones. So, the enlarged-prostate diagnosis became more feasible and the TURP operation was a step nearer. The man with the funny hat and frightening surgical instruments was waiting for me.

The so-called urodynamic test, which I did after a morning's teaching in Milan the following week, pointed in the same direction. This test was actually rather fun. You pee into a funnel and the urine swills down into a device that measures volume released per second. The results are then expressed as a graph showing flow rate over time of urination.

I drank as much water as I could an hour or so before the test, in the hope that this would improve my performance. It's curious how one does these tests to establish firm facts, yet still tries to get the best result. To cheat almost. Obviously there is something virile about a copious, vigorously splashing pee, and I did not want to seem too pathetic. It crossed my mind that pulling back the foreskin entirely, which compresses the urethra a little and intensifies the jet, might alter the results further in my favour. Then I reflected that this was like putting your thumb over the mouth of the garden hose to get the water to reach the bushes behind the flowerbed. The jet looks better and goes further, but the flow rate is the same.

Standing in a curtained-off cubicle, then, I produced my melancholy, rather lengthy and intermittent pee into the white plastic funnel, while, at the other side of the room, a clever needle traced a tormented, broken-peaked zigzag onto a roll of moving graph paper. As soon as I had zipped up, the young, rather handsomely moustachioed doctor who was supervising tore off my Alpine-arc result and, by way of explanation, sketched over it the trajectory of a normal person: the line he drew showed a smooth pinnacle of healthy urinary performance.

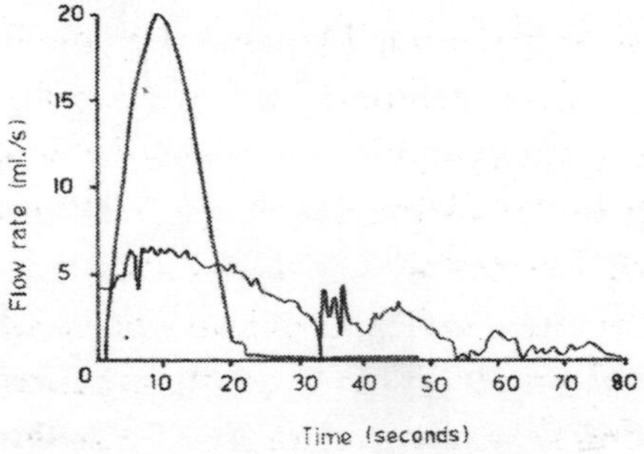

Looking at the two curves, the one vertiginously graceful, the other stunted and stuttering, I was aware that the graphs were telling me something I had actually known for a long time. Perhaps a year before, my son and I had been preparing for a kayaking trip together in Austria. Before getting in the car, we both took a pee in the two loos on the first floor of our house and, being two men alone, we didn't close the doors. What I heard then – a brief Niagara thundering around the tiled walls, preceded and also followed by the tinkling stop–start of my own silted trickle – was the acoustic and far more *felt* equivalent of the superimposed urodynamic graphs. Now, I knew the same thing in a colder way, with numbers.

Voiding time 68 seconds
Flow time 66 seconds
Time to max flow 19 seconds
Max flow rate 11.4 ml/s
Average flow rate 6.7 ml/s
Voided volume 447 ml.

Wonderful, as Samuel Beckett's Molloy remarks after counting his farts for 24 hours, how mathematics helps you to know yourself! I placed the superimposed graphs in the medical file I'd been advised to keep. The sight of the healthy curve did not cheer me the way the sound of my son's explosive performance had.

'I've seen worse,' Carlo smiled when I showed him my piece of paper in the hospital cafeteria.

'So,' I asked, 'diagnosis confirmed?'

'It could still be the bladder sphincter rather than the prostate.' A normal sphincter, he said, opened almost to the diameter of this doughnut – we contemplated the soggy, sugar-coated ring he had ordered – whereas mine might only be opening – what? – to this: he pointed to the fifty-cent coins he had placed on the counter.

'That would explain it.'

As he ate and talked, wiping jam from his lips, his eye glancing round at the bodies of pretty nurses, I became aware that despite my miserable urinary performance I was enjoying a faint sense of superiority. Whatever my problems, I was trim and slim, at fifty-one, whereas Carlo, who could hardly be more than forty, was a good twenty kilos overweight and growing jowly. Every time I saw him, he was eating: a doughnut, a sandwich, a pizza. The nurses, I decided, were much more likely to look at me, especially if I managed to straighten my shoulders a little.

In the car driving home I smiled at this vanity, but revelled in it none the less. It was true that my body and I weren't the best of friends these days; we hardly communicated except through pain. All the same, the flesh could not help but testify to my impressive strength of character: *I wasn't eating jam doughnuts mid-morning*. I had *self-control*.

Thus one might be cheered, I reflected, to find oneself cutting a figure, so to speak, on the operating table.

Later still, Velázquez came to mind again. I was standing at the computer and as I lifted a cup of tea to my lips, my hand trembled. Was it really possible, I immediately wondered, that the boy and man in the painting at Apsley House could hold that water so perfectly still as they passed it from hand to hand? Would a glass in the streets of Seville really have been so crystal clear? Shouldn't the painter rather have shown the two of them spilling a few drops from a more clouded glass? Everything else in the picture seemed so authentic. And was there a link, perhaps, it even occurred to me, between this no doubt deliberate anomaly and the more famous one in the same painter's nude Venus where the lovely woman with her back to us has a cherub hold a mirror so she can gaze at her face; only, given that we see her face in the mirror, she wouldn't have been seeing herself at all, but us, or rather Velázquez.

Both pictures, I thought, calling them up on Google, seemed to have to do with looking, with bodies and minds; and at the centre of both, focusing our attention and tying our mental activity to that of the figures in the painting, were deceptive images of glass and transparency. Why were the boy and the waterseller looking neither at each other nor at the water, yet apparently communing through it?

I went back and forth between the paintings. The exchange of water would have been a commercial transaction – the waterseller sells – but it didn't *look* commercial. It was rapt, or meditative, as Venus and her cherub were rapt. But the real question was: why had I – quite absurdly – started to think of the dark fig at the bottom of the glass as the prostate, the prostate in a state of perfect health, but only thus because beautifully submerged in that transparent, strangely mental water? The water was more beautiful because of the fig, and the fig was darkly perfect because of the water.

I get angry with myself when my mind meanders in this oddball fashion. This is the merest self-referential vagary, I muttered. Crotch-gazing. Probably any picture would have set it off. You should give up writing books, I told myself, and accept straight journalistic commissions that would force you to think more purposefully.

On returning home, I opened a letter with the results of the so-called three-day urine cytology test and discovered that they had found pre-cancerous cells in my bladder.

Deterritorialisation

The nights were unpredictable; I was growing used to that. My wife and I slept in the same bed, but more apart than before. Discomfort formed a shell around me. My wife was careful not to enquire too much, or she was growing bored. She was walking the dog later. I was going to sleep earlier, after a whisky, of course. Then the counting began. How many bathroom trips? At what intervals? Sometimes I thought I should write them down. Perhaps I would see a pattern in the numbers. But what could the pattern tell me that I didn't already know?

Basically, each night divided itself into segments: two or three of one and a half hours, followed by two or three of one hour. These must be the famous sleep cycles. Sometimes, but more and more rarely, I would skip one of the breaks and not wake for a whole three hours. Opening my eyes, then, I was intensely and pleasurably aware that I had slept for longer than usual.

On the bedside table was a digital clock that lit up when you tapped it. It glowed dimly and emitted a faint electronic whine. Waking, I would feel pleased that I knew what time it was even before checking, as if this little achievement cancelled out the defeat of needing to wake so often.

Wearing just a T-shirt, I shivered barefoot down the stone stairs. Only the dog would see me. A Border collie. His basket almost blocks the bathroom door. Invariably, he opens an eye as I step over him. What did he think, I wondered, about me getting up so often, leaning on the wall over the loo to pee?

Then there was the question of whether to flush. Six times three hundred and sixty-five would be two thousand one hundred and ninety flushes in a year. That's a lot of water in a country with over-stretched resources. I let the bowl stew till around five. No one would be using the bathroom before six.

You're becoming a creature of the night, I thought, climbing the stairs again. You and the dog. Sometimes, I rather liked this feeling of making the small hours present, being around when no one else was. My mental life was changing. In bed, I could lie and think about what I was writing. I had learned not to worry about sleep; it always came. Thoughts were richer and more bizarre in the night, rarely useful if remembered in the morning, but more pleasurable. Almost a sensual pleasure. Rousseau was constantly pushing catheters into his penis, I remembered. To pass his stones. He writes about it in the *Confessions*. At one point he bought a lifetime's supply of catheters. At least I had been spared that. Montaigne also suffered from stones. Was it something to do with writing in French?

In the second half of the night the dreams came. I dreamed my wife and I were walking through Verona by the river, but the water had dried up, there was only a muddy trickle, and the solid bourgeois *palazzi* along each bank turned out to be built on wooden stilts rotting in the sludge.

At five the pain woke me. It was ferocious. I went downstairs, peed again, flushed the smell away, ate my cereal, and once again got on the net to look up *cellule uroteliali* and *strutture papillari*, *nucleo ipercromico*. I had taken urine samples to the hospital three days running. They had centrifuged the samples and carried out a cytological analysis. There were precancerous anomalies.

'Could be anything or nothing,' the lady doing the ultrasound scan said. 'Let's see what we can see.'

I was paying privately now. This *dottoressa* was the only person in Milan whose scans he and his colleagues trusted, Carlo had told me. She slid the scanner slowly across Vaseline on my stomach and I asked her if she saw a lot of cases like mine.

'Sure, lots of guys your age. It's standard stuff.'

She was in her mid fifties, grey-haired, a small pouty mouth, pretty.

I asked her if she noticed similarities between the men she saw with these symptoms. She worked while we talked. Her right hand moved the instrument back and forth across my belly in sweeps, some fast, some slow, halting a moment, then off again, searching, intent; her eyes were focused away from me on a computer screen. The left hand tapped on a keyboard. She was concentrating. I could just glimpse phantom shapes in a dark turbulence on the screen.

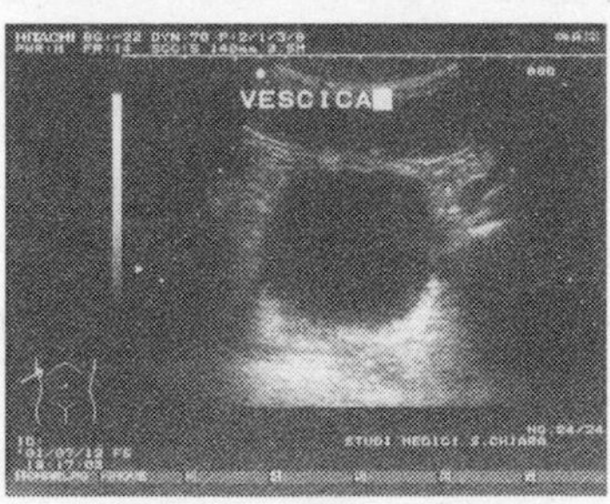

'Well, they are all *busy* people,' she said. 'It's always difficult to make appointments. Now, if you could go and pass water, please.'

I went to the bathroom, peed and came back. She was

clicking through images on the screen, making notes.

'That was quick,' she observed.

'Quick?'

'Too quick. Go back and finish. I have to measure how well the bladder voids. It won't be empty yet.'

I had peed my normal pee with no impression at all of having hurried. Obedient but sceptical, I went back to the loo and found that, though I had no impulse, there was still a fair bit to go. Weird. She knew my body better than I did.

'Thirteen ccs,' she said. That's how much was in there now. 'It's nothing. You void fine.'

I was foolishly pleased, but then vaguely wondered if she hadn't been cheating sending me back again. Did that mean I could always pee more when I thought I'd finished? I also wondered if she would be candid with me if a tumour appeared on her screen. In a kidney perhaps. But I wasn't going to put her on the spot by asking. It would all be in the results.

I waited while she pressed the scanner lower down my belly, then thought, why not put her on the spot? Why this heavy silence around illness? I was paying. It was my body.

'So where are the tumours?'

She smiled. 'Hiding so far.' She understood my mood exactly. 'If there is something, it's probably in the bladder wall. You'll need a cystoscopy to see that.'

I had to turn on my side and pull my underwear down. She switched instruments for the anal scan. It's strange how we let these things be done to us, casually, as if they happened every day. I tensed.

'Relax.' She pushed the thing in.

'The doctors think I need the TURP,' I said.

I stared at a glass cabinet full of small white boxes. The word TURP, I thought, seemed to give the operation an acrid turpentine smell. She said nothing. I was sent to the bathroom to wipe off the Vaseline. When I came back she was sectioning shadows on the screen and measuring them. If I would wait five minutes outside, she said, she would type out her report. I could then take it to my doctor for his assessment.

'Just tell me straight,' I asked. 'I won't understand the medical stuff.'

She frowned at the screen. 'The prostate isn't enlarged at all, actually it's rather small for a man of your age. All I can see is some faint calcification. Within the norm.'

Not enlarged! It must be cancer then, I thought. In the bladder wall. That was the rock in my belly, the constant, nagging pain. All the same, I was oddly pleased that the 'official medical version' had been proved wrong.

I called Carlo. 'Afraid not!' he laughed. 'The prostate can be small, but fibrous inside round the urethra. It's complicated. We have to wait till all the tests are done. Then I'll send you to the best surgeon.'

About a week later, I had a disquieting experience in a restaurant. A university colleague and I had invited a visiting professor to dinner. We had been sitting together talking about translation, the subject I teach. The visitor was American, a real academic with a penchant for Walter Benjamin and Derrida. He grew earnest, insisting on what he saw as a deterritorialisation of the signifier despite the essential stability of the signified in a shifting translingual pattern of *différance*, doing his best to emphasise the anomalous 'a'. Edoardo and I encouraged him to eat *ossobuco*, the local speciality, and he did, but without interrupting his description of the various projects he had in hand. He was balding, bulky and intensely solemn, to the point that I began to wonder whether he had noticed what was on his plate at all. He ate with embarrassing, almost infantile appetite, but his mind was entirely taken with himself and his *différance*. Edoardo, who is slim and elegant, smiled politely, occasionally trying to change the subject. I stood up and announced I had to go to the bathroom.

Since the experience with the ultrasound doctor, I had been trying to slow down my peeing, waiting a while after finishing to see if there was more. Naturally, my hope was that this little encore would reduce the number of times I had to go. It didn't. Apparently there was no relation between the quantity I needed to pee and the impulse to go. So what difference would it make, I wondered, if they 'cored me from the inside', and I 'emptied better', as Carlo had put it? I walked through this rather quaint Milanese *osteria*, found the bathroom, turned on the light, went in and locked the door. The pee was slow in coming. When I'd finished I waited a little more and . . .

The light went out.

It must be on a time switch. I was in the dark. There wasn't so much as a chink. And the switch, I now recalled, was on the *outside*. Obviously they didn't want people hanging around in the loo, shooting up, masturbating, making love. But had I really taken so long? I zipped up, turned, and found I couldn't locate the door. I banged into a washbasin. The corridor light must be off too. There was no window, just a vent humming, sounds of dishes and footsteps, but distant. It was pitch black. Talk about deterritorialisation. I reached out to feel the wall and, as my hands met first a tiled surface, then plaster, then a pipe, I felt intensely present, intensely aware of being alive, here, right now, in this idiotic situation, stuck in the loo in the dark.

I still couldn't find the door. Would I have to yell? How foolish I would seem!

Then I had the door, but couldn't find the lock. What kind

of lock? I couldn't remember. A latch? I started to feel panicky, as when you go upside down in your kayak in a rapid and you can't roll up and then can't find the tab to pull your spray deck and escape. You only have so long. The length of this breath.

Got it. I'd been looking on the left of the door instead of the right. There was a small button that turned inside a knob. I pulled the door open and at once was immersed in normality. Food smells, laughter, warm air, photos of Milan in the '30s. How wonderful. Forget hand-washing, though. I hurried past a full-breasted woman leaning across a table. A waiter winked. It was so convivial! Just as I sat down the American pronounced with great indignation: 'People really don't want to accept that the language they live in is only one of many possible worlds.' He hadn't noticed I'd been away too long. Edoardo was nodding. I poured myself a glass of wine and drained it in a gulp. This is what it will be like, I thought, if I ever return from illness. Nobody will have noticed I was ever away.

Remember Life?

'Signor Pax, could you just tell us whether you need to pass water or not?'

There was a note of exasperation in the young doctor's voice.

What struck me, on my back under a huge grey X-ray machine, was the distance between the medical staff and myself; however sophisticated their equipment, they were a million miles away from the stewing confusion in the organs they were photographing, the mesh of unease inside my head. Perhaps they were a million miles away because of the equipment.

'Signor Pax…'

'No, I can't tell you,' I snapped. 'And if I could, I wouldn't be here.'

One of the pretty nurses almost giggled and had to turn away with her hand over her mouth. Or maybe she'd just had enough of looking at my nether parts.

The urogram is one of those medical tests of which one says, if you're not feeling ill before, you will be afterwards. But I *was* feeling ill before. The previous week, on a promotional trip to Germany, I had barely been able to sit through the evening presentations. The pain was hot, fierce, constant. I needed to walk. I couldn't concentrate on the public's questions. I simply had to *move*. Released, I hurried outside to find a freezing wind and slushy snow that swamped my shoes.

Frankfurt was cold and gritty and full of building sites. And I felt worse. For the first time walking was as painful as sitting. You're a zombie, I told myself. The only thing to do was to finish these tests and let the doctors operate.

Do it. Get it over with.

The urogram is a series of X-rays of the abdominal area. After the first pictures of your belly as it ordinarily is, they fill you with a radioactive contrast medium by intravenous drip so that the X-rays can record the liquid's passage through kidneys, bladder and urethra. The day before the test you have to take a laxative, then eat nothing afterwards. The intestine must be empty.

This punitive preparation guarantees you arrive stressed. While Rita and the girls were eating roast chicken the evening before, I was sitting in front of an oily, lemony-tasting electrolyte. Two litres of it. An hour earlier, the first mouthful had seemed almost pleasant but after a pint or so the stuff grew sickly, heavy. It was physically hard to force it down.

Retiring to the bathroom, still with a full jug of laxative to get through, I took the cordless with me. I phoned Carlo to thank him for making the appointment at the hospital. He wouldn't be around personally, he said, but he would arrange for the hospital's best surgeon to meet me afterwards to look over the results together. 'Actually the best surgeon in Italy,' he added. 'Bar myself of course!'

In my bowels something dissolved.

On impulse, why?, I phoned Mum in London. She was in a cheerful mood despite her breast cancer which we didn't mention. Your mum is much worse off than you are, I thought. People all over the world were far worse off.

The door handle rattled as one of my daughters tried to burst in. I covered the mouthpiece to yell out my presence.

'Nothing serious, love?' Mum asked jollily.

'I was thinking about Dad.'

There was a silence.

'I just wondered if he ever had problems, with needing to go to the bathroom a lot at night.'

'Oh.'

Mum thought about it in her tiny London terraced house, a sort of bed-sit on two floors.

'He did go to the toilet a lot when he was nervous.' She added, 'Like all men, I suppose. Is there anything the matter, love?'

Tectonic plates shifted in my fundament.

I told Mum it was probably just a phase. Why on earth had I chosen to call her at this of all moments? I hung up and spent a truly unpleasant hour emptying my gut. Laxatives are unnatural, I decided. Passing water through your anus is extremely unnatural.

Towards nine, when it was all done and I'd cleaned up, I went downstairs and Googled 'urograms' to find out exactly what was in store for me at the hospital. Almost at once I turned up a research study claiming that 'laxative preparation does not improve imaging during intravenous urography. Radiology departments still requiring laxative administration prior to the urogram are not practising evidence-based medicine.'

It was not encouraging.

Around eleven the following morning, I lay down on a thin mattress beneath a monster of an X-ray machine while a nurse set up a drip with the iodine contrast medium, then strapped a thick belt over me. She pulled it tight. Then tighter.

'To keep the fluid concentrated in your kidneys while we X-ray, we have to compress the lower abdomen.'

'It has to hurt, I'm afraid,' an older doctor chipped in.

'It's doing its job,' I assured him.

The photo shoot began. Every time they took an X-ray, all four staff scurried to a door behind me and watched through a glass screen. X-rays are dangerous of course. After half an hour, the belt was released and I was sent off to walk around, 'until you're ready to pass water, Signor Pax'.

The problem was the word 'ready'. I was already dying to go. There was a festering heat down there that might erupt at any moment. After ten minutes I hurried back only to be told that I couldn't possibly be 'ready' yet. Anyway, they had another patient.

'You won't be ready for at least an hour,' the assistant doctor said rather sternly, over-pronouncing as a concession to my foreignness.

All the same I felt desperate to go.

'Walk around,' they said. 'Relax.'

The imperative 'relax', like the over-pronunciation for foreigners, is something that drives me crazy.

I walked. The hospital has a main block and two wings, each with dauntingly long corridors. The walls are a light grey, the floors, blue linoleum, the lighting an insomniac fluorescence. Hospital staff hurry by in white coats, green trousers, clogs. Less sure of themselves, patients and visitors stare at signs: Oncology, 5th floor, west wing; Cardiology, 2nd floor, main block. The body is divided up into floors and wings. The vital organs are kept well apart. People lose their way in between, clutching large yellow envelopes with technical information about their innards, much as they might clutch VAT returns and invoices at the tax office. All in all there is little to distinguish the place from other government buildings. It's not a house of reassurance or healing; not if by healing we mean wholeness. It's a grand industrial and bureaucratic enterprise. You come here to get your body serviced, to have bits removed, prostheses installed, medicines administered, in the separate and appropriate parts of the building. How could it be otherwise? There's a queue at the window for making appointments, another queue for collecting results, another queue for paying. Here and there, rows of chairs have been bolted to the floor. A young man is sitting with his head in his hands.

They had told me I could have a coffee, so I went to the cafeteria. The big window panes were steamy against the cool air outside. It was overcrowded but friendly. I sat down, found it too painful and drank standing at the counter, watching MTV. The volume was so low you could hardly hear the beat that three girls were moving to. Their gestures were elaborately erotic, their clothes spectacularly impractical. I gazed, amused and perplexed. The girls gyrated and shook. The body has become a parody of the body, I thought. This dance was a spoof of sexual allure. All around me people's postures were neutralised, resigned, mechanical. On screen, the girls rehearsed a pantomime of exaggerated vitality. For money. They didn't care whether we believed in it. Remember life? their young hips said, Remember sex? What a joke!

To while away the rest of the hour I walked in the gardens, so called. A gravel path made aimless twists and turns between winter shrubs dwarfed by walls of illuminated windows. The benches were empty. The only other visitors advanced no further than the first frosty flowerbed. They had come out to smoke. The soil was littered with stubs. The vegetation was grey. This garden is no more than a *reminder* of gardens, I decided, just as the music video had been a harmless reminder of eroticism. The present is cytology, radiography, ultrasound, cigarettes, anxiety.

'Signor Pax, could you just tell us whether you actually *need* to pass water or not?'

I was on my back, squeezed under the X-ray machine again, but this time without my underwear. On my stomach I had what the Italians wonderfully call a *pappagallo*. Ordinarily, the word means parrot, but in this case it referred to a small white plastic urinal. 'Slip your penis, Signore, into the opening,' one of the nurses instructed me, 'then hold the parrot still with your left hand, but without blocking the photograph.'

'No, like this.'

She smiled as she reorganised my hands and genitals.

Once that was sorted, all I had to do was lie dead still and… pee. At that point the grey apparatus looming above me would take a snap of the contrast medium seeping its radioactive way through my iffy plumbing.

'*Siamo pronti*?'

The staff retreated.

'Just shout when you feel the urine coming, Signor Pax.'

At last. I had been waiting ninety minutes for this release. I had been praying for it. I pushed to pee.

Nothing.

Relax, push gently.

Nothing.

The minutes passed. Eventually a door opened and the radiologist's young assistant hurried over.

'Signor Pax, you can pass water now. Just shout when you're starting.'

He repeated the instruction, speaking more clearly. I could have killed him.

He retreated. Through the glass wall all eyes were on me. Evidently the star of the show, I tried to relax and pee. Nothing. The needing-to-pee pain remained exactly as it was, a boiling swamp in the bladder. But nothing budged.

The young doctor came back.

'Signor Pax, could you just tell us whether you actually

need to pass water or not. We are behind with our schedule.'

'I beg your pardon?'

'We are behind schedule and—'

'No.'

He looked at me. There were a couple of days of dark beard on his cheeks.

'No, I can't tell you whether I need to pee.'

He looked perplexed.

'I don't know,' I repeated.

'Signor Pax, perhaps—'

'Do you actually realise why I'm here?' I asked. 'I presume they told you what my symptoms are.'

'Signor Pax—'

'If you had read the referral papers you'd understand that most of the time *I have no idea at all* whether I "need" to pass water or not, OK? Nor whether, needing to, I can. If I knew those things, I wouldn't be here. I'd be happy, perfectly happy.'

Even as I was indulging in this shameful sarcasm, I was acutely aware that the real object of my anger was my body.

The older radiologist came over and explained that we are all taught from earliest age not to urinate while lying down on our backs. 'It's just a psychological block,' he said. He would turn a tap on. The sound of running water would help.

If ever there's a myth, it's that the sound of running water helps you to pee. I now felt a complete invalid, and criminally crotchety to boot. My tackle, I'm sad to say, looked pathetic, lolling limp and wrinkled on the rim of the white plastic urinal.

Not that anyone was interested.

'Just give me time,' I said.

We tried again. The doctors ran off behind their screen, I concentrated and pushed and waited and pushed and tried to relax and waited and pushed and… at the first hot feel of pee arriving, yelled, '*Viene!*' Coming.

As if we were making love.

Exactly as the X-ray machined buzzed, the pee stopped. We had wasted an expensive photographic plate.

The rigmarole began again.

'As many times as it takes,' the radiologist reassured me.

And again.

The pee wouldn't come.

The radiologist shook his head. 'We'll have to try standing up, Signor Pax.'

As I swung my legs off the table, I heard one of the nurses explaining to another that I was a personal friend of one of the doctors in urology.

They stood me up against a white plastic curtain and started setting up a machine to photograph me front on. Meantime, I was supposed to drink glass after glass of water to 'keep things moving'. After a few minutes it occurred to one of the nurses to bring me a towel to cover myself. She smiled. I smiled back. Then at last something eased, something opened. I peed – oh not spectacularly, nothing to be proud of, but I produced the goods, they got their photo.

'All's well that ends well,' the radiologist laughed.

'All's well that ends,' I replied.

No sooner was I out of the X-ray room than I stopped at the first bathroom and peed at least as much again.

At ten past two I met my designated surgeon, a lean, dark, earnest man with disquietingly prominent veins on wrists and neck. Together we went to the radiography viewing room where he introduced me to the head of radiography, a Romanian in his late forties.

'Stefan, this is Tim,' my surgeon said, 'Carlo's friend.' As if this relationship explained everything. To me in a low voice, the doctor muttered: 'This man is brilliant, probably the finest radiologist in Europe.'

Despite being anxious to know the worst, I couldn't help but be amused by how Italian all this was. The surgeon was the best surgeon in Italy, the radiologist the best radiologist in Europe. And by purest chance we were all the best of friends.

Let's hope it was true.

The big grey X-ray plates were slid up onto the illuminated viewing panels. It was rather eerie. My body had been reduced to the two-dimensional black-and-white of the biology-book illustration. I could study myself as a separate phenomenon.

Or I would have been able to, if they had given me time enough to understand what I was looking at. No sooner had he put up one plate than Stefan was taking it down again with barely a glance. The surgeon wasn't even looking, but reading through the radiologist's typed report. I wondered how much detail the brilliant Stefan could be seeing. One image followed another. Filled with contrast medium, the kidneys floated up like white lilies in a weedy underwater of muscle and bone.

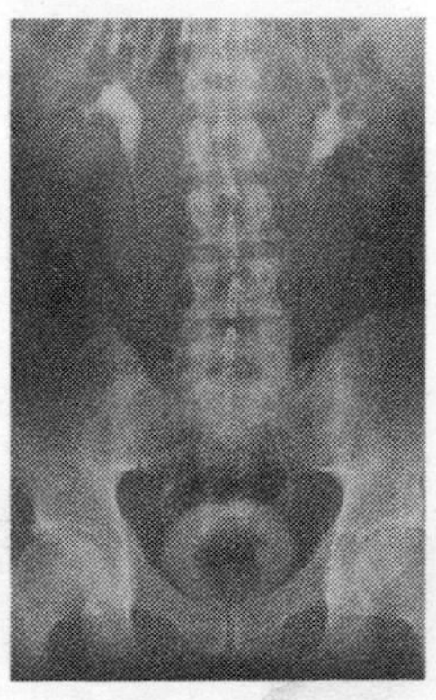

'These next ones are where you're passing water,' the surgeon said.

Now he was paying attention. The two men gazed at length at five small plates, arranged one beside another; Stefan took a pen to follow the line of the urethra in each.

'Marked restriction at the sphincter,' the surgeon observed, 'and narrow through the prostate.'

The radiology man didn't reply. He took a magnifying glass to examine one of the images.

Neither of them invited me to look at the points in question.

Stefan shrugged. 'Nothing dramatic.'

'Since we're only getting two dimensions,' I suggested, 'couldn't it be that the urethra is pinched along the plane we're looking at, but not in the other dimension, if you get me?'

Nobody replied.

'Calcification in the prostate,' the surgeon remarked.

Stefan smiled and took down the plates, shaking his head. 'Nothing,' he announced. '*Niente di niente di niente*.' He had a strong accent. 'If Signor Tim had no symptoms, I would say from these X-rays he was perfectly fine.'

A Tussle in the Mind

Language splits the world up into thousands of discrete units, then puts them back together again in unexpected ways. In a hotel in Agra, Uttar Pradesh, I was thinking about the word psychosomatic.

I had come to India for ten days to talk at a conference in Delhi on storytelling and translation. By the time I appreciated that my approach to the subject was not welcome it was too late. For more than a century now, I said from the podium, writers had been suspicious of the values encoded in their languages and in the kind of stories people told each other. They altered the stories to expose convention, they forced words into surprising combinations to challenge the unthinking conformity of their languages. That was the modern novel. But the translator's culture was constituted with different stories, his language was a different straitjacket. How could you translate Lawrence's description of Gudrun's mental state after lovemaking – 'She was destroyed into perfect consciousness' – in a language where consciousness did not have the strong positive connotations it had developed in the West. The provocation would be lost. How can you convey the strangeness of 'destroyed *into*', if in your culture nothing is ever truly destroyed, but only transformed?

As the public began to ask perplexed and indignant questions, I realised that in India people were wonderfully excited by translation, by becoming part of a globalised world where everyone reads everyone else's books and imagines they're getting the real thing. They didn't want to hear my cavils. Perhaps they weren't obsessed, as I was, by the problem of being inside or outside a particular story. The one about the operating table, for example. Talking to one of the organisers after the presentation, I found myself asking if she could direct me to a respectable ayurvedic doctor.

'They are all respectable, as far as I know,' she said and gave me the phone number of a friend who used such a doctor.

India was decidedly cooler than I had expected. I hadn't realised that Delhi had a winter. Incongruously wearing a sweater beneath a linen jacket, I sat in an auto-rickshaw as it fought its way across town. Finding a goat or a cow in the road is normal here, I realised. Here, you would have to slip rather different spanners into the works to bounce people out of their mental routines. What was I doing, consulting an ayurvedic doctor, if not trying to bounce myself out of my medical dilemma? I had never given any credence whatsoever to alternative medicines. I prided myself on being rational, sceptical, modern and Western. I believed in *evidence-based medicine*. I had always made fun of homeopathy, aromatherapy, crystal healing and the like. It would never have occurred to me, I realised, to consult someone like this, if I weren't, by the merest chance, in India, if there wasn't the excuse of the travel-writer's curiosity. I hesitated for some time before pressing Dr Hazan's bell.

It took me a while to tell the whole story. The doctor wore a shirt and tie and listened attentively; his wife and secretary (thus he introduced her) was sitting beside him.

'So, the urologist still wants to operate on me, but having heard the radiologist's comment on the urogram I'm not convinced. There's no evidence that there's anything wrong with the prostate at all. On the other hand, the symptoms are getting worse. The only test still to do is the exploration of the bladder. For cancer.'

The wife nodded, making notes. She was modest, attractive, wearing Western clothes. Dr Hazan waited some moments before responding. Had I seen him in the street, I would have imagined he was a young executive in one of Delhi's booming software companies.

'Well, for immediate relief, we could address the symptoms,' he eventually began. 'For that I would prescribe an enema of sesame oil and various herbs to be held in the colon for as long as you can manage, certainly not less than forty minutes.'

I was silent.

'On the other hand…' He sat back and looked me in the eyes. His face was frank. 'This is a problem you will never get over, Mr Parks, until you confront the profound contradiction in your character.'

I can't recall being more surprised by a single remark in all my life.

'Ah,' I said at last.

'There is a tussle in your mind.'

I sat still. I had wanted a different story, to challenge the 'official medical version'. I was getting it.

'What actually causes all this pain?' I asked.

'It is blocked *vata*.'

'That is an energy that flows in the body,' his wife explained. 'One of the five elements. It balances others and needs to be balanced by them. When the balance goes wrong, then the *vata* is blocked and causes pain.'

'It is this mental tussle that blocks the *vata*,' the doctor said.

I reflected. 'So, what is the tussle about?'

'Good question!' The doctor smiled.

'A tussle like this is not really *about* anything,' his wife explained. 'It is part of the *prakruti*.'

They began to explain what *prakruti* was: the amalgamation of inherited and acquired traits coming together to form the personality. If those traits were at odds and the two couldn't mix, you'd be in trouble.

'In that case a person may get the impression that his life is a series of dilemmas. He may think: If only I could resolve this or that dilemma, I will have resolved my problems. But each dilemma is a only a manifestation of the deeper conflict.'

It was an elaborate theory.

'Let's assume that you are right,' I said. 'How would one go about, er, sorting out something like that?'

I sensed as I spoke that 'go about' and 'sorting out' were the wrong terms. Somebody who knew ayurvedic medicine would not have used them.

Dr Hazan was weighing me up. 'There is no prescribed cure, as such. It is hard to treat the *prakruti*. But a good way to start would be with a birth chart.'

I had noticed some publications on astrology in the waiting room. The doctor could see my scepticism.

'You don't believe in our connections with the stars, Mr Parks?'

I shook my head.

'It is a shame. I have been able to help many people in that way.'

He began to explain that one of his specialities was helping businessmen with dilemmas: perhaps a man has been trained in one field but is offered an interesting job in another. He doesn't know what to do.

'That sounds more like a question of convenience and good sense.'

'To you, perhaps, yes. But he doesn't experience his dilemma like that. For him it goes deep. It threatens his health.'

There was a silence. Astrology was a bridge too far for me. I was eager for new stories, but they had to be stories I could believe in, or at least such that I could suspend disbelief.

'Let's go back to the physical side.' But I stopped myself: 'Or are you telling me it's entirely psychosomatic?'

A slow smile spread across the doctor's face. 'That's not a word we have much use for, Mr Parks.'

I looked at him.

'You only say *psychosomatic*,' his wife explained, 'if you think that body and mind are ever separate.'

It was a fair point. 'Diet then,' I said. 'Could it have to do with diet?'

The doctor laughed openly now. But when I told him what I was eating he grew more reflective.

'It is difficult without getting to know you better,' he said. 'I mean without understanding the balance of the various elements in your body. But looking at you, listening to you, I would say you should eat less raw food, less salad, more cooked vegetables. And, in general, you should eat *more*.'

'The last thing I need is to get fat.'

'I have the impression that at present you are starving yourself.'

'Not at all. My weight is more or less what's recommended for my height and age.'

'We have that impression,' the wife confirmed.

I wondered if they always shared the same view of their patients. They seemed very sure of themselves. I couldn't imagine my own wife and I reaching the same opinion about anyone, never mind a person we had only known for half an hour.

'Masturbation can be an important factor with these kinds of pains,' the doctor said.

Again I was surprised. It was the ease with which he introduced the subject. The Harley Street doctor, years ago, had warmly recommended the habit while carefully avoiding the word. Hazan's wife seemed relaxed.

'Tell me.'

The doctor began to say that recently he had treated another man with similar problems. A man much younger than myself. In his late twenties.

'He had all kinds of worries. About his life and his job. His *prakruti* was very troubled. He had split up with his girlfriend, he wasn't seeing a woman; when I questioned him, he admitted he was masturbating very frequently.'

I waited.

'When I suggested to him he should get over that, he found it helpful.'

I asked, 'As you see it, Doctor, how often is very frequently?'

'As often as twice a week,' the doctor said.

Now it was my turn to laugh. 'I'm sorry,' I shook my head, 'but for a man in his twenties, without a girlfriend, even twice a day would hardly be considered excessive, in the West. A Western urologist would have told him he wasn't masturbating enough.'

The doctor wasn't put out. 'Perhaps our worlds are so different in their assumptions that it is difficult for me to advise you. But...' he reflected, 'what matters is not really how often someone masturbates, but in what spirit.'

I listened.

'When a boy or young man is naturally moved to masturbation from excess of vitality, this is normal and healthy. His physical energies must find a release. But if a man constantly works himself up, neurotically as it were, because he is unhappy, because something is missing, then his masturbation will upset the balance of elements in his body and his *vata* may becomc blocked.'

Here it seemed to me that Delhi was making more sense than Harley Street.

The doctor now spoke to his wife in Hindi. She stood up, went to a cabinet full of small drawers and began to make up two small polythene bags of pills. The doctor was writing a prescription. 'These herbs may be a help for the pain you have,' he explained. 'I have written down dosage and instructions. In case you wish to pursue a serious treatment, I shall give you my card with our email address. We can send birth chart, advice and medicines to Italy with no problem. We supply many people in Europe.'

The translation conference had three more days to run, but the meeting with the doctor and his wife had captured my mind and I found it hard to concentrate on what my colleagues were saying. If you were born and brought up, I thought, in a family that had always been into ayurvedic medicine (which after all only means Knowledge of Health), this story of *vata* and *prakruti*, inherited and acquired characteristics, would all make sense. You would do your birth chart, you would ponder the position of the stars, who you were originally, what you have become, and react accordingly. And you would be able to distinguish this ayurvedic doctor from others, know which school of thought he was coming from, how he compared. As it was, the unfamiliar words and explanations I had heard soon fell away; just two remarks continued to echo in my mind: 'You will never overcome this problem, Mr Parks, until you confront the profound contradiction in your character.' What was it in me that had prompted the doctor to make that observation? Then his wife's comment a few moments later: 'You only say psychosomatic if you think that body and mind are ever separate.'

Since I had a day and a half free when the conference was over, I arranged for a driver to take me to Agra so I could see the Taj Mahal. The man was a Sikh, burly and brazen. About halfway along the road I asked him if he could show me a small village since so far I had only seen Delhi. He found a dirt track and, waiting at a level crossing, we were besieged by beggars. The driver had his window down waving them away. At a certain point, when a small child was particularly insistent, he yanked his shorts down and tried to grab his tiny prick. The child was away like lightning. The driver laughed. 'Pretty boy,' he said. Then we drove up to a temple that marked the birth place of Krishna. It was strange to see religious images with brightly coloured clothes and big grins stamped on lacquered lips. One is so used to Christ suffering on his cross, the martyred saints. The driver pointed to some tall barbed-wire fencing, armed men in uniform and a mosque about two hundred yards away. 'For the Muslims too this is a holy place,' he said. 'There has been a lot of fighting.'

Why, I wondered, in bed that evening, did almost everything I heard and saw seem obscurely relevant to my condition? I kept recalling the young boy's perfect body as he wriggled from the driver's heavy hand.

The sheets were damp. We had arrived in Agra at nightfall to find the town under thick fog. The Sikh's car had no heating and my hands and feet froze. Mostly unlit, the streets were a ghostly play of headlights, cooking fires and dense bluish shadow. The major hotels were full. There was a festival of some kind. My driver found a small place with a damp room and a loo that didn't flush. I had to pile more or less everything in the room onto the bed to get warm. Suitcase, pillows, floor mat. How strange this was, in India. Yet I felt oddly cheerful.

Dr Hazan's wife was right, I reflected, when she said that only a culture that tried to keep body and mind separate would need to use a word like psychosomatic. To put Humpty together again. And this word was always associated with sickness, in particular the sort of sneaky, stubborn sickness that Western medicine can't cure. So body and mind are only one when the anxious mind makes the body-machine ill. Or makes it think it is ill. Or makes the mind think that the body is ill. When actually it isn't. And because it isn't really ill the doctor can wash his hands of it, or send you to a psychiatrist. 'If Signor Tim had no symptoms,' the radiologist had concluded, 'I'd say he was fine.'

The fact that your condition is psychosomatic, I told myself – and it seemed amazing to me that my feet could be so cold in India – is amply demonstrated by the way it never really stops you from working or doing the things you want to do. You talk about chronic pain but you always deliver your books on time. You travel to Milan every week to teach. The lessons are two hours long but you never have to go out to the bathroom. You never miss a book presentation. You accept invitations to Germany and even to India, you eat and drink healthily and you fulfil all your obligations. *Obviously* your condition is psychosomatic. Why else would I spend time trying to find obscure significance in a painting by Velázquez while feeling mainly indifferent to the results of blood and urine tests?

On the other hand, one frequently reads of people who keep working, keep pretending there is nothing wrong with them, then drop down dead.

Every time I got up to go to the loo that wouldn't flush – but perhaps the filthy bucket had been put there to flush it – I had to rearrange the suitcase and pillows and floor mat on my legs in the hope that the circulation would finally come back. Could cold feet, I wondered, also be psychosomatic? And if my condition was psychosomatic did that mean that there was *absolutely nothing wrong with me*, or, on the contrary, that my mind had somehow created *a genuine physical condition*, even if it wasn't showing up very clearly on the medical radar.

That said, of course, it was still possible that the cystoscopy would reveal that the inner wall of my bladder was riddled with cancer. Then everything would be clear. Actually, following Sherlock Holmes's assumption that once you've drawn a blank with the most likely solutions the answer to a puzzle must be the one explanation, however improbable, that remains, I ought to be terrified.

Every now and then, as I lay waiting for my feet to warm, a loud humming started up, rattling the thin panes of the window. It was the hotel's electricity generator clicking in when the mains went down. Each time it began the sound shocked me a little, sending a sudden strong pulse throbbing through my body. My father had also been extremely sensitive to noise. He could hear the faintest of sounds very far away, as indeed can I. One evening, as a child, when I told him that the living-room clock was ticking more loudly than usual, he immediately said: 'That means you have a temperature, my lad.' He liked to call me my lad. And he was right. I had a high temperature and was packed off to bed. After he died, as I was the only child living close by, I was made executor of his will, and thus discovered that for some years he had been making a regular donation to the Noise Abatement Society, this despite leaving less than 2,000 pounds in assets and having always given his tithe to the church. My mother used to get upset, I remembered, when people would suggest that cancer 'had a psychosomatic element'. 'As if it were Dad's fault he was ill!' she protested. Having never touched a cigarette, he died of lung cancer at sixty.

The generator fell silent. What a pleasure sudden silence is, as when a harsh light goes out and your eyes can attune to the friendly dark. I picked up faint noises of plumbing, cries from the street, and I reflected that most people feel ashamed if told their problem is psychosomatic. They feel accused, guilty. It's acceptable to have a sick body, that's not your fault, but not a sick mind. The mind is you, the body is only yours. Choosing to go to an analyst because you're unhappy is another matter. There is a respectability about being unhappy in a complicated way and most people would agree that to recognise you need professional help shows humility and good sense. But someone who makes his body ill because *he doesn't want to acknowledge his mind is in trouble*, because he's repressing his fears and desires and conflicts, is just a loser.

At exactly the moment I formulated this view, I realised that I was actually extremely eager for my problems to be psychosomatic. I was more than willing to countenance the idea that my pains only existed in my head, or that trouble in my head had brought them into existence in my body. I want to change, I told myself, returning from the bathroom. Why else would I have gone to an ayurvedic doctor? I want *everything* to change, inside me.

The following morning I felt let down by the Taj Mahal

with its determined whiteness and oppressive symmetry. It was too much the photos I had seen of it, enclosed and regimented and wilful. But the view of the Yamuna from behind the Taj remains to this day one of the most powerful images I have of India. You lean on a parapet and look down. The river is a few hundred yards away, slowly meandering across a broad brown floodplain. Beyond, low hills stretch into emptiness. From left to right, nothing obstructs the eye as it follows the stream's wintry drift through a sea of sand. The sun was hazily bright that day and here and there spots of intense colour marked where women were turning the soil for springtime. Very slowly, three camels forded the stream.

Experiments with Truth

You unzip your fly, point your penis to the bowl and out flows a stream of dark blood. This happened to me sometime in my early forties; I did not suppose it to be psychosomatic. I had been out running on a stifling July afternoon. The temperature was in the thirties. Climbing the hills, I could barely breathe. Back home, I took a shower, dried off, then went to pee. The deep dark red electrified me.

I stood and stared, then called the doctor at once. Discomfort, even pain, I might ignore for years, but blood propelled me to the phone.

'How much water did you drink before running?' the doctor asked.

I couldn't recall.

'And you didn't take a bottle of water with you?'

I hate carrying water. I hate the way it sloshes at every step.

'Dehydration can do this,' the doctor said. 'If there's a serious problem, you'll see blood frequently. If not, just remember to drink enough before running. And don't go when it's too hot. Why punish yourself?'

It's curious that despite all my efforts, in that miserable winter of '05–'06, to trace my problems back to their origin, I didn't recall this particular experience until, following the cystoscopy, I went to the bathroom for the first time and tried to pee. How long life has been, it occurred to me then, seeing the bowl once more splash red! You try to structure it in a story that will hold all your experiences together, but so much is left out and forgotten. The blood that July afternoon of years ago had been a ten-minute fright. I had put it aside, forgotten it, a random incident that had nothing to do with the main plot. Would it ever be possible, I wondered, to say the same of these stupid pains that plagued me now?

Flying home from Delhi, I had been very aware that within forty-eight hours of landing I would be anaesthetised in hospital with a rigid instrument skewered through my penis. 'About as thick as a pencil,' one website had said. At least it's the last experiment and we'll have the final truth, I thought.

In the corridor seat I'd asked for, near the bathroom, I read Gandhi's autobiography, appropriately entitled *The Story of My Experiments with Truth*. Since I was visiting India it had seemed right to read Gandhi. I was struck by the book's obsessive references to diet. Gandhi seemed to remember what he'd eaten, or more often hadn't eaten, every day of his life. 'Soon after this,' runs a typical sentence, 'I decided to live on a pure fruit diet, using only the cheapest fruit possible.' He imposed these regimes on those around him, his long-suffering wife in particular. No meat, no eggs, no alcohol, no salt, no cereals, no food at all after sundown.

The autobiography is also unusually up front about embarrassing ailments. 'As a result of the attack of dysentery [brought on by eating groundnut butter] my anal tract had become extremely tender, and owing to fissures I felt an excruciating pain at the time of evacuation, so that the very idea of eating filled me with dread.'

This unhappy situation creates a dilemma: should Gandhi accept his doctor's advice and drink goat's milk to build up his strength, or should he hold true to his vow never to drink milk again, a promise made in reaction to the cruel way cows and buffaloes are treated. In the end, he drinks the goat's milk and recovers, then bitterly regrets it. What betrayed him, he reflects, was the 'subtle temptation of service'; he was too eager to serve his fellow men to allow himself to die.

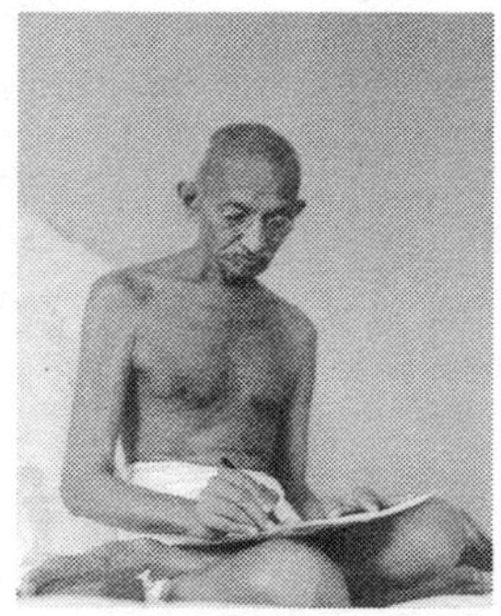

I puzzled over this strange story as the plane made its steady journey west: almost every aspect of Gandhi's relationship with his body became a means of imposing his will on others, yet he thought of himself as striving only for purity and universal love.

'The carnal mind,' he writes, 'always lusts for delicacies and luxuries … Instead of controlling the senses, it becomes their slave.'

So he rules out sex with his wife from age thirty-seven; she must also renounce her jewellery.

'I explained that it was always a good thing to join with others in any matter of self-denial.'

Accordingly, he doesn't allow a desperately sick child to be given meat broth. He doesn't allow his dying wife to be injected with antibiotics. Injections are impure. She dies.

Again and again, Gandhi uses the spectacle of his own

self-starvation to force his political enemies onto the back foot. The experiments with truth in the book's title often seem to involve searching for the most mortifying of diets, the one that will cause most concern in those around him. His enemies can't hit back because everyone agrees that self-denial is a positive quality that leads to purity. Meantime, Gandhi acknowledges his desire for service as a *temptation.* His only impurity is generosity.

'Carnal mind' was an odd construction, I thought, going back through the book to reread the sentences I'd underlined. Like 'psychosomatic' it blamed the mind for something going on in the body, in this case ordinary appetite rather than chronic pain; the mind rebels against its own yearnings and punishes, or purifies, itself through the body, to which it is ever superior.

Was this healthy?

Those ayurvedic doctors could say what they liked, I reflected, but my own dietary denials were laughable when compared with Gandhi's whom everybody admires. Nor were my experiments aimed at purification, a concept that meant nothing to me. I had simply hoped to identify some link between diet and pain. Certainly I never imposed my renunciations on others; and they would never have succumbed if I had. My wife, for example, eats far less than I do anyway and almost never the same things.

But was I in some subtle way using my ailments and dietary fussing to manipulate people, or at least to come across to them in a positive light? There are those, after all, who see eating disorders like anorexia as a way of controlling others by presenting a suffering, self-denying image.

No. I could not accuse myself of this. If anything I did my best to hide my troubles. On the plane I used three different bathrooms so as not to be seen going too often.

Approaching Rome in the early morning, I remembered a connection between Gandhi and Italy. In the early twentieth century, a certain Vinayak Savarkar had translated a biography of Giuseppe Mazzini, the Risorgimento revolutionary, into Marathi, formed a group called Young India (after Mazzini's Young Italy) and launched a campaign of violent insurrection against the Raj not unlike Mazzini's rebellion against the Austrian Empire. Gandhi responded to Savarkar by devoting a chapter of his manifesto *Hind Swaraj* to comparing India and Italy; he dwelt at length on Mazzini's love of humanity and presented him as a non-violent visionary who had redeemed his country by 'his strength of mind' and 'extreme devotion'. It was the warrior Garibaldi, Gandhi claimed, who, distorting Mazzini's pacifist message, had got involved in the Satanic business of shedding blood.

This was an outright lie and one that would have infuriated Mazzini who untiringly preached the virtues of violent action in a good cause and himself yearned for martyrdom in armed struggle. Gandhi must have known this; pacifism, then, was more important to him than truth. Yet Gandhi was right that Mazzini never shed blood. Blood frightened him. In his teens he had switched from studying medicine to law because he couldn't bear the dissection lessons. Later, every time he set out to join some revolutionary uprising – insurrections that he himself had instigated – he fell ill: lumbago, rheumatism, stomach pains. Psychosomatic stuff. He never made it to the field of battle, whereas the arthritic Garibaldi rode into the fray even when he had to be lifted on his horse and strapped to the saddle.

Gandhi, Mazzini, Garibaldi. I make no claims to being a positive force for change in the world, as these three great men no doubt were: on the other hand, I would never distort historical fact for ideological ends. Nor, try as I might, could

I see a connection between my bouts of illness and those duties I found onerous or frightening. I never used my condition to skip classes, or extend delivery deadlines, or even avoid domestic chores. I was in no less pain on days I was looking forward to and would enjoy, nor any greater pain on days I was dreading. If my troubles were psychosomatic, they were driven neither by phobia nor by megalomania.

On the train from the airport, I at last started worrying that it might not be psychosomatic at all. Which left only cancer.

The Difficult Target

I was to meet my surgeon in the urology ward on the fifth floor, then proceed to the operating theatre for the cystoscopy. He was busy when I arrived and to pass the time I studied a number of posters hung at intervals along the corridor advertising conferences. In each case, there was a title, a subtitle and an image to illustrate the topic. A crude cartoon of a dripping tap represented the problem of female incontinence. More imaginatively, a conference on erectile dysfunction was advertised with Magritte's painting *The Double Secret*: against the backdrop of a nondescript sea part of a man's face has been lifted off like a mask to reveal, inside the head, what seem to be bundles of bamboo with strangely split spherical joints. Evidently, male problems were more interesting than female, or sexual problems than urinary.

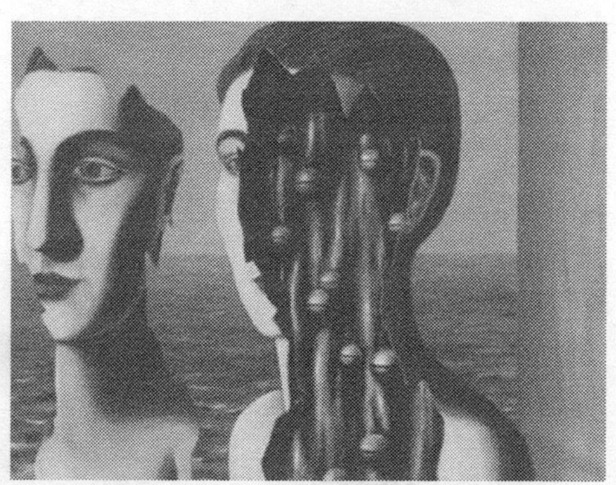

Magritte's face in this painting, it should be said, or rather, the face Magritte painted, is decidedly androgynous. How were the conference-goers to interpret that? In any event, there seemed no doubt that this ailment at least could be considered in intimate relationship with the psyche.

But the most disturbing of the posters referred to a conference entitled **LA PROSTATA: IL BERSAGLIO DIFFICILE**: the difficult target. To illustrate the idea, the poster presented a frontal outline of the male body with arms and legs outspread. At the crotch was a red bull's-eye with concentric yellow lines (of pain?) radiating outwards as far as the knees and the chest.

I was struck: the prostate, or prostatitis, was an enemy to aim at, an interesting enemy because hard to hunt down, like some devious terrorist who avoids open confrontation and holes up where he can't be got at. A military challenge.

My surgeon arrived and quite unexpectedly put a friendly arm round my shoulder. How wonderful Italy was, I thought, the way knowing just one person made a whole group of people so well disposed towards you, and protective. 'You do realise,' the doctor was saying, 'that if we wanted to I could burn out a bit of that prostate while I'm inserting the probe for the cystoscopy; and open up the sticky sphincter too, if you like. We use the same instrument for both jobs, you see. It would only add five or six minutes to proceedings and save you a second trip. What do you think? No more tests, no more anaesthetic. Get it over with.'

I was taken by surprise and reacted vehemently. 'No, No and no, *no*!'

'Ah, I just thought you ought to know that that is an option. It's a very simple procedure. While we are in there, so to speak.'

I turned to look him in the eyes. 'Absolutely not. OK? We're just looking, it's just a test.'

I was surprised by my own intensity.

'Don't worry!' The man was amused but taken aback, as if it was extraordinary that I should care so much.

You strip and put on a long white nightshirt, then half sit, half lie, on something that looks like a birth-chair with a plastic bowl beneath your butt to gather the blood. Everywhere there are straps and buckles to hold the work-piece – yourself – absolutely still so that radical things can be done to you. The thick smell of chemical cleanliness is one with gleaming surfaces and sharp tools. You surrender your body to their science.

I smiled and said hello to everyone.

'Good morning, Signor Pax,' someone said. 'How are we feeling this morning?'

While the team were setting up their instruments, the surgeon asked me if I had heard that Carlo had discovered he had diabetes. It had happened while I was away in India.

'Almost passed out in his car, came right away for tests and found his blood sugar was way over. Stratospheric.'

'Given what he was eating ...' I said.

One of the nurses was now strapping my feet into two large boot devices way up in the air and a good metre apart. There is always a part of me, at these moments, eager to rebel. Yet I never do. I imagine it is the same at executions.

'In fact, they put him on a diet,' the doctor chuckled rather lugubriously, taking his place between my feet. 'No more doughnuts, I'm afraid.' He had a mask over his face now and what looked like a plastic bag on his head. 'Not to mention the medications.'

Then despite the situation I was in, with a nurse tying rubber round my forearm to inject the anaesthetic, I said the real problem with Carlo was, why did he feel the need to eat so much? There must be some sort of psycho problem if he couldn't keep away from the sugar. Especially being a doctor and knowing the risks.

Pulling rubber gloves on those heavily veined hands, the surgeon shook his head. 'Carluccio just loves his food', he said.

A nurse lifted the white nightshirt to prepare the approach to the difficult target. I was aware of something long and metallic in the doctor's hands and at the same time I felt intensely concerned that this man who was about to push something hard and far too wide into the tip of my penis could not see the plain truth that our friend Carlo had serious problems.

'If ever there was a case of physician heal thyself!' I protested. 'He's always got something in his mouth. That can't be—'

I passed out.

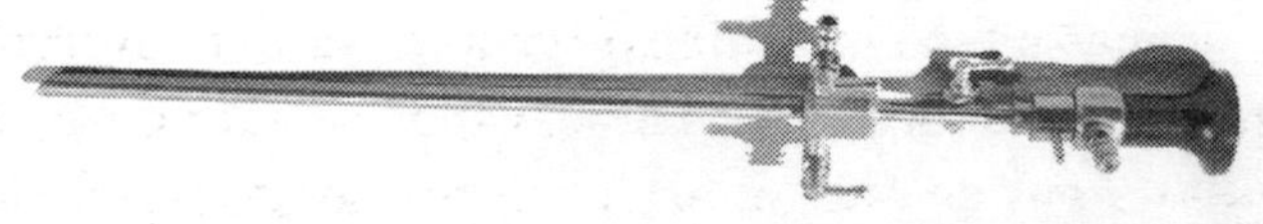

A curious thing about anaesthetics is that when you come to you have no sense of time having elapsed. With sleep, as I said, I know within ten minutes or so how long I've been unconscious. Here the film cut abruptly from feelings of anxiety, distrust and humiliation on the operating chair, to the sound of echoing footsteps and low, urgent voices. I opened my eyes and judged, from the ceiling, that I must be in a corridor. It was a trolley bed. Turning my head, I saw another bed being wheeled past me. The occupant was entirely covered by a sheet.

I breathed deeply.

I will know now, I thought. Now I will find out that I have cancer of the bladder. Then I can forget all the psychosomatic crap and start fighting it. Chemo, surgery, radiation. I was ready.

I waited. The minutes passsed. I thought back to the operating room and realised I could hardly remember it. I had only the vaguest image of that chair; in retrospect it looked like a Meccano-built torture instrument assembled by a provincial serial killer. There had been a woman and two or three other people around me, but I had no recollection of them. Did the doctor tell the nurses what he was seeing through the probe as it pushed up the urethra, past the prostate and urinary sphincters into the bladder? How did they get you off the operating chair and onto the bed afterwards? How long had I been unconscious in the corridor here? Why did no one come to check on me?

More beds were wheeled by: a boy sitting up smiling; an elderly woman's face in profile, grey and wasted. Everyone wore gowns, white or green. There was a constant buzz, not unpleasant. I felt no pain at all. Then the doctor was beside me. His hollow, dark face smiled down. A perplexed, ironic smile, I thought.

'Bladder clean as a baby's,' he said. 'Pink and pristine.'

Passing water and blood in the loo two hours later was the most excruciating pain I have ever felt. I remembered the time I had gone running and passed blood and it had been nothing. Nothing. I felt jubilant.

6,820,000 Hits

My husband has been diagnosed with an enlarged prostate for the last 3 years now. He's only 29. He's seen one urologist several times. Is there anything else he can do? Any other antibiotics or anything? Second, would these problems affect his fertility or sex drive?

It's 5.30 in the morning. I have typed 'prostate pain' into Google.

I don't go out any more. Every time I go into any place I have to locate the bathrooms. I won't go anywhere where I won't be able to pee at least once an hour.

There are 'approximately' 6,820,000 hits for this search. Most lead to other links. Some open chats that fill screen after screen.

I've been taking alpha blockers for a while now but I've lost all sexual stimulus.

My uro has diagnosed me with 'multiple prostate stones' as the main reason for my almost constant pain and discomfort. He has prescribed Cipro and then Floxin, both without success.

Until the cystoscopy I had only used the net to check up the medical procedures that they had prescribed for me. Now I have to decide what to do.

> *A year ago my husband was in great shape. He was mountain climbing, kayaking, and backpacking. Although he is only 27 years old, his health has drastically declined in the past year. he suddenly had difficulty urinating, and we found out that he has an enlarged prostate. We've been to 3 doctors reguarding that and they don't know what is wrong. He had blood work done and they don't think it is cancer. Beyond that, they don't know why it is enlarged.*

I realise now that before completing the medical tests I had imagined that, if they all came out negative, I would automatically start feeling better and my problems would subside: finding there was 'nothing wrong with me' would itself be a cure. Instead, things are worse. I can't stay in bed after five. I go down to the computer until it's time to take Lucy to school.

> *I have pain in my anal area. I am a little embarrassed to go to see a doctor. Well, and not sure if it is anal pain or prostate pain. Is there a difference?*

> *Your husband is rather young for this problem. Antibiotics can dampen down the infection but never seem to eradicate it, and it can go on for years I am afraid to say. Certainly the pain will/can affect his sex drive. It's like getting your hand slapped every time you reach for the sweet tin! There must be a ? about fertility.*

The net is not encouraging. But it seemed important to find out how other people were dealing with the situation.

Anyone any ideas on how to lesson the irritation and long-term lubrication of the part of the catheter outside the penis?

We just learned this week what went wrong. After the green-light surgery his prostate swelled. It got so large it cut off its own blood supply. The loss of blood supply caused his prostate to swell even more. It got so big it pushed against his lower rectum, pinching it shut. He couldn't poop solids.

I try to bring some method to my research but for the first few days I'm just shocked and fascinated. I read at random, losing myself in the unhappy crowd.

I had not thought the prostate had undone so many.

After what I've been through, I think I would sooner have disturbed nights than take another medication with more potential side effects.

I did not have erection after 1996 except twice after the surgery. The pills and the pump do not work and I have to inject myself.

The 'certain procedure' turned out to be that I would have to catheterise myself three times a day!

Then the doctor inserted a balloon to stretch my bladder and later they put in a stent to keep my urethra open only it got infected.

In the 1940s, when Alfred Kinsey was putting together his report on sexuality in the USA, interviewing thousands upon thousands of men and women about their experiences, there came a point where he was overwhelmed. It was too much. He began to lose his sense of identity. On the net, it only takes a couple of days to realise you are in danger. You start to mix up your own story with other people's. You imagine symptoms you don't have.

> *Dear Dr. Motola: My husband was told that his urine was being forced sideways into the prostate duct and it was that that was causing the swelling and the pain.*

> *Prostate fullness, slight pain, extending into penus on occasion … had fistula in the past, have hernia … Can anyone help?*

> *Pray for Linda and Her Husband who has severe chronic prostatitis: 'My husband and I have been trying for a baby for 4 years now but he has pain during sex and after. The doctors …'*

I rarely finish reading a thread. I never write down my own symptoms or respond to anyone else's. I'm reminded of Nathanael West's novel, *Miss Lonelyhearts*. A male journalist is asked to write the agony column in a New York newspaper under a woman's name. He starts out with the idea it will be a joke but eventually drowns in oceans of anxiety.

> *hello yes ive been masturbating since the age of 14 and starded smoking pot at 17 and im now twenty having problems with pelvic pains, stomach pains bladder problems off and on headaches my scrotun has serousily shrunk and ive been having penis and testicle pains i would go to the doctor to get checked out but im very scared on the bad news im going to get what should i do and is there any hope of me having kids*

The curious thing as I scroll down entry after entry is that I feel I am both the agony aunt *and* the letter writers. These lives seem interchangeable. We're all in the same boat.

I'm getting up 4 to 5 times a night sometimes more to go to the bathroom, evidently their must be some other reason for it other than enlarged prostate as ***I had the operation almost two years ago now!***

Taken singly, none of the entries seems to offer much wisdom; taken together they read like a life sentence.

It went from an ache in my lower back in the morning to a sharp stabbing sensation in my pelvic area, groin and testicles. Eventually, I would be doubled up in agony and would have to go back to bed. Then I'd get up a few hours later to find the pain had gone, thinking 'what was that all about?'

... 70% of men over fifty ...

This is driving me nuts, if it's goes on forever I'll kill myself. I really will.

The net is so promiscuous. There are those who can spell and those who can't, those who are suffering and those who are selling. Today's threads run alongside messages a decade old. This man is writing from China.

I was ever been a prostatitis patient for seven years. The prostate expand and pain sharply. My waist pain, dizzy and weak. I had seen many famous doctors in china, had used the microwave, infrared ray scan, acupoint injection, squeeze medicine into anus to cure the disease.

The cancer patients get mixed up with the enlarged prostate sufferers. They discuss their post-operative incontinence problems.

I'm a commercial service tech. Finding a restroom on a forty acre factory rooftop can be a challenge. Can't use pads because of the leakage, and changing a pull up on the job with other guys around is a real pain in the buttocks.

Rant your ass of brother! I listien to alot of Springsteen and Neil Young. It helps.

Hey, why not try condom catheters? Here's the link!

There are those convinced that prostate pains are the result of an autoimmune disease, those who believe in a mystery virus. It comes from too much sitting and a sedentary life. It's sexually transmitted. Masturbation helps. Masturbation makes it worse. All you can do is wait for science to find the cause and the cure. No, you must be proactive! Take hot baths, do yoga, avoid spicy food, stop smoking and drinking.

If I type in 'pelvic pain' rather than 'prostate pain', I find the women are going through exactly the same thing. It's uncanny. Here is Marion:

I'm 22. I use the bathroom right before I go to sleep at night, but then about 5 minutes after I lay down I get the urge to go, and only a little tinkle comes out. And then again and again and again. But there's no infection. And only at night. What is happening to me?

And here is Helen:

This went on for more than thirteen years, until in the end in desperation they took my bladder out, yeah, believe it, my bladder, and had a bag put in. And the pain went on just the fuckin same !!!

The long-term sufferers are inured. The young are dismayed.

I've just started this new job. If the pain goes on I don't think I can stay with it.

My girlfriend's trying to be nice but I can see she wants out.

Suddenly my semen got clumpy and discoloured. I also experienced pain in my testicles and back. I'm 23. In addition the sensation during ejaculation has changed completely. I get these really bad headaches for hours afterwards. And this sort of dull pain in the groin.

Reading these posts, I start thinking about my own children, presently fast asleep upstairs. I start to think it's bound to happen to them. They'll wake up to this misery one day. But these are dumb, defeatist thoughts. Here at last is a success story.

After eight years of taking medication for constant **prostate pain**, *antibiotics for* **infections** *destroying my immune system, and frequent time consuming costly visits to numerous urologists, a surgeon at the Cleveland Clinic referred me to Dr. Krongrad. He referred me for surgical prostate* **removal**. *When I came out of surgery, I was laying on my back for the first time in many years without the pain of feeling as if I had a golf ball in my rectum. One month later, I was able to resume my passion of playing drums and gigging with my band.*

Ten minutes later I find this.

My case is very simple, at forty-three I was mutilated, they did that operation they call TURP, man it was the biggest mistake I ever made, when I decided to have that procedure.

Going back to the triumphant post-surgery post, I realise it makes frequent references to Dr Krongrad and his clinic. Could the guy really have felt so good as they wheeled him out of the operating room? After a while you realise that most of those claiming dramatic cures are pushing you towards a product or a clinic. Prostatitis is big business.

I have found Saw Palmetto to help expel urine completely. Orgasms are getting closer to normal. Pains declining. I've been on Saw Palmetto (85% fatty acids & sterols) for about two weeks. I have noticed improvement within three days. I got the Saw Palmetto from Trader Joe's for only $6.99 (100 tabs). This is about $15.00 cheaper than most other brands.

A man with his own site on prostate health directs you to the Aneros anal massage and sex toy.

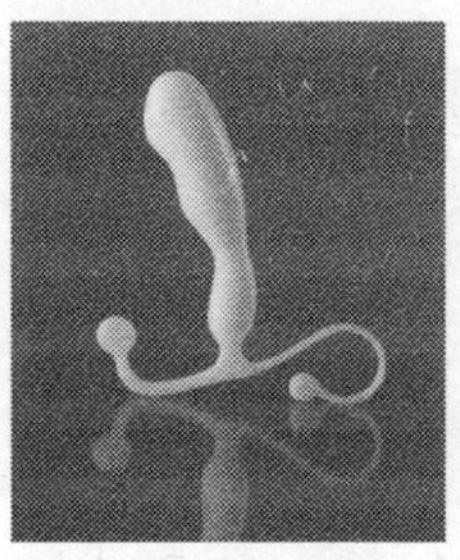

It's a must!

A woman writes in:

I am a prostate massage therapist who has been practising for over 9 years helping gentlemen who have prostate issues. Remember, just because the prostate is tucked away doesn't mean it doesn't need attention!

I wonder if 'prostate issues' was meant to be a joke.

Sometimes a contributor doesn't realise what kind of chat he's in:

God knows why the male G spot was put up the arse but there we go, if it's done correctly along with stimulation of the penis the orgasm is out of this world! Try it!

This time there's a link to:

The ***PS New*** *is our flagship prostate massager. It has a long body with two nodules on the end for direct contact on the prostate. The ridges add stability and the fixed perineal acupressure arm provides an external massage. Made of medical-grade, impact resistant, non-porous plastic.*

Occasionally an expert puts someone straight.

I am glad that Saw Palmetto worked for you. A recent study showed that it does improve symptoms. However, patients on placebo also have the same kind of symptom relief. Therefore, I don't think there is a scientific proof at this time.

An American medical site claims that 50 per cent of enlarged prostate patients respond to placebos for periods of two to four weeks. Considering this statistic, it occurs to me that 'placebo', like 'psychosomatic', suggests a perverse relationship between body and mind, something muddying the waters of scientific research, putting the wayward psyche between an expensively certified substance and a carefully analysed condition.

Still, to say 'only a placebo effect', as one expert complains of a product called 'silver water', seems to me the wrong approach. The important thing, surely, would be to stretch out the placebo effect ad infinitum. Then who cares if the medicine's just a sugar cube? All the better, in fact. That said, I am one of the 50 per cent who *never* get a placebo effect from anything, whether it be ayurvedic herbs or powerful adrenalin receptor blockers. Is this because I don't have faith in my doctors, because when I take a medicine I actually expect things to get worse rather than better? Or could it be that in my case psychology has little say on the matter, which would be ironic given how willing I am to embrace that version of events?

After a week and more of these early-morning browsings, I realise that the sheer abundance of 'cures' can only mean there are none.

> *My cure method include seven parts.*
> *1. Eat four kinds of nature product every day. Bee honey, royal jelly, bee pollen and propolis.*
> *2. Take the following Chinese medicines . . .*

> *I've read that some people take a magnesium/zinc supplement to clean out the prostate stones. Does this actually work? And if so what is the recommended daily dose rate of magnesium and how much zinc must I take to balance out the side effects of the magnesium?*

> *Fresh parsley juice. You gotta try it!*

I don't even take mental notes, never mind written ones. Less and less am I planning to try anything anyone suggests. If these solutions worked, everyone would be using them: there'd be no chat rooms and no problem.

So what am I doing at the computer? I'm not enjoying

myself, I'm not getting anywhere, but I can't stop. It seems to be a common condition. All these sufferers are interminably surfing the net.

> *I started some very extensive and exhausting research on prostate pain and prostate problems. Since modern medicine was telling me there was 'nothing really wrong with me', I decided to research every other avenue I could find.*

Isn't this an updated version of the 'restless, worrisome, dissatisfied individual' described in that urologists' manual so many years ago? 'Dragging his miseries about' from onc website to the next. I'm being drawn back into that story again, the one that ends on the operating table. Almost infallibly, the guys with symptoms like mine seem to be obsessive types, anxiously weighing up the pros and cons of surgery. Some of them are still going over and over the problem even after taking the plunge.

> *I look at data for a living. I build information programs and systems to help decision-makers do their jobs. I am used to looking at incomplete, contradictory information and constructing analyses out of it. So I thought I was well-suited to work through the process of choosing a surgical methodology, and I continue to think I did a good job. But when it came to outcomes – how fast I would become continent and regain my sexual capabilities – I now can recall to mind how circumspect were those I queried, how hedged were their responses. Nevertheless, like so many, I suspect, I fell for the best-case scenarios and rosiest anecdotal accounts.*

'You should still do the operation,' Carlo tells me.

It's about two weeks after the cystoscopy. He is drinking orange juice and there's no doughnut.

'I know you'd feel better,' he insists.

I can see my friend is trying to help and however blind he might have been about his own condition, the fact is that he and his colleagues treat hundreds of patients like me every year. They know what they know. I start to tell him about some recent Japanese research I've seen that uses three-dimensional imagining and shows that poor flow during urination can be caused by poor interaction between the two urinary sphincters, rather than by any actual physical obstruction through the prostate.

Carlo nods. 'That's why we open the top sphincter permanently, then only one sphincter has to work.' He hesitates. 'The fact is, if you go on as you are, the bladder wall will thicken with the effort you're making every time you go to the bathroom. It will age prematurely.'

I haven't seen anything about bladder-wall deterioration on the net. After a pause, I sigh. 'It's too bad they can't do all these tests at night, you know, because then it's so different from—'

'Listen,' Carlo interrupts. 'It's your call. You decide.'

He has realised I'm not going to do it. He's not exactly offended but something in his voice tells me I mustn't ask him for any more advice from now on. I am no longer his patient.

The Pilotòn

'I'll have to stop. You go on.'

The thing my wife and I do most together is walk. We live in the hills just outside of town. Within a few minutes you're on paths through vineyards and cherry orchards, following stone walls thick with ivy. One path negotiates a steep gulley round a place called the Witches' Well, then climbs up to a ridge. At the top, there's a whitish stone column, the Pilotòn. This is where all the paths meet and you can see for miles in all directions.

I lean on the stone.

'I'm sorry. I'm too uncomfortable.'

We're only about fifteen minutes out from home.

'You've got to sort this out somehow,' Rita tells me. 'It's been months.'

'It's just a bad day.'

She walks on to exercise the dog and I rest on the grass. This has never happened before. We have always walked, ever since we met thirty years ago. Our relationship *is* walking. Now I find it too uncomfortable.

The Pilotòn is about two feet in diameter and ten feet high and dates back to Roman times. Once it was twice the height but in the Middle Ages they put an iron crucifix on top and it was struck by lightning. The stone shattered. Absurdly, the circumstance reminds me of that word *prakruti*, the complex amalgamation of original and acquired traits. Appropriated to Christianity, the pagan phallic column split apart. The tension was too much. Now it's a relic, with neither the cross on top, nor the virile thrust it had before.

Since the operation, I get a kind of tickle and fullness, but haven't been able to achieve a proper . . .

This is silly. Like when I started thinking of the waterseller's fig as the prostate. Yet I notice that my mind is more at ease with these eccentric analogies than with the information onslaught of the net. I have the impression they bring me closer to some truth about my condition, but in the way dreams do. Something important is staring you in the face, only you can't decode it. It won't come out in words. That's the fascination of dreams. And certain paintings. There is truth that can't be said, knowledge you can't access or use. My mind wanders off in these enigmas and after a while I find I'm feeling a little better. Is it a placebo effect? One day, I suppose, I will discover the meaning of Velázquez's painting. Or maybe that would spoil it. It's such a quiet pleasure, lying down with closed eyes, trying to recall that glass of clear water with its dark fig.

I sit up and look across the valley towards Verona. I've lived here, or within a few miles of here, for almost thirty years. Could it be, it comes to me, that Italy, Italian, is the acquired trait that clashes with my original English inheritance? Is this the long tension that undid my health? A smile spreads across my face.

I came to Italy because I met an Italian girl in the States. She assured me she would never go back to Italy to live. A year in England changed her mind. When we arrived together in Verona, I spoke not a word. I knew from school that languages were beyond me. I struggled. Now I lecture *in* Italian. On translation, *into* Italian. And every moment, every word I speak, I'm on my guard against mistakes, I'm listening to correct my accent. It will never be quite right.

Is this the sort of structural conflict the ayurvedic doctors were talking about? Italy versus England (always an impossible game for me). I love Italian. It has become my destiny. My whole life is tied up with Italy. And I hate it. I hate it for having become my destiny. For taking up so much space. Would I get better, I wonder, if I went back to the UK and lived a monochrome English life? Or would I just have the same problem the other way round? Yearning for Italy. Most likely the damage, like the benefits, is irreversible now.

It's pleasant on an April morning to follow odd thoughts to the point where you shake your head and laugh. I'm put in mind of two essays I've been working on, one finished and one in the pipeline. Thomas Hardy was born more dead than alive into a family of masons, builders. He was thought too weak to follow his father into the profession. So since he was bright they pushed him at school and he moved up in the world to become an architect. That meant leaving his village home to study in Dorchester. Eventually he went to London, worked in an architect's office and won prizes for his designs. Just when things appeared to be going well, he fell ill, or, as he put it, 'felt weak', abandoned his career and went home again. This might seem like a disaster, except that at home he completed a novel he had started in London. Writing allowed him to link his ambitions for city celebrity with security among his village roots.

Later, having married an upmarket woman from Cornwall, Hardy started to oscillate between life in London and life in Dorchester. He never really knew where he wanted to live. And his books are frequently about young people who leave their homes, always country homes, too early, feel overwhelmed, frightened, exploited, and beat unhappy retreats to their roots, their mothers. It's never clear how far they are victims of society or flawed in themselves. A great walker (like my wife!), his characters are forever traipsing back and forth between village and town, infancy and adulthood, security and adventure. Often it seems they'd rather walk for ever than arrive.

Hardy's wife got mixed up in this uneasy character trait. Having married in 1874, the novelist began to drag her back and forth from London to Dorchester. Seven moves in eight years. The children they wanted did not arrive. Encouraged to help with his writing during romantic betrothal, the childless Emma was now frozen out of his professional life. She did not mix well in London, where she preferred to live, or at all in Dorchester, which he now seemed to prefer.

But in 1880 their relationship was suddenly transformed when Hardy fell ill and, taking to his bed for many months, allowed Emma to run his life for him. His recurring mystery illness, vaguely described as a 'bladder inflammation', did not prevent him from meeting the gruelling demands of serialised novel publication. He wrote reams. On his recovery, Emma was sufficiently reassured about her role in the partnership to agree to the building of a permanent home not far from Dorchester. Or alternatively: when Emma was sufficiently reassured about her role in the partnership to agree to the building of a permanent home not far from Dorchester, Hardy recovered.

Could it be, then, I wondered, that the secret purpose of Hardy's bladder inflammation – and the few symptoms described in the biographies would not look out of place among Google's six million and more posts for prostate pain – was to reset his relationship with his wife, turning her from an embarrassing would-be literary helper into a traditional carer? And simultaneously to sort out the interminable question of where to live, in city or country? Needed again, albeit in a different way, Emma was willing to move back to Dorchester, on condition that they build their own posh home. Hardy got his father and brother to do the building to his, Hardy's, design in a place near to, but nevertheless separate from, the family's village. In terms of relationship and location, he was realigning the inherited and acquired aspects of his personality.

With an illness.

So, in what way has my mystery condition altered my relationship with my wife?

Or my situation in Italy?

I frown and tear up a couple of tufts of grass beside the solid Pilotòn. It's easy to come to conclusions about someone whose biography you can study. Not to mention the novels, poems and letters Hardy left. You can go backward and forward through the pages, checking dates and events. But how can I hope to understand my own situation when I don't even remember when these pains began? Was it shortly after I arrived in Italy? Is that possible? As I see it, there's no question of the condition's having changed my wife's role in any particular way. She is not one of those anxious women who write to the chat rooms on behalf of their husbands. Nor would I want her to be. She doesn't have more power because I'm not well. Or less. Nor has the problem altered where I work, or live, or plan to live. Perhaps it has *frozen* things, though. All decisions – holidays, home improvements – seem to have been put off until I'm well again. We are living in a kind of limbo. Now we can't even walk together.

About a kilometre to the north of where I'm sitting, as the ridge rises gently towards the Alps, there's a convent. And to the south, where the path winds down towards the plain, there are the three towers of the Castello di Montorio, which, in the Middle Ages, was a monastery. It seems that at night there was quite a back-and-forth of lusty nuns and monks along this ridge-top path; it's not hard even now to imagine them in their hoods and habits hurrying to moonlit liaisons. Eventually, the scandal reached such proportions that the monks were kicked out and sent elsewhere. I wonder if the nuns laid cool fingers on the virile Pilotòn as they passed, whether the monks somatised the conflict between vows and libido in prostate problems. Some psycho-site on the net claims that pelvic pain is often a guilt response to adultery, which was a sin, funnily enough, that became quite an obsession, for Thomas Hardy. 'Eastern ideas of matrimony secretly pervade his thoughts,' wrote the ironic Emma. But though the author was almost always in eager correspondence with young female admirers, all the information we have suggests that he never broke the deadlock of wedlock.

Could bladder pain be a way of keeping yourself true?

The other essay I'm writing is about Mussolini. The man could not be more different from Thomas Hardy yet, as always, I have a habit of making connections. Mussolini's parents were famously poles apart. His father was a blacksmith, an aggressive socialist activist gaoled on a number of occasions, once village mayor, almost the only man in the community never to go to church, not even on Christmas

Day. His mother was a much loved, very devout Catholic schoolmistress. The young Benito oscillated between periods of exemplary piety and episodes of rebellious violence. In late adolescence he formed a habit of more or less raping a girl, then doing everything he could to have her love him. He was happy to be sentimental, if he could dominate. Eventually, after his mother's death, he married the daughter of his father's long-term mistress. Married is not quite the word. They pledged themselves to each other for ever, but without being officially married. Benito didn't believe in formalities. Meantime, every institution he was involved in – schools, newspapers, political parties – kicked him out, until he started a movement of his own that all Italy would be obliged to join.

Preaching violence, Mussolini was never involved in it himself. On his desk he kept a loaded pistol, but never used it. He preferred reading, writing, translating. Threatening parliament with draconian reforms, talking about how radically he could and some day would impose his will on Italy, for more than a decade he actually left things much the same. His wife accused him of not living up to the severity of his rhetoric, of postponing a more brutal manifestation of himself to some indefinite moment in the future and meanwhile letting his enemies off the hook. 'You should be tougher, Benito!' she told him. Occasionally he followed her advice: in 1924, shortly after the murder of socialist MP Giacomo Matteotti, the first high-level political assassination of the Fascist period, Il Duce was afflicted by violent stomach pains. He was reduced to writhing on the floor. He couldn't function. He then arranged for the murdered man's widow to be given a state pension.

These pains came and went intermittently throughout the rest of Mussolini's life. Physicians diagnosed an ulcer and he settled down to a diet of mostly warm milk. Like a baby. Another severe crisis occurred after his visit to Berlin in 1937. He had seen at first hand how successful Hitler was and how ruthless. Here was a man who had no hesitation in keeping his violent word, who didn't put off his purges and massacres or revert to a sentimental maternal piety. On returning to Rome, Mussolini got serious and introduced the race laws and the goosestep. 'Trying very hard to be wicked,' says his biographer, Richard Bosworth. At once he was paralysed with stomach pain. After his death, an autopsy could find nothing wrong with his stomach at all. There had been no ulcer.

One of the curiosities of Mussolini's life is how abjectly and comprehensively this habitual bully eventually surrendered power and prestige to Hitler, a man he had previously despised, allowing the German to make all the important decisions in their alliance. Perhaps this surrender spared him some stomach pain. However, and despite the fact that his own survival had come to depend on Hitler's, Mussolini would always rejoice when the German army was defeated. At some deep level he couldn't wish the ugly side of himself to triumph. It was a mental tussle he never resolved. Captured and summarily executed, he offered no resistance.

'What are you up to?'

It was Rita's voice. I opened my eyes to find her standing over me.

'Just reflecting that a guy with bladder pains is unlikely to become a serial rapist.'

Walking home, I found the pain had gone. I felt fine. It was strange.

Maybe a week or so after this aborted ramble, I had my first experience of impotence.

Harley Street

Sometime in May, I ordered an American self-help book on line. It's the kind of thing Tim Parks doesn't do, and I was at pains to stress to my wife that the book was *medical*, nothing loony or mystical. I had found it during one of my purgatorial dawns on the net. It was called: *A Headache in the Pelvis*. The title at first seemed incongruous, silly even, of a nature anyway to guarantee that it could never appear on the first page of responses to any question typed into Google's search engine. Later, I realised it was precisely this superimposition of head and belly that had drawn me to it.

My ayurvedic enquiry had been a traveller's whim. It was one thing idly to speculate on the concept of *prakruti* and quite another to embark on a programme of sesame oil enemas or to follow recommendations from a study of the heavenly bodies as of 11 p.m., 19 December 1954. Willing to be fascinated, I retained an intense distrust towards any treatment that wasn't underwritten by Western science.

Yet Western science was letting me down. I had a further demonstration of this when, London-bound for a conference, I got in touch with friends and had them recommend a urologist in Harley Street. Once again I would appeal *in extremis* to the most prestigious combination of science and upper-class tradition that England has to offer.

In the event, the encounter was so similar to that of twenty years before as to be uncanny. The waiting room at the London clinic was polished and quiet. The secretary was discreet, polite. I was ushered into the doctor's surgery only three or four minutes after the appointed hour. My seat was comfortable and the elderly doctor, on the further shore of an impressively old-fashioned desk, was lean, accommodating and avuncular.

The doctor listened to my story with attention. He looked carefully at the various test results that I had brought and remarked on the excellent quality of the X-ray images. Having absorbed all the facts, or as many as anyone can absorb in just a few minutes, he took me into a small side room, invited me to remove my trousers and performed a manual inspection of testicles and prostate. The finger he inserted was experienced and respectful. He then had me lie down and carried out an ultrasound scan. Well-equipped and diligent, he was doing as much as one man in a single appointment can possibly do. Yet when we sat down again, each side of his leather-topped desk, I knew he had nothing to tell me and that I had come, in fact, precisely to confirm that this experienced man at the top of his profession would have nothing to tell me. Or just in case, as it were. I had come *just in case* by some miracle he had something to tell me.

He didn't.

I was right, the doctor said, to hesitate before undergoing surgery. Aside from some mild calcification, the prostate seemed healthy. My *problem*, judging from his ultrasound and the hospital X-rays, was *very likely* one of bladder-neck dyssynergia, a failure, that is, of the urinary sphincter to relax and dilate fully on urination. How this then provoked the many pains I was having he couldn't say. He smiled. The solution, he went on, despite my previous unhappy experiences, was an alpha blocker; this would encourage the sphincter to relax; and he suggested I try first Alfuzosin and, if I wasn't happy with that, Tamsulosin. He wrote a legible prescription. Both drugs could cause retrograde ejaculation and mild postural hypotension (call it dizziness), but I would get over that and could carry on taking them indefinitely. I could also use saw palmetto, if I so desired, and should achieve orgasm daily 'in one way or another'. Occasional impotence, he reassured me, was a passing phenomenon and typical of these conditions and the anxieties they aroused. Tall and erect, he shook my hand firmly and told me not to hesitate to be in touch were my condition to alter in any significant way. It was probably the most civilised encounter I ever had with a doctor. And the most expensive.

Outside, instead of heading towards the pharmacy his secretary had courteously directed me to, I crossed the Euston Road and found a seat in Regent's Park, feeling extremely uncomfortable. 'Medicines are not the answer,' I said out loud. I was depressed and resigned. At no point, as I recalled, had the doctor suggested that the medicines he prescribed would reduce the pains I was having, only the night-time trips to the bathroom. Without evidence of organic damage, pains were perhaps unimportant. At least to doctors. 'That is the last time,' I said, even louder, '*the very last time* that I will go to a doctor about this condition.' Hadn't everything I had read on the net confirmed the pointlessness of such visits? Wasn't it weird, in fact, the way everybody imagined that when you were ill all you had to do was go to a doctor and get yourself prescribed a medicine? How did that happen? Dr Piggott was the name of our family doctor in Blackpool. He wore a large overcoat and pulled a gleaming stethoscope from the traditional black bag. I can remember its cold touch on my chest. When you had measles, or chicken pox, or bronchitis, he prescribed a medicine and you got better. Whether you got better *because* of the medicine was another matter but the sequence of events was dependable. Even my brother had got better from his polio, in a way, despite the damage it left him with. This was because the body was something that could be represented by diagrams in textbooks and the doctors had understood everything about it.

My evangelical parents reinforced this belief in conventional science and medicine. My father, in particular, was eager for his children to study the sciences and was intensely disappointed when first my sister dropped out of school, then my brother abandoned maths and physics for art, and finally I dropped all sciences after O levels and studied literature. A matter-of-fact believer, my father didn't trust literature. Science was a manifestation of God's unerring, rational laws; it was respectable to study those laws and manipulate them to the benefit of mankind. Literature all too often was the product of man's interminable bellyaching about his fallen condition. 'Bellyaching!' he fumed. It was the word he used to dismiss any attempt to quibble with the perfection of creation. I wondered whether, alive today, Dad would associate this bellyache I had with my agnosticism.

There was, of course, another kind of intervention which could cure an illness if medical science failed. When I was in my early teens my parents became involved in the 'charismatic movement'. They were 'baptised in the spirit', 'spoke in tongues', were 'given prophesies' and 'words of wisdom'; they performed exorcisms and celebrated the laying on of hands. Perhaps, trusting firmly in science, they were well-disposed to acknowledge miracles, if only to cover those occurrences that official medicine can't account for. Like the doctor's syrups, divine healing required no effort or self-knowledge on the part of the sufferer; neither my father nor mother paid much attention to their bodies. On the other hand, it was not available on the National Health and you couldn't get it on demand. It was up to God. You could pray, intercede, beseech (what lovely words), but you couldn't *count* on God's intervention, nor systematise it afterwards. The thing about a miracle was that it left nature's (rational) laws unchanged. 'Rational' was a very important word for my father, and absolutely beyond criticism. So was faith. In the best Cartesian tradition, these two mental dispositions divided the world between them, without needing to communicate with each other: science was not invited to cross-examine the miraculous, nor did the miracle seek to force its way into anyone's academic publications. Each ruled supreme in its separate dimension. Everything else – astrology, yoga, hypnotism, dream interpretation, meditation, mesmerism, marijuana, rock music, psychedelic design, the whole of the paranormal or the merely oriental – was the work of the devil.

In this regard, I remember how once, in a fit of adolescent enthusiasm, I tried to read my mother some lines from *The Four Quartets*.

'To communicate with Mars ...' I began – she was on the sofa knitting and I at the table doing my homework – '... converse with spirits,

> To report the behaviour of the sea monster,
> Describe the horoscope, haruspicate or scry,
> Observe disease in signatures ...

I had chosen the passage carefully, sure that when we got to the closing lines

> ... are usual
> Pastimes and drugs, and features of the press:

she would be pleased with Eliot's irony at the expense of pagan superstition and thus reconciled to the study of literature. I was looking for Mum's approval, trying to bring our worlds together, not seeking to provoke.

We never got to those lines. '... evoke Biography,' I read on,

> from the wrinkles of the palm
> And tragedy from fingers; release omens
> By sortilege, or tea leaves, riddle—

'What a lot of hocus-pocus,' my mother interrupted. She shook her head over a dropped stitch. 'Very unhealthy, Timothy.' No, she didn't want to hear any more T.S. Eliot, thank you very much. Just the naming of these irrational practices had upset her. I should never have studied literature.

On the bench in Regent's Park I smiled, remembering my mother's impatience and those troubled charismatic years. Failing at school, my sister had taken my parents' side, was more fundamentalist than they. Hippy-haired and rebellious, my brother made ferocious fun of them, pretending to be demonic, pronouncing curses and casting spells with a wave of the arm. I oscillated. At school there was much sniggering over page three of the *Sun*; on the way home I played football in the twilight, sweating and swearing. Then, closing the door behind me, there would be the commotion of an exorcism in the sitting room, my mother speaking in tongues, my father praying loudly, my sister's fingers pounding blind belief on the piano. I might join in, or I might hurry upstairs to play Subbuteo with a friend and listen to Leonard Cohen. When I withdrew from it all, at sixteen or seventeen, science seemed to me the sole sane explanation of the world. Literature was our response to the fact that, thus explained, life had no meaning. I had fallen in love with Beckett. He seemed a man inoculated against all religion.

The charismatic gifts did not serve my parents well. They

tried to exorcise my brother and heal his polio. He was not changed. My sister gave birth to a severely handicapped daughter. The power of prayer did not transform her. Nor a trip to Lourdes. My father's cancer was not healed by the laying on of hands. He lost his mind and died in pain. Afraid of anything that reminded us of their spiritual aberration, my brother and I counted entirely, perhaps aggressively, on official learning and official medicine; perhaps the only opinion we now had in common with my mother and sister was that all alternative therapies were boloney. Even today, if you mention acupuncture to my atheist brother, he will declare it hocus-pocus. Just like my mother.

So where was I to turn, now that I had washed my hands of the doctors and they of me? The previous week, at the university, I had had to interrupt a lesson; for the first time the pain had obtruded on my teaching. On Sunday afternoon at the stadium – for I was still an avid football goer – I was barely able to sit down during the second half of the game. I had to keep jumping to my feet as if excited by what was going on on the pitch. '*Arbitro di merda!*' I yelled, when nothing much was happening. My stadium friends laughed, but someone behind asked me to sit down.

On the bench in Regent's Park, among the pleasant trees and lawns, I shouted: 'Something's got to change! Please!' and a young man turned and glanced at me and hurried on.

That evening I went out with an old friend, drank heavily, talked about the two girlfriends he was playing off against each other and didn't visit the bathroom once or speak a word of my troubles for three or four hours.

This was another thing about this odd condition, a symptom almost: I was absolutely determined *not to talk about it.* I wanted to come out of it *without anyone having known.* Aside from Carlo in Milan. With 'a clean record', as it were. My manhood intact. Only to my wife had I confided everything, making her swear she wouldn't mention it to the children. The attraction to the net, I'd often thought, was so strong because this was the only place where people could, in anonymity, get together and *bellyache.*

Il bell'Antonio

Everything conspired. On my return to Italy, having landed in Milan and gone directly to the university to teach, I opened an email inviting me to write a preface to a new English edition of Vitaliano Brancati's novel *Il bell'Antonio.* I should have turned this work down. Between writing and going back and forth from Verona to Milan, not only to teach but to run the whole degree course, I was doing too much. I wondered at what point, with this intensifying condition, something would finally give: I would miss an important deadline, start forgetting appointments, take to my bed like Hardy, writhe on the floor like Benito. Instead, I accepted at once. I love these commissions. They allow me to extend my knowledge of matters Italian while making some extra money. I was aware that *Il bell'Antonio* was considered a masterpiece. I knew the film had starred Marcello Mastroianni and Claudia Cardinale, but I had no idea what it was about.

Impotence.

Who would have thought there was an Italian novel about impotence?

With a mixture of amusement and dismay, I read the book over the following week on the train back and forth to Milan. Sicilian Antonio is gorgeous. Sent by his parents to make his fortune in Mussolini's Rome, he finds men and women flocking to him; the women to drool, the men to be near the drooling women. Everybody assumes Antonio is enjoying a hectic sex life and that this explains his failure to make a career for himself in the Fascist bureaucracy. Eventually, his parents recall him to Catania; they have found a girl for him to marry. Antonio isn't happy, he had wanted to choose his own bride. But Barbara is ravishing and he falls in love. To the chagrin of other hopefuls, the couple marry and go off to live together in the country.

Brought up by nuns, Barbara is as innocent as she is irresistible. It is a year before she realises why the babies aren't arriving. At last the scandal hits town: Antonio can't get it up. The bride's parents are outraged and demand an annulment. Antonio's father is so ashamed he makes well-advertised visits to prostitutes to 'save the family's honour.' The book is a brilliant comedy and, for any man, a disquieting reminder of just how much hangs on your sexual potency. Once the truth is out, Antonio can forget a political career. 'He never had the stuff of a real Fascist,' comments a local official. 'My son is dead,' his father declares.

But why does Antonio have this problem? It's not that he has *never* had sex. There's nothing physically wrong with him. Is it because the women who chase him are so predatory and demanding, his parents and in-laws so pushy, or because Sicilian culture is drenched in a crass male pride? 'My son's got a planting stick could punch holes in rocks!' Antonio's father raves in the presence of his embarrassed wife; 'I support the regime because it's led by a man with a real cock,' says one of his friends. Is it, then, that Antonio's beautiful body (and beautiful mind) refuses to participate in this ugliness? Or is the Church with its insistence on purity and virginity partly to blame? When the still adolescent Antonio turns all the ladies' heads at mass, the priest invites his worried mother to pray that God may 'call the boy back to Himself as soon as possible'. He'll cause havoc.

Brancati doesn't spoil the novel with easy answers. When Antonio emerges from shamed withdrawal to explain himself to his dying uncle, it is not a criticism of this or that aspect of society he offers, but a long, complex, highly personal story, full of odd incidents and relationships. He describes a moment when he had begun to make love to a beautiful German woman who had at last decided to betray her fiancé with him.

> We said nothing more, turned out the light and embraced. A little later, she almost fainted from happiness, opening slowly like a rose in the sunshine. Nearly out of my mind with an even greater joy than hers, I just was telling myself to tone down the cry about to explode from my throat, when … when a sudden dread chill crept into my flesh, starting right where I'd least have wanted it . . .

This really wasn't a good moment for me to be reading *Il bell'Antonio*; the descriptions of lost libido discouraged me even from trying to make love. I couldn't stop thinking about

Antonio. What was Brancati saying? Perhaps that when a sufferer's complaint is one with his psychology you can never say that the cause is just this or just that, as you might with a virus or an infection: you can't say, oh, it's the overwork, or the long-term cross-cultural tension, or some trauma from his childhood, or this or that difficult relationship. No, a condition like this is a unique amalgam with a history all its own; it's an enigma to pore over, and so, in a way, not unlike a work of art. Something to contemplate, over time. A puzzle without a solution. The waterseller of Seville.

The idea of an illness being a work of art was immediately fascinating to me. Wasn't Kafka's *Metamorphosis* a case of sickness and aesthetic superimposed? The same was true of a hundred tales of Gothic decline. Don't many novels feed on a hero with a mystery malady which in a certain sense *is* the book? I had perhaps *created* my chronic condition over the years, the way I had written my novels, or become part of a family, or changed my home and language and culture.

This made a kind of sense and everything seemed more interesting.

Then I was furious. What was the point, what on earth was the point, of congratulating oneself on such a sick combination of navel-gazing and literary reflection? There was, I realise now, at this worst moment of the story, a strong temptation to give up. Accept it. Aestheticise it. This is you. Your life will always be like this. The interrupted nights. The constant abdominal pains. Stop looking for a cure and get on with it. Then if it helps to pretend it's something fascinating, go ahead.

Behind this there was also a curious fusion – confusion – of complacency and guilt: you *deserve* it.

Why?

I would reach a state of resignation, queerly gilded with

self-importance, then suddenly jump to my feet, kick the wall and shout no! No no no! An illness is *not* a puzzle to contemplate in eternity. I want to get better. I WANT TO MOVE ON! I want a sex life, for Christ's sake. You have none of Antonio's excuses for impotence, I told myself on putting the novel down: you have neither the stunning looks nor the women constantly throwing themsclves at your feet, neither the crass Sicilian father boasting about his sexual prowess nor a mother and wife in adoration of the Virgin. Why should this chill have entered *my* flesh?

Antonio's friends love to give him advice. Remember, they tell him, the days when you did make love and try to picture how it was. To give yourself confidence. The healing powers of positive visualisation. Returning in my frustration to the net, I found people on line offering very similar solutions for pelvic pain:

Hi Everyone,
Here's a common male problem that's relieved easily with EFT! No drugs or surgery involved.

EFT? Electronic Funds Transfer? Surely not.

'Emotionally focused therapy,' Wikipedia told me, 'proposes that emotions themselves have an innately adaptive potential that, if activated, can help clients change problematic emotional states or unwanted self-experiences.'

'Clients' sounded ominous. All the same, I thought there might be something in this. The internet post went on to offer an anecdote.

My husband and I recently visited some old friends of his and stayed over. 'David' (who is 59) went to bed early because he was having pain from his prostate problem.

Concerned, the narrator 'works' with David to construct a series of encouraging formulas he can repeat to himself when things are bad. Standing balefully over the loo, for example, he must say:

> *Even though my pee might come out slowly, I deeply and completely love and accept myself and my penis. I forgive myself and my penis for anything that I may have done.*

There was something very funny about this. I have never thought of my penis as a separate entity to be loved or forgiven. But was I in a position to be ironic? I read on.

> *Reminder phrases (I had David alternate these phrases while imagining positive images):*
> *Even though it may come out in a dribble*
> *And then again it may come out like a race horse*
> *And sometimes just a dribble*
> *I relax and let it flow like Niagara Falls*
> *And sometimes it's slow and I relax*
> *And let it flow like a fire hydrant*
> *I just let it flow and go easy on myself*
> *If I feel angry because it isn't flowing, I just let the anger flow easily out of my penis*

After a week or so, David gets huge benefits from this rigmarole. His pain declines, his urinary flow improves, he feels altogether better about himself, reactions compatible with the short-term improvements frequently described when administering placebos to prostate pain sufferers. Absolutely against the grain, I decided to take the approach seriously. Or at least to *try* to. It's an easier route than faith-healing, I thought. David is encouraged to open up the bathroom taps full blast, the better to visualise a rumbustious pee. Despite all my scepticism, not to mention the fiasco during the urogram, I opened up the taps. Rather than Niagara (which for me evokes images of kayaking catastrophe), I remembered the happy plash of my son peeing that morning before we set off on holiday together. And I invented a few determinedly optimistic formulas to repeat…

I shall spare you the formulas. All I can say is that doing all this stuff at two in the morning and at three and *again* at four and certainly at five is no joke. You have to feel gung-ho. To keep at it you'd need to get quick results. Unfortunately, the only effect it had on me was to wake me up to the point that I couldn't easily get back to sleep. Lying in bed, I wondered whether David hadn't exaggerated the positive effects of EFT because he liked having his friend's wife hanging out in the bathroom with him, the sound of those taps covering any hanky-panky they might have got up to. Impotence was not among David's listed symptoms.

On the last pages of *Il bell'Antonio*, after Catania has been bombed and Fascism overthrown, Antonio gets his libido back. Sort of. Outraged by the news that Barbara has married an ageing but wealthy rake, he imagines giving her a good thrashing. And finally something stirs. But I had no such violent feelings to turn me on. Nor wanted them. Who did I have to be angry with? Why does one have to be angry to have sex? The truth is, that after all this time, all these doctors, all this research, I *hadn't the slightest idea what was happening to me.*

Lives of Quiet Desperation

I was on Blackpool beach with friends. They were hesitating. So, show them how it's done! I stepped back, whipped off my clothes and started a heroic run to the sea. But I'd forgotten my trunks. I was naked! Far from impressing them, I was making a fool of myself. Plunge into the sea then! My feet pounded across the sand. No sea. The tide must be miles out. Suddenly, incongruously, in the huge expanse, I was running into a small barrier, the kind workmen set up round a hole in the road. It appeared from nowhere and I went over it and fell in. The hole was deep and dank with black, evil-smelling mud. I woke and hurried to the bathroom.

I was dreaming a lot. Almost every time I woke I had dreamed. Six times a night. And more and more these dreamscapes seemed to be telling me something. Why was I always dreaming of water? Or rather, of water that had run out, of mud and sand and slime. And why the constant element of embarrassment? I dive excitedly into a lake, only to find underwater weeds so thick and woody that I can walk on them, but awkwardly, foolishly. These watery scenes seeped into my nights. On more than one occasion, waking, I recalled the winter view of the Yamuna, trickling through broad sands behind the Taj.

It was on a morning like this, in the slightly hallucinatory state dreams leave you with, that that vast ocean that is the internet tossed up a dry page that I almost felt I had written myself, so accurately did it describe my condition and state of mind. It was by the authors of *A Headache in the Pelvis*.

In a few hundred words they gave their take on pelvic pain or so-called chronic prostatitis. What they offered was neither the official medicine of the hospitals nor the New Age alternatives. It was neither psychosomatic nor unaware of psychology. Neither mechanical nor mystical. It did not give importance to dreams, star charts or works of art, but nor did it propose to drive a motorway through my urethra or radically alter my body chemistry. There were no obscure herbs or expensive drugs. No difficult diets. It did not promise a quick recovery. It did not *promise* recovery at all. It said recovery was possible, up to a point, if I worked at it. Above all, it described my symptoms *accurately*. All of them. Even the ones the urologists had written off as irrelevant. It took the pains *seriously*. And it was the first thing I had seen written by doctors with Ph.D.s that accepted the glaring discrepancy between official explanations of this complaint and reality. It addressed itself to women as well as to men. So this was *not* a prostate problem. In short, in just a few minutes, I realised I had stumbled across a completely new story, a different version of events, one I could perhaps believe in, and that might even be true. Or at least helpful. That said, I had no idea at the time what it would mean to engage with this vision of things, nor how much I would be expected to change in myself. Nor did I understand how it could have taken me so long to find this page; if it really was a valid approach, why wasn't it the first hit on all the pelvic pain searches?

Their names did not inspire confidence. David Wise and Rodney Anderson. Together they had the ring of a charlatan double-act dreamed up by *Mad Magazine*. And what a mistake to dub their treatment The Stanford Protocol, which immediately suggested a pompous bid for patent status, the better to sell. But perhaps this was just an innate resistance on my part; I don't give trust easily. On the web, they wrote:

> *95% of patients who are diagnosed with prostatitis do not have an infection or inflammation that can account for their symptoms... the prostate is not the issue.*

Just to read this was a considerable relief. Not only had I not gone crazy, I was not even an unusual case.

> *Once the condition starts, the symptoms tend to have a life of their own.*

I had never formulated the thought quite like this but there was definitely something capricious going on: intense pains came and went without relation to external circumstance; urinary frequency varied enormously irrespective of what you drank. Doctors had never wanted to go into detail over this, as if afraid that an exhaustive description of symptoms would mean losing themselves in a labyrinth of highly nuanced but irrelevant sensation. Inevitably, this made you feel more alone with the problem. You were complaining about things that had no objective referent nor any apparent consequence beyond the pain itself, you weren't wasting away. As far as others were concerned you might perfectly well be making it up. So you learned to keep quiet. It was weeks since I had bothered my wife with the latest developments. She was growing tired of it all. Understandably.

'Symptoms may be intermittent or constant,' wrote Wise and Anderson, 'and few people will experience all of them.' They listed twenty-three. I had sixteen. Nor was there any symptom I had that they didn't mention. What most impressed me was that they included 'relief after a bowel movement'. Nobody else had corroborated this impression of mine; I felt like printing off the page right away and driving straight to Milan to slap it down on the urology ward operating table.

'The effect on a person's life,' the authors continued, 'has been likened to the effects of having a heart attack, angina, or Crohn's disease... Sufferers tend to live lives of quiet desperation.' Depression, anxiety and 'catastrophic thinking', they said, were the norm.

It may seem strange to say that I was cheered on reading this grim assessment. I would certainly never have made such comparative claims for my sufferings, nor did I consider myself desperate, not yet. But it was definitely a plus to be told that I hadn't been wildly exaggerating. My father, I remember, confided something of the like to me in more dramatic circumstances when the doctors finally told him that the radiotherapy had not cleared up his cancer and his condition was terminal. Previously informed, in order to 'keep his spirits up', that he had been cured, he was made doubly miserable because any expression of what he was feeling seemed like whining. Told he must die, he knew that everybody could stop wondering why he wasn't more cheerful. In literature too, I'm convinced, a clear-sighted pessimism is always more exhilarating and liberating than soft soap and denial.

But Wise and Anderson were not bringing bad news. They had an entirely new theory as to what caused this condition. Here I began to doubt. It seemed too simple to be true. It also seemed to be leading very directly to my spending money on their book and visiting their no doubt expensive clinic in California.

Basically, they took the view that *the entire problem was muscular* in origin, then, consequently, neurological. It was a well-recognised, instinctive human reaction, they claimed, particularly on the part of males, to raise the muscles around the pelvis in response to excitement and stress. A defence of the genitals. Some people did this constantly, compulsively, with the result that the muscles of 'the pelvic floor' never relaxed. A sedentary life and, in particular, a job that meant sitting day after day at a desk exacerbated the problem by restricting blood flow to these contracted muscles, which, as a result, suffered fatigue and eventually lost their natural elasticity, tightening and pulling in areas where they shouldn't, compressing the complex bundles of nerves that threaded the area.

I wasn't sure what to make of this. I had never seen the expression 'pelvic floor' before. What was this thing? All the medical diagrams I had studied restricted themselves to showing the relevant organs – bladder, prostate, kidneys – floating inside a transparent skin and linked by nothing more than the thin tubes that shifted fluids from one to the other. None of the doctors I had spoken to had said anything about how these organs were held in place or what lay in the spaces between them. Rather they took on the quality of heavenly bodies, miraculously fixed in emptiness. Finding it difficult to visualise what was being talked about, I went on Google images, typed in 'pelvic floor' and found this:

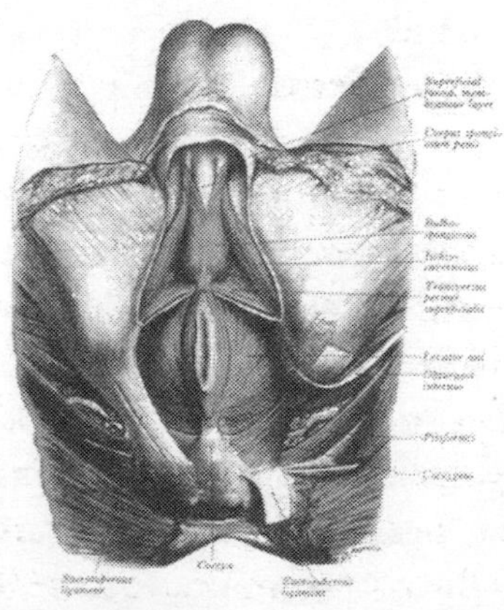

It was decidedly unattractive and hardly helpful. On the other hand, this business of getting relief after a bowel movement suddenly made sense: the big muscle round the anus relaxed, allowing all kinds of other things to shift and resettle. Each muscle, each area of muscle, Wise and Anderson maintained, if frequently and unnecessarily contracted over many years, could spark off pains in places that might be some distance away.

I thought about this. It was true that I had spent many hours of many days of many years sitting on my butt. There was a general consensus that I was a tense guy. When I write, for example, my body is far from relaxed. I might have one hand thrust hard into my hair – what's left of my hair – while my right knee is constantly bouncing up and down on the ball of my foot and my jaw working open and closed, open and closed; because I get excited about what I'm writing and I get frustrated when it's not going well. On the other hand, I had no *sensation* that the muscles in my body were tense. It all felt pretty normal to me.

But if chronic muscle fatigue was the problem, what was the treatment? Again the answer was suspiciously simple.

Relaxation and massage.

Nothing else. No drugs. No operations. '*We have never seen a satisfactory surgical intervention for these pains*,' the authors claimed. Just relaxation and massage. It was true they gave fancy names to these things – *paradoxical relaxation* and *myofascial trigger-point release massage* – but that, I feared, was merely to create the impression that you couldn't be expected to achieve relief without direct help purchased from Wise and Anderson Inc. The massage was highly specific. *And included anal massage.* It required trained experts. The relaxation procedures were so complex, the authors insisted, that they would not sell tapes to guide you because you'd never be able to make use of them without expert assistance; the last thing they wanted was for sufferers to give up in frustration and write off The Stanford Protocol along with all the other cures they had tried in vain. This was a treatment that took many months, even years, and required considerable effort and commitment on the part of the patient.

I was deeply suspicious. What could be so damn complicated (or 'paradoxical') about relaxing? What effort could possibly be required to get yourself massaged! Financial effort, obviously, EFT as we know it. I looked through the book's endorsements, most of them from doctors and Ph.D.s. Friends no doubt.

> *A Headache in the Pelvis* is a lamp in the dark human suffering of chronic pelvic pain.

If there is one virus a writer is naturally immune to, it's blurb-talk.

> *A Headache in the Pelvis* is a very important contribution to understanding and treating pelvic pain. It is also an illuminating discussion of the relationship of mental and physical interaction in the production of disease, and an approach to a truly comprehensive treatment of illness that has relevance to a whole range of contemporary morbidities.

This sounded more interesting. Particularly 'contemporary morbidities'. I realised that what I liked about this new paradigm was the way it accounted for a psychological component – the years of tension and bad living habits – without saying that my condition came in manipulative response to a specific psychological need (I fall ill to alter my relationship with my wife, for example, or to have an excuse for going back to England). There was also something fascinating about this clumsy title – *A Headache in the Pelvis* – as if it might have been precisely the thinking too much over the years that was the root cause of the pain. This reminded me of Leopardi's beautiful line about thoughts drowning in immensity. Perhaps those desiccated dreams were telling me they couldn't find water enough to wash away my arid lucubration.

But among a dozen endorsements it was the next that swung it.

> This is the book to read before you contemplate surgery, drugs or resign yourself to continue to suffer with chronic pelvic pain. Return to health is possible. Drs. Wise and Anderson have developed an innovative clinical protocol that works.

I needed to believe this and clicked on the purchase button.

A Cat on Board

It takes about ten days for a book to arrive by post from the States. Before it does and my life begins to change, I want to sing the praises of the only product that gave me some relief in this unhappy period. Benzodiazepine.

Here is a detail I had forgotten. When I had seen that Harley Street doctor, the first one, over twenty and more years ago, he had prescribed, along with the antibiotics, a milligram of benzodiazepine every morning and evening. I was offended. Why was he prescribing a tranquilliser for a prostate condition? 'We've found it helps,' he said. I never considered following his advice. How can a writer work on tranquillisers? The mind has to fizz like a firework. You have to be a fury of creative attention. But at the worst moment, in that spring of 2006, I tried it.

The frequency of my night-time trips to the bathroom had increased. Seven. Eight. Nine! I began to suffer from insomnia. I would lie in bed for half an hour, my mind raking back and forth over this and that, then go to the bathroom again without having slept. Then after another half-hour. Then another. There is a curiosity about our house that I haven't mentioned. It's a semi-detached and every now and then, from the party wall with our good and quiet neighbours, we hear a low, as it were electronic voice that speaks for no more than a few seconds. It has very much the sound of those battery-operated games for infants where you press different buttons to get nursery rhymes, or animal sounds, or jokes. But the words are muffled by the wall and I can never make out what is said. My daughters laugh and argue about it. It says, '*Un gat-to è sa-li-to a bor-do*,' Lucy claims, mimicking the mechanical sound. A cat has climbed on board. But Stefi, who was first to notice it, is sure that it sometimes says, '*Tro-va la chia-ve!*' Find the key. Or an indistinct, 'Maw maw maw.' The neighbours claim they know nothing about it.

Occasionally I had heard this voice in the middle of the night. It starts very abruptly, like those robotic instructions that surprise you in elevators or Japanese cars, repeats its six or seven muffled words, and stops. Now I began to hear it more often. Sleepless, I tried to make out what the voice said. The kids had got it wrong. They were imagining what they heard. We all make up things we've only half understood. Why would it produce words that were nonsense? The house was haunted perhaps. Stefi had floated that idea. The ghost was seeking to give me a message; *tro-va la chia-ve*, find the key. To my dreams? To my illness? Except I wasn't sure it really did say '*trova la chiave*', but something else. I listened. The problem was it spoke only rarely, briefly, and without warning. You couldn't prepare for it.

I lay alert, uneasy. The church clock chimed the hours and half-hours. Streetlamp and moonlight sheened the dark. Over the hill, a scooter droned. My mother had been perfectly willing to believe in ghosts, I remembered. She was sure she had seen my father after he died. In his robes. For a while she had been enthusiastic about the idea of exorcising haunted houses. The spirits of the dead must be healed to allow them to move on. Perhaps this is a sophisticated, post-modern ghost, I thought, playing to my paranoia, mocking my obsessive attention to language, saying muffled words that might be meaningful but can never be deciphered. A poet, in short.

If anyone needed to move on, it was me.

Some nights I became extremely agitated. Breathing softly beside me, my wife had never seemed more distant, more healthy. I was becoming withdrawn. I was losing interest in intimacy. How many lunches and dinners had I cancelled because I found it uncomfortable sitting down? People were accusing me of being aloof. I found it hard to explain myself. There was a crucial part of my life that couldn't be talked about, except by allusion, perhaps, in my novels. My characters were also growing manic and withdrawn. Inexplicably Harold Cleaver abandons his whirlwind life to retreat to mountain solitude. Inexplicably Albert James withdraws into idiosyncrasy and death wish. These stories didn't quite satisfy. Or at least, they didn't satisfy me. They didn't really *say it.* Nothing could.

In bed, my leg twitched. I couldn't sleep. There. A nerve just above the knee. And now I felt thirsty. I needed water. My father, I remembered, had always had a thing about air, fresh air. Whenever he got out into the country he would go through a rather cranky routine of deep breathing and sighing and saying how wonderful the fresh air was. Perhaps he felt constricted in his ecclesiastical life. My father had wanted to be a missionary in Africa or Asia and ended up suffocating in the stale air of an ugly, fake-Gothic suburban church. 'Ah! Fresh air at last!' he would exclaim, when we got out of the train at some holiday destination. 'How marvellous! Sea air! Mountain air!' We made fun of him. And he died of lung cancer, choked to death, having never smoked. 'Breathe on me, breath of life', he loved that hymn. Would I die dried out in some way, I wondered? Bereft of water, in the low tide of my dreams? I had started to drink a lot during the night.

Every time I went to the bathroom I needed a gulp of water. From the tap. That was new. My mouth was always dry.

Is this what Dr Wise means by catastrophic thinking?

Maybe you should have had the operation after all, I thought then. Maybe the hospital doctors were absolutely right. Anderson and Wise were not urologists. Wise was a psychotherapist and Anderson a neurologist. What did they know? Carlo was a good man, a trained urologist, who saw dozens of patients like me every day. I couldn't believe he and his colleagues were operating on people unnecessarily. It was your foolish pride stopped you doing it, I told myself. Some kind of mad male vanity about the integrity of your wedding tackle. To what end, if we never make love? And it was pride stopped me asking my mother to try faith healing. Give it a whirl. Why not? Stoop!

But how can you, I wondered – and again I was furious with myself – how can you hold such different interpretations of your situation *simultaneously*? How could I think I'd got it wrong about TURP *and* about faith-healing? 'This is a problem you will never overcome, Mr Parks, until you confront the profound contradiction in your character!'

'*Un gatto è salito a bordo.*'

The voice spoke, abruptly, from beyond the wall. A cat has climbed on board. I was going nuts. The truth is we know nothing about our bodies, I thought. Nothing. What's in there, what's going on? Each research paper contradicts the next. Every discipline is scathing of the others. A second opinion. A third. The web is an ocean of confusion. Above all, every story told in words, every medical story in particular, is always a thousand times clearer than reality. However unhappy, narrative is, of its very nature, reassuring, gives the illusion of knowing, when all anyone ever really knows is how he's feeling now, now, now and *now*, in this instant.

I was feeling terrible.

I got up, went to the bathroom and took three milligrams of benzodiazepine.

That will sound easy enough but in Italy this drug is mainly distributed in drop form under the product name Lexotan. Ten drops per milligram. In the dead of night every drop took an age to fall from the small brown bottle glinting in the light above the bathroom mirror and down into the battered tooth glass. Thirty times I watched the drops form. Even slower than my peeing.

Thirty times.

The effect was hypnotic. But I mustn't look away or I'd lose count. And all the time my hand trembled as it held the bottle. You are old old old, I told myself. Older than the waterseller.

Catastrophic thinking.

I tapped the bottom of the bottle. Hurry up! Hurry up! The drop quivered but wouldn't fall.

Twenty-one – pause – tremble – twenty-two – pause – tremble.

Why does it have to be so achingly, achingly slow?

To discourage suicide. With Lexotan, you'd die of boredom before killing yourself.

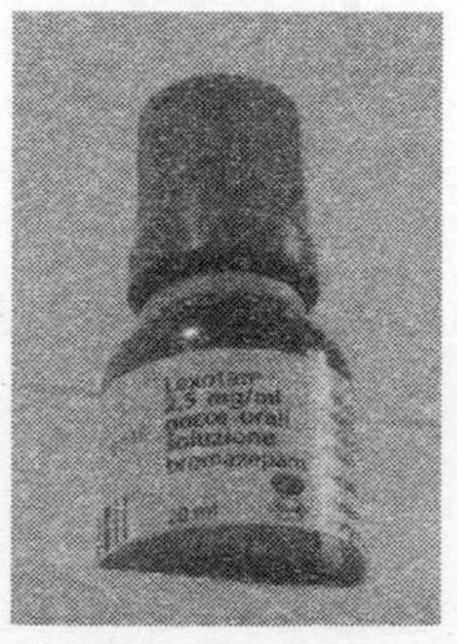

Back in bed I reflected that maybe I was trying to make something serious happen with this insomnia. I had begun to envy people who were indisputably ill. I wanted to be seriously, *seriously* ill myself, so that people could see my condition and it would all be out in the open and someone would finally have to *do something.*

Eventually, a narcotic calm stole over me. It was a huge pleasure, like sliding into a warm bath. Then I slept for four solid hours. That was longer, I realised on waking, than any other sleep for a year and more.

Thank you, benzodiazepine. Thank you, pharmaceutical research.

The one drawback was that if you used the drug three nights in a row the effect wore off. But not the morning drowsiness. To each night, then, its elusive antidote.

PART TWO

Be Silent, Oh All Flesh

One late afternoon in June, I closed a door, placed two pillows under my knees, lay back and took a deep breath. I had a book in my hand. It was open at the heading: **Respiratory Sinus Arrhythmia breathing in preparation for Paradoxical Relaxation.**

Daunting.

It was a strange book I had pulled out of its mail-order cardboard a couple of days before. On the net it had seemed the cover was simply the cumbersome title writ large. Now I saw that the brownish background behind the words was actually a faded reproduction of a Renaissance painting – something famous I'd seen before but couldn't recall where – showing a seated saint with a splendid beard immersed in a book. At the reader's shoulder, apparently equally interested in what was written there, were two blond cherubs.

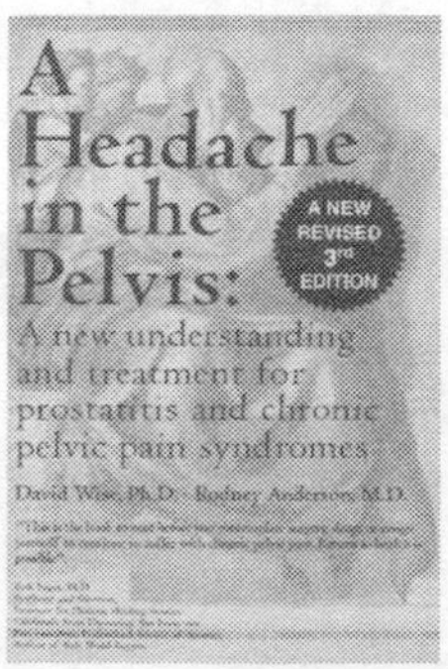

What on earth had possessed the good doctors to front their ideas with such an image? Were you supposed to assume a parallel between the book in your hand and the tome the saint was reading, presumably holy, perhaps even the Bible? Was this why the orange sticker declaring 'A NEW REVISED 3RD EDITION' was placed right beneath the ancient book?

Surely even the most ambitious authors wouldn't claim as much.

Or were Wise and Anderson suggesting that this was precisely the kind of man who typified the headache in the pelvis: an avid, elderly reader with bad posture and rounded shoulders? It wasn't easy to see what the saint was sitting on, but it looked uncomfortable. If not marble, then at least hard wood. Still unable to recall where I'd seen the picture, I wondered if it mightn't be St Jerome, patron saint of translators, since he is usually depicted as mortifying the flesh with his mental toils. Did St Jerome have chronic pelvic pain syndrome? Did he have to steal a moment's inattention from himself before he could pass water? Certainly the Renaissance painter wasn't teaching *mens sana in corpore sano*. I studied the credits, but they merely said 'Cover Design, Bob Lee Hickson.'

In any event, I took it that the idea had been to foreground the obsessive mental world of the CPP sufferer, something the authors frequently commented on. Their patients, they said, were over-achievers who had little time to look after themselves, tensing their pelvic floors year in year out while they worked their butts off to satisfy aspirations that had nothing to do with healthy living. On the first page it emerged that Dr Wise himself had once been such a man. 'As someone who suffered for twenty-two years with pelvic pain and dysfunction ...' his preface begins. And he goes on: 'More times than I can remember I would wake up in the middle of the night weeping because my pain was so great and I saw no solution for it.'

Twenty-two years! Respect.

He describes his obsessive, pre-internet researches: 'I would go to the library at a local hospital, or the medical library at the University of California Medical Center, and pore over old medical journals ...'

So was the frescoed saint the archetypal prostatitis sufferer searching for a cure, and the book some ancient medical treatise? Dr Wise made a list of all the treatments he'd tried in vain: antibiotics, diets and renunciations (alcohol, coffee, spices), reflexology, zinc supplements, 'acupuncture, psychotherapy, guided imagery visualisation, hands-on healing and prayer'.

That made me sit up. Throughout *A Headache* Dr Wise, who appears to be the main author, hints at a side to his character that has to remain mostly hidden if he's to keep the sceptics on board. I began to warm to him. There seemed to be profound contradictions in the man.

And in his approach. Again and again the book makes the double gesture of first explaining very carefully to you how to get well, then warning that the recommended procedure is far too complex for you to undertake on your own. It was harder than learning the piano, he insisted. Hence impossible without a teacher. This was not, or not only, I realised now, to lure you to his clinic, but out of a genuine, control-freak's anxiety that if he, Dr Wise, wasn't there in person, there was no way you, Tim Parks, would get things right. It was a position I understood because I often feel the same way myself when I give advice to my students.

'This guy thinks like me,' I told Rita. 'Let's hope this is the breakthrough.'

'Can I see?' she asked. She picked up the book, looked at the cover and immediately pronounced: 'Michelangelo, Sistine Chapel, the prophet, Zechariah.' My wife's effortless erudition can be chastening. Then, while she was looking, and despite the fact that this business of the painting must be entirely irrelevant, I Googled the good Zechariah and discovered he was famous above all for his obscurity:

> The prophecy of Zechariah is exceedingly opaque, for there are contained therein dreamlike visions which are given an interpretation, but we are unable to pronounce definitively regarding its interpretation until the advent of a 'true teacher' (*moreh tzedeq*).

It was uncanny. Was Dr Wise presenting himself as the true teacher who would interpret my dreams? Or the prophet who would bring difficult truths to a recalcitrant, stiff-necked people? Or stiff-bladdered people? And why did I care so much about the cover and keep referring it to myself? Was paranoia a character trait of pelvic pain sufferers? Opening my battered Bible, given to me by my parents at my baptism and bearing, in my father's scrawl, the ominous dedication/exhortation, 'Hold fast the form of sound words, which thou hast heard of me (II Timothy 1:13)', I looked up Zechariah and read the whole first chapter until the following verse stopped me in my tracks:

> Be silent, O all flesh, before the Lord.

Sound words and silence. They were taxing and conflicting imperatives. Meantime, I was in pain and eager to put *A Headache* to the test; if I couldn't have the Californian myofascial anal massage, exhaustively described and somewhat grotesquely illustrated, I would nevertheless try the book's relaxation technique.

Now.

At once Dr Wise raised a barrier. The paradox in paradoxical relaxation was soon explained: having stretched out on the bed and got yourself calm, you focus on some tension in your body and *don't* try to relax it. Just concentrate on it. Let it be. That way, eventually, it will relax itself. But only if you genuinely *don't try* to relax it. Paradox.

OK, I'll try, I thought.

Or rather, not try.

I'll try not to try.

However, before doing that, the doctor insisted, I must first get into a state of 'respiratory sinus arrhythmia breathing' and this complicated process should be done, of course, 'under the supervision of a professional'.

Damn.

However, Dr Wise then offered precise instructions on how to do it, knowing full well that you wouldn't have a 'professional' in your bedroom. Still, if it didn't work, you would know it wasn't his fault.

Basically, the idea was to align the heartbeat with the breathing so that the pulse was a little faster on inhalation than exhalation. Six deep abdominal breaths a minute was optimum, Wise suggested.

I had never really figured out what abdominal breaths were.

There were now nine numbered paragraphs of instructions.

'Take your pulse,' paragraph one begins.

It always spooks me to take my pulse.

Paragraph four reads:

> ... count up to five heart beats (if your heart rate is 60, as in the example above) as you inhale raising your abdomen and then count to five heartbeats as you exhale. If your heart rate is 72, you would count up to six beats as you inhale or exhale.

There was no way I could do this. The whole rigmarole reminded me again of Beckett's Molloy calculating his farts per minute over twenty-four hours. How could anyone begin to relax while checking his pulse, counting beats and trying to breathe in response to computations? Harder than learning the piano, indeed. I had never got anywhere with the piano. And I had had a teacher for that. Discouraged, I put the book down.

Perhaps I should say here that the one previous experience I'd had of breathing techniques for relaxation had been an amusing fiasco. When my wife was pregnant with our first child, some twenty years previously, we had attended classes in autogenous training; they were supposed to help mothers deal with the pain of childbirth. The doctor was a charming eccentric in his late sixties whose broad smile and glassy eyes sought to radiate a jovial calm. He gathered together about a dozen couples, had us sit down, eyes closed, on straight-backed wooden chairs and began to intone in a sonorously hypnotic voice: '*Ognuno si dica, io sono calmo, io sono tranquillo* – everyone say to themselves, I am calm, I am relaxed.'

I found it hard not to burst out laughing.

As soon as the good doctor thought he'd got the class into a state of deep breathing, he invited us on a mental tour of our bodies, but speaking as if we were all mothers-to-be, with the result that I had the confusing experience of being encouraged to explore my womb and baby. After about the third lesson, as we were leaving, the man took me aside and said, as if needing to unburden himself: 'Signor Parks, I don't believe I've ever seen a person *as completely unable to relax as yourself.*'

It was like the moment when the debonair pensioner with the white cowboy hat stopped me on the street and ordered me to 'stand up straight, for God's sake!' I had the strong impression that I was being singled out as a freak. People couldn't refrain from telling me I was uptight.

Remembering both these occasions now as I baulked at the hurdle of respiratory sinus arrhythmia, I couldn't help seeing that they corroborated Dr Wise's theory that my troubles had to do with excessive, unrelenting tension. So perhaps I should at least try the relaxation technique even if I couldn't do the complex ten-minute breathing routine beforehand. No doubt this made it even more unlikely that I could succeed without a trip to Stanford. All the same, two simple and effective pieces of advice earlier on in the book had encouraged me to believe that it might be worth at least trying to follow Dr Wise's programme. To check the position of the pelvic floor, *A Headache* had said in its opening pages, make as if to urinate, but without actually urinating, and feel if the muscles move. Tentatively, since I'd never made as if to pee without peeing before, I did as asked. Abruptly, a tight girdle of muscle between navel and pubis slid down, as if settling into its proper place. At once I felt more comfortable.

That was odd.

I waited five minutes and did it again.

There.

I caught myself out in the kitchen preparing lunch and did it again.

Yes!

I was astonished. You go to three or four urologists and pay hundreds of pounds only to get the first piece of useful advice, *the first instruction that makes a tiny difference*, from a self-help book. It definitely felt good to do that.

Your defensive reaction to pain, Dr Wise went on, is to pull away from it. This is particularly true in the abdominal area where the muscles pull up in defence of the genitals and away from your pain. Don't. Push *towards* it.

There was no shortage of pain to experiment with. I pushed, waited, kept pushing. It definitely felt different. There was still the same smouldering, pulsing soreness, but it felt safer somehow, more manageable.

I was excited. It was the first time I'd been able to make anything happen with these pains. Instead of the arrhythmia breathing, I decided, I would just take a dozen deep steady breaths, then start the relaxation, paradoxical or no.

I lay on my bed. I placed pillows under my knees, as instructed. Was I ready? No, the neighbours' dog was barking, and Stefi was playing her guitar. I found my earplugs. Good.

At last I shut my eyes.

I took a deep breath.

Goblin Fires

Silence.

More or less.

How strange, I thought, after the fourth or fifth theatrically deep breath, this closing oneself in one's body, not to sleep or snooze, but to pay attention.

Attention to what? Eyes closed, I felt disorientated.

There was an itch at the corner of my mouth and I scratched it.

You're not supposed to move, I remembered. Your hands must be still. But where? Wise had spoken of them being spread out, palms up, but this felt weird. Anyway, I was on my side of the bed, so one arm hung over the edge. I put them side by side on my abdomen.

Now there was an itch at the base of the ear. I tried to ignore it; it itched more fiercely. Wise hadn't talked about itches.

I was supposed to be paying attention, to tension.

Attention, tension!

But not verbalising.

Don't verbalise.

I couldn't feel any tension. Just the itch. Otherwise, what surprised me was a growing sense of space. Being very awake, inside myself, determined to pay attention to I didn't know what, it was as if I were surrounded by a large expanse, though I couldn't see it. I was alone in a strange, brooding landscape; under a low sky, I thought, damp hills perhaps, but invisible.

Absurdly, I remembered Doctor Who's Tardis: small on the outside, spacious when you went in. If only I could open some inner eye I would find my body, inside, was roomy.

You are not supposed to be thinking.

Silence. Eyes closed.

Be silent, O all flesh, before the Lord.

It seemed Michelangelo had painted Zechariah with the face of the Pope in order to flatter him, the Pope that is. Of course, everybody knew that the whole Sistine Chapel was a complex coded message which—

You are supposed to be concentrating *wordlessly and thoughtlessly* on tension.

Concentrate thoughtlessly.

There was no tension.

That I could find.

The minutes passed. No, they didn't pass. I had set the alarm on my phone for an hour hence, but there was no way I would last an hour like this. I had so much *work* to be getting on with! The itch at the top of my ear wouldn't let up. My hands were eager to get at it, eager to *move*.

And the pain. The pain was a fire smouldering in mud, as in some hot volcanic land. Hot belly mud. It had become steadier than it used to be; less maverick, fewer fireworks, dour.

Dour dour dour.

The pain surged to the fore. It was strong. You deal with the pain by keeping in constant motion, I realised now. That was the truth. Even when I was still, I moved. My knee jerking. Scratching. My fist clenching and unclenching. That kept the pain at bay. And when my body was still my mind moved. My mind was in constant motion. All day every day. The thoughts jerked back and forward like the knee that twitched. The difficulty when I was writing was not to come up with thoughts, but to give them direction and economy.

Like a climber plant that must be pruned and tamed, pruned and tamed. Above all pruned.

You are supposed not to be thinking.

Or not supposed to be thinking.

Or supposed to be not thinking.

I moved the not. Language is always on the move.

Even when I slept I moved. To sleep I needed to be on one side with one knee pushed forward. Then I switched to the other side. Every time I went to the bathroom I turned myself, like meat on a griddle. And I switched my earplug from one ear to the other. I can't bear having an earplug pressing the pillow.

I pulled the earplug out, turned over, put the earplug in. Six times a night.

In the silence, eyes closed, I remembered a documentary I'd seen years before about some kind of desert lizard that stopped its feet from burning on the hot Sahara sand by constantly and rapidly lifting and dropping the right front foot and back left foot, then the left front and back right. Alternately. They lifted and fell in the blink of an eyelid, almost too quick for the camera to see. A sort of purgatory, I had thought, when I saw the images.

Downstairs someone answered the phone. Even the best earplugs have their limits.

So where was this famous tension I was supposed to be full of?

No sign of it. *Niente di niente di niente.*

Perhaps Dr Wise was right that there was no point in trying this on your own.

Should I give up?

If you couldn't find any tension, he said at one point, try contracting a muscle for a moment, then let it go. There would be a residual tension you could recognise.

I wasn't sure I saw the sense in all this. I had begun to feel that I'd be much more relaxed doing a spot of reading for an essay that was due.

The pain was growing stronger.

Drs Wise and Anderson have developed an innovative clinical protocol that works.

You are here because of the pain.

Wise had said not to concentrate on the pain. I would be too eager to make it go away. I wouldn't be able to concentrate on it without trying to change it.

He was right.

Do not abandon hope until you have given these methods your most sincere effort. This signed by somebody who claimed to have recovered.

What was the word 'sincere' doing there? Why would anyone be insincere about stuff like this? Was that 'abandon hope' a deliberate allusion to Dante? Did the healed man—

Stop thinking!

I tensed the muscle above one knee. The one that jerked. And relaxed it.

Well?

Nothing.

Then my mind latched onto a glow. Yes, there was definitely a low glow, a buzz from the muscle. So that must be residual tension. It was quite pleasant. Concentrate on it, Wise said. No problem.

There.

And I started to congratulate myself. I'm getting the hang of it already. Performed the old trick of matching words – 'residual tension' – to experience – the glow of above the knee. Then fastened my mind onto it. Well done, Tim!

What did Wise mean, this was too demanding?

Already I'd lost it. The pain in my belly flared.

Start again.

I did the trick again, contracted the muscle, let it go, found the tension again. Don't think. Don't congratulate yourself. Then the corresponding muscle on the other side began to sing too. Without my contracting it first.

Interesting.

I held on to the glow. This feeling. This feeling. This feeling. Instead of the tension dissolving, it grew. Quite suddenly and rapidly. Actually it grew enormously, grotesquely. All at once the muscles on my leg were bursting with tension. Damn. I'd have to move them. They were blazing.

Why hadn't Wise mentioned this?

Other fires lit up around my body. Close by in my neck. Far away in a calf. Not fires, but flickerings of red heat in the dark expanse of the flesh. The backs of my hands smouldered. A muscle in my cheek sparked. The darkness that had seemed deserted was full of life. Goblins. Havoc.

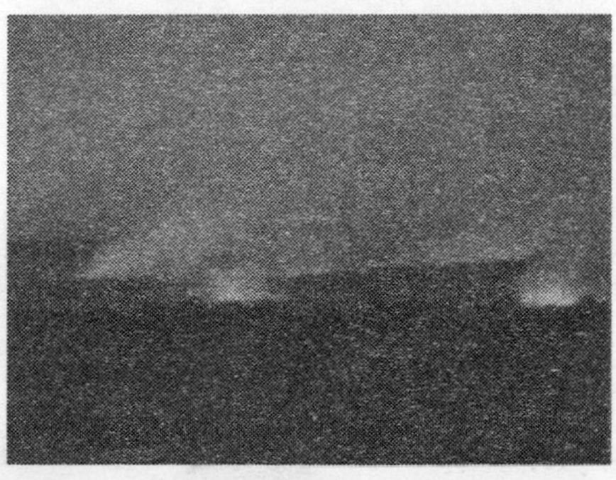

I was shocked. This is me. Bonfires under a night sky. It was so strange. Then I was reminded of that scene in Buzzati's *The Tartar Steppe* where, desperately eager to find an enemy in the emptiness, scrutinising the vast desert around the isolated fort, one of the soldiers starts to see campfires lighting up along the horizon. In just a few moments he has conjured the Tartar army into existence.

The Tartar Steppe, I remembered, was another book about mental paralysis, about wishing to move on and not being able to. Never finding the enemy.

The fires faded. I had lost them in the Tartar Steppe.

Try again.

So the mind went back and forth, concentrating on tension, watching it flare and grow, losing it in wayward thoughts. It showed no signs of dissolving as Dr Wise had promised. Sometimes it was too intense. It would drive me mad. The mind turned elsewhere. I forced it back.

Then I noticed the pain in my stomach had *gone*.

What? Check.

Of course, it hadn't gone. It was there, but as a shadow, a ghost of itself.

I was suspicious and went to investigate. It roared up.

But it had definitely gone, *been gone*, unnoticed, as it were. For a little while. As though when I slept. But I hadn't been sleeping. I'd been awake with these goblin fires in the dark and the pain had subsided.

Without waiting for the alarm to sound the hour, I jumped out of bed. The pain was back to normal.

'So?' Rita asked.

'Interesting,' I told her.

Ineffable

Two things. However briefly, I had made the pain go away. Done it myself, with no drugs. Presumably it could be done again. Maybe for longer.

Second. My body was different from what I had imagined. The problem was: time.

'Many of our patients are simply too busy to dedicate themselves to our treatment,' Wise and Anderson observed. These people, men and women, were not yet suffering enough. They still saw their pains as an irritating waste of time, a distraction to put behind them as quickly as possible. Hence they were drawn to accounts of their illness that saw a rapid solution in drugs, or a surgical operation. No personal energies need be expended. It could be paid for. Hopefully by the State.

This described my thinking, at least until very recently, with ominous accuracy.

'We strongly advise sufferers,' Wise went on, 'to accept these pains as part of the main curriculum of their lives.'

The main curriculum!

Would I have to stop referring to my pains as 'stupid'?

Wise's position, a little pious-sounding to my ear, was that this chronic and worsening condition was trying to tell me something about myself, about the way I had been living, and I was supposed to listen. I would have to give my pains the time of day.

An hour, to be precise. Every day. At least for the first two or three months.

Where am I going to find an hour a day?

'But you have oceans of time,' Rita laughed. Having always complained that I am 'too driven', too interminably focused on my 'precious work', this was a big told-you-so opportunity for my wife. She was loving it.

'Aeons of time!' she insisted.

Rita was right. I was lucky. Aside from the university, no one was breathing down my neck. I wasn't running a major multi-national, or standing for parliament, I wasn't on piece-work with an extended family to feed. All I had to do was to sacrifice an hour a day of writing. Turn down a few essay commissions.

The main curriculum of your life. No sooner had I read that phrase than I kept repeating it, mulling it over. Wise had scored a direct hit there. I saw at once that, far more than the time itself, the hour count, what was at stake here was a major principle. Instead of taking my work with me to hospital waiting rooms, dealing with my troubles as if I was getting the car fixed, my eye on my watch and my hand on my wallet, I would have to accept *a radical shift of priorities.* The pain must be allowed to come on board and take equal status beside my writing, beside my family, as part of the core curriculum.

A cat has climbed on board.

Six months previously I wouldn't have been ready for this. Even now it galled.

OK, so, perhaps after lunch, I thought, an hour might be found, when I usually yawned my way through the papers online.

Or shortly before bedtime, when I leafed—

'To be effective you must give it your best period of the

day,' Dr Wise warned. 'Otherwise you won't have the attention and concentration required properly to relax the pelvic floor.'

Every time I turned to *A Headache*, it seemed the good doctor had the measure of me. He closed my bolt-holes. I took a blanket and a couple of pillows to the office and made up the bed there.

Prime work time.

Again and again the hour would start with a feeling of time-wasting and humiliation. Why did it take me so long to settle down? I'd forgotten to remove my glasses. My watch. I'd forgotten to set the alarm. There was sleep in my eyes. My underwear felt tight. Take it off. Start again. Now the sheet – because I'd got between the sheets – was irritating my chin. My toes wanted to twitch. At this point I may as well abort. At this point it's a lost cause.

But I lay still. 'Your most *sincere* effort,' I remembered.

It came to me now how difficult it had always been for me to sit still, to *be* still in any way. 'Sit still, Timothy!' My mother's voice. I was squirming beside her on the pew. I couldn't sit still through my father's sermons. (Why is it always so tempting to imagine my troubles started with my father's sermons?) Or even worse his long prayers. I *hated* prayers. I couldn't sit still in church, couldn't kneel still either. '*Parks!*' A piece of chalk whizzes past my cheek. That was school. 'Stop fidgeting, boy. Sit *still!*' Happy days, when a teacher could throw chalk at a kid. What if he'd got me in the eye? Later in life it would be lectures, conferences, readings, faculty meetings. I couldn't sit still to listen to my colleagues. I fidgeted through a fellow author's reading. No doubt I've offended many. Parks isn't listening. He's drawing attention to himself. When I teach I have to move around. It's essential. Otherwise everything dries up. I can't teach sitting down. It's fun in Italy,

I've always thought, that you can gesticulate as you talk. You keep moving.

'By all means move a little in the first few minutes,' Dr Wise conceded, 'to make sure you are quite comfortable. But then we would advise you to try to stay absolutely still for the full period of your paradoxical relaxation.'

The first few minutes have passed now. However excruciating, I must lie still. I breathed deeply and remembered Eliot. 'Teach us to care and not to care. Teach us to sit still.'

Don't verbalise.

Then after a while something would happen. A breath breathed itself and I slid down into that dark landscape with its low sky and damp hills. At once the muscles of my face buzzed and sang with tension.

I say 'something *would* happen', as though these sessions were all the same. Certainly there was an element of repetition, particularly at the beginning: the itches, the fuss, the trivial adjustments, the mill of defeatist thoughts. But from this point on, from the moment I entered my bodyscape, as it were, every day was different. And as the first week moved into the second and third, things grew more intense, more – here was a real paradox – *exotic*.

There were curious pulsations. In my wrists perhaps. Not a regular wrist pulse of the kind you can check and count. Rather it might move along my right wrist, from hand to forearm, then ripple over into the left. Faster than an ordinary pulse. More fluid, mobile. The wave was picked up by a ticking in the stomach. Then a leg too. A sea swell of pulses were criss-crossing the muscles. The tension in my cheeks was exactly superimposed over the tension in my calves. The two seemed to be the same. Both were growing and changing, glowing and noisy. Suddenly, it was all so *interesting* that the mind found it easy to concentrate. More interesting than thoughts. As when you surrender yourself to strange music. It was so *busy*. Parts of the body were calling back and forth to each other with little rippling pulsations, as if the tide was lapping in and out across underwater weeds.

Stop describing it!

Concentrate.

Suddenly my belly drew a huge breath, absolutely unexpected, and a great warm wave flooded down my body from top to toe.

I nearly drowned. Shocked and tensed, I sat up and opened my eyes.

'What in God's name was that?'

The feeling had vanished at once. It was gone. But so too, I realised now, was the pain. The pain had quite gone. Not even a shadow of a pain. Not a ghost. I was lying still, *painless*.

I then spent half an hour trying to make this bizarre thing happen again. It must be the famous abdominal breathing, I thought. Though Dr Wise hadn't said anything about the effects being this dramatic. I was so excited now that the fact of the pain's disappearing seemed rather secondary.

I knew it would soon be back.

I tried and tried to conjure up that wave again; it wouldn't be conjured. I was hugely disappointed. I'm a far more reliable companion, the pain sniggered. The proverbial bad penny was back.

I tried the next day. And the next. Nothing. I actually lost ground.

Perhaps a week later when I'd almost forgotten about it and had begun instead to concentrate on the muscles of my face, begun to realise that the muscles of my face formed a fierce knit of tensions that urgently required releasing, it happened again.

It was violent and very sudden. A great warm wave burst from the dry, knitted muscles of my cheeks and forehead to surge across this low landscape. Dyke after dyke gave way in its path. Nothing resisted. I was swamped, submerged from head to toe.

This time I managed to keep still. I felt it flood over and through me. But I was too excited. There! There! The wave again! The wave! *You did it*!

It ebbed.

Afterwards, back at my desk, I was reminded of a passage from *Women in Love* that I had sometimes used in translation lessons. I Googled it.

> After a lapse of stillness, after the rivers of strange dark fluid richness had passed over her, flooding, carrying away her mind and flooding down her spine and down her knees, past her feet, a strange flood, sweeping away everything and leaving her an essential new being, she was left quite free, she was free in complete ease, her complete self.

That wasn't quite it. The experience had been more sudden. More violent. But the business of the mind being flooded away, flooded *clean*, was definitely the same. It felt good. And 'lapse of stillness', I realised, must mean lapse in the sense of thoughtlessness, unexpected unawareness. As in 'lapsus'. You had to be still to make it happen. I started to read around the passage.

This is a bizarre and embarrassing moment in *Women in Love*, one of those that prompted critics to jeer at the book. Birkin and Ursula have just had a big argument, then made up, during a country walk. An engagement ring gets tossed back and forth in fine melodramatic style. Afterwards, the two find a pub, ask for lunch and are shown into a back room where the landlady leaves them alone for a few minutes while she prepares the food. Here they have some kind of weird sexual–spiritual experience which involves Ursula kneeling open-mouthed at Birkin's thighs. He is one of the 'Sons of God' and she one of the 'Daughters of Man.' Thus:

> She traced with her hands the line of his loins and thighs, at the back, and a living fire ran through her, from him, darkly. It was a dark flood of electric passion she released from him, drew into herself. She had established a rich new circuit, a new current of passional electric energy, between the two of them, released from the darkest poles of the body and established in perfect circuit. It was a dark fire of electricity that rushed from him to her, and flooded them both with rich peace, satisfaction.
>
> 'My love,' she cried, lifting her face to him, her eyes, her mouth open in transport.

Hmmm.

Still, you have to admire Lawrence for taking on this stuff, in 1922. My idea, I remembered now, when I showed my students this lapse passage, had been to compare it with an earlier moment when Gerald and Gudrun first make love and afterwards Gudrun spends a tormented night with her thoughts racing and churning away destructively. That's the passage that has the untranslatable expression 'destroyed into perfect consciousness', which I had talked about in India.

> But Gudrun lay wide awake, destroyed into perfect consciousness. She lay motionless, with wide eyes staring motionless into the darkness, while he was sunk away in sleep, his arms around her.

What I was trying to show the students was the way the states of obsessive thinking on the one hand (Gudrun), and 'thoughtfreeness', we might say, on the other (Ursula), seep into the syntax. The provocative thorniness of that 'destroyed into consciousness', the serene elision of 'lapse of stillness', the smooth rearrangement of linguistic furniture in 'in complete ease', rather than 'completely at ease'. Along with this analysis, I confess, there would be a fair bit of banter with the students at the expense of the pompous pseudo-spiritual psychodrama of the passage. It goes on:

> There were strange fountains of his body, more mysterious and potent than any she had imagined or known, more satisfying, ah, finally, mystically-physically satisfying. She had thought there was no source deeper than the phallic source. And now, behold, from the smitten rock of the man's body, from the strange marvellous flanks and thighs, deeper, further in mystery than the phallic source, came the floods of ineffable darkness and ineffable riches.

But florid prose or not, it now seemed that I had had an experience that matched the one Lawrence was describing. Minus the sex, of course. I had not been up to sex for some time. In that regard I was the smitten rock without the fountains. All the same, and even though I would never have put it like this, 'floods of ineffable darkness and ineffable riches' made sense. That was what it had felt like. We were talking about the same thing.

Ineffable.

The only time I'd ever used the word was singing that hymn: 'Oh worship the king, all glorious above'. One of the verses starts: 'Oh measureless might, ineffable love'.

What did it really mean though? Much the same as measureless, presumably. I went to the dictionary.

Ineffable: too intense to be uttered.

So, something you can only speak by saying you can't speak it. And when you did try to speak it, at least with this experience, you found yourself talking water – it was the obvious metaphor – abundant, flowing, crashing water, ultimate antidote to thought, essential requisite for Leopardi's sweet mental shipwreck.

The water at low ebb in my dreams.

But that wasn't the end of Lawrence's scene. A few lines later, when the food arrives (hopefully the couple have rearranged their clothing), Ursula serves her lover tea, and we have:

> She was usually nervous and uncertain at performing these public duties, such as giving tea. But today she forgot, she was at her ease, entirely forgetting to have misgivings. The tea-pot poured beautifully from a proud slender spout. Her

eyes were warm with smiles as she gave him his tea. She had learned at last to be still and perfect.

Learned to be still and perfect! Are such things possible? I wasn't so ambitious. But I did hope that one day I might 'forget to have misgivings '.

And so I did. Only the following week in fact. Waking at 5 a.m., pain miserable as ever, I brewed a cuppa and decided that, rather than surfing the net, I might as well use this dead but wakeful time for the famous paradoxical relaxation. I lay on the sofa. Afterwards, six thirtyish, I returned to bed. At which, my wife rolled over and, quite without thinking, we made love.

Perfect.

Verbiage

I wasn't cured, much less healed. I wasn't whole, or an essential new being or lapsing into complete ease. I hadn't learned to sit still or to stand up straight, nor was I having visionary sex every day or surfing the crest of a perfect wave. The pain dragged on. The nights were interrupted five or six times.

But the change in my life was enormous. Little pools of comfort had begun to ripple out from the relaxation exercises. I recall vividly the first time I walked downstairs and realised that the usual burning sensation had not returned. More than that, my belly was miraculously calm, *positively* comfortable. My bladder was *comfortable.* It came as quite a shock and I stopped and checked it. Like a child's. I remembered that little Indian boy my Sikh driver had grabbed. His perfect body. And I realised: *This is the first time you have felt like this for many years.*

I was sure now that it had been many years.

And I had done this *myself.* 'Empower' is a verb I dislike, easy currency of those who tyrannise us with their piety. But I felt inclined to use it now. I had been empowered. However imperfectly, I could do something I wasn't able to before. Feelings of deep gratitude towards Drs Wise and Anderson welled up in me. It was true that they talked of anything up to two years to recover. Two years' perseverance, sacrificing precious time every day. Even then, they admitted, one hundred per cent recovery was unlikely. 'Flare-ups are always possible,' Dr Wise warned. I didn't care. A door had opened; lying still, I had moved on. I had made love again. After each session for a few minutes I felt absolutely normal. Or rather, I felt infinitely better than what had for a long time seemed normal, to me. It lasted fifteen minutes, then, a week later, half an hour. As long as the trend was positive I honestly didn't care if it took ten years. Or even if I never got there.

A Headache in the Pelvis was determinedly pragmatic about what was happening inside me. Relaxing the pelvic floor, I had allowed blood to flow; muscles could begin to heal. As they did so, a more 'hospitable environment' was created for the nerves passing through them, which thus ceased to transmit pain. For a short while.

To what extent this description corresponded to *reality*, I have no idea. There is no way of measuring such things. Wise spoke of experiments introducing electrodes through the anus into the muscles to measure tension as electrical intensity; and again through the urethra to measure the tone of the sphincters. Who wouldn't be tense with a bundle of wires up back and front passages? Who would ever sign up to such an experiment? If the doctor's version was true, one can only say that nature was being very generous. Mistreated – as Wise and Anderson saw it – for decades, my body had reacted with exemplary promptitude to a fairly limited effort on my part. As if a dog cramped for years in a tight kennel were suddenly to become a cheerful walking companion.

For my part, I had the impression that the changes taking place were more profound. On the one hand I had been forced to make the concession of allowing these pains into my life alongside the things I cared about; in return, my 'illness' had been drastically cut down to size, emptied of fear and menace. What self-respecting illness would allow you to halt its hitherto inexorable advance with a few deep breaths?

I felt sure now that the worst was behind me and this conviction altered my state of mind and the texture of each passing day.

More than that, I wasn't even *interested* in the pains any more. Or not for themselves. I had taken them on board. I was learning to go towards them rather than pull away, to feel them fully as I lay with eyes closed. This way they lost rather than gained in fascination. They no longer seemed a deep enigma, some contorted Gothic construct holding clues to my conflicted character. Their day was up. I no longer trawled the net for new insights, new tales of woe, new cures. Instead of seeing the future as a life sentence to be served in a narrower and narrower cell, I was looking forward to adventure and exploration.

In the space of a few weeks, then, the mystery of this ugly, wearying condition had given way to the positive and inviting mystery of the body, the same body I had hitherto *studiously* ignored. Ignored *studying*. Ignored in favour of interminable, overheated mental activity. This new (to me) mystery was something that opened out rather than closing in. Something you would be happy to explore without feeling an urgent need to solve. An ocean, not a leak.

There were at least two sides to this. The small successes I had scored with Dr Wise's paradoxical relaxation had opened my eyes to the eyes-closed silence where mind meets flesh. I appreciated at once that there was much, much more to be done here and many discoveries to be made. Except that you couldn't simply set out, guidebook in hand, to find them. Like the wave that sometimes swept over me, any discoveries would present themselves when *they* wanted, when I was *ripe for them*. So it was a question – and, extraordinary as it may seem, this had never occurred to me before – of cultivating a mental discipline that might allow new things to happen, a discipline in which, for the moment, I was a complete novice.

And for the first time in my life it was a mental task that had *nothing to do with words*. For decades now, I realised, all purposeful mental activity, for me, had been linguistic: writing, thinking, reasoning, teaching, talking (I had given up *numbers* the day they let me take maths O level a year early). When I did a sport, I turned all the mental side of it into words. I tried to work out *in words* how to do everything. How to head a goal in football. How to spin my kayak on its tail. What length of steps to take when running downhill. As opposed to uphill. Same with love-making even. I worked it out in words. And I honestly imagined that everybody did this, that everybody explained every action to themselves in words. After all, I had grown up listening to sermons more or less daily (there we are again), studying the scriptures over the breakfast table. *Exegetics!* My father loved to talk about exegetics. He loved to read the Bible at breakfast and elucidate. It was an inexhaustible puzzle. Etymology, philology. When I saw a painting, or a film, I immediately tried to sort out its pleasures and failings *in words*. My mind rattled off a review, a critical essay. Most of the pleasure in films and paintings, was precisely this verbal activity afterwards. Even *during*. I was writing the review *during* the movie, *while looking* at the painting. Everything had to be lived through language, or it wasn't lived at all; to the point that I hadn't really *seen* a painting or a film (or a game of football, for that matter) until I had thought about it in words, or preferably talked about it, or better still written about it, in carefully organised, purposeful, self-regarding words. Then I *possessed* it. In this, I suppose, I was not unlike those unhappy people who haven't really been on holiday unless they can show themselves the photos. The photos *are* the holiday, even when they're on the beach, or in the bedroom. And if I never took a camera on holiday, it was only because I was doing the same with words. What mattered was not the experience itself, but the experience *described*. My notebook, my laptop. And when I wanted to understand something new, I bought the book, of course, or books. I taught myself, with a book. Like Manuel in *Fawlty Towers* – 'I can speak English, I learn it from a book.' When I travelled, there was a guidebook. I had *faith* in books. I had a whole shelf-full of books on kayaking technique. I bought them compulsively. One day one of them would finally explain to me how to make that elusive manoeuvre round the slalom gate.

One consequence of all this verbiage was that I never really appreciated that there could be hard mental work that *did not involve words*, work for which, on the contrary, words might prove an obstacle. And this business of relaxation – but the term seemed quite inadequate now – was clearly work, of a kind. I had to labour at it. I made heavy weather. Under that low interior sky. It required effort, skill, determination. *Harder than playing the piano,* I kept repeating to myself.

Equally clearly, the big obstacle for me with this discipline was the constant chatter in my head. How could it ever be stilled so that I could focus on physical sensation, as Dr Wise insisted I must? Yet, however daunting, I was excited about this challenge. I sensed it was *timely*. These pains had come, I even found myself thinking, because I *needed* this. And without really knowing, or caring, where it would take me, I began to see the silence of these hours I had so grudgingly conceded to my condition – these hours of paradoxical relaxation – opening up before me across the months and years ahead like a vast new continent, a territory more arduous and gratifying than anything that foreign travel, or even reading, could offer; a journey that would take me far beyond the solution, or otherwise, of my pelvic pains and peeing problems.

Away from those relaxation sessions, though, what a physical wreck I discovered myself to be! What a bundle of twitchy nerves, poor posture and bad habits. The tension I had initially struggled to locate, eyes closed in the dark, complacently convinced that I was *not* tense, turned out to be *everywhere* in *every moment*. Not an inch of me, not a sinew or muscle, that didn't clang with tension, constantly. No sooner had I stumbled on the tiniest corner of it, clenching and unclenching a muscle at random, than it reared up and overwhelmed me. I was *nothing but* tension.

How could I ever have let myself arrive at this state? I brushed my teeth ferociously, as if I wanted to file them down. I yanked on my socks as if determined to thrust my toes right through them. I tied my shoes as if intent on snapping the laces. When I pushed a command button, I did so as if it was my personal strength that must send the lift to the sixth floor, or raise the door of the garage. While I shaved I tensed my jaw, while I read I tensed my throat, while I ate (too fast) I tensed my forehead, while I talked I tensed my shoulders, while I listened I tensed my neck, while I drove I tensed *everything*. My grip on the steering wheel was set to crush it. My spine was hunched rigid. My stomach turned to rock. And yes, my pelvic floor was hoist up tight, like a trapdoor against a besieging army below. It was as though, as far as my body was concerned, I was forever accelerating and braking in first and second, when I might perfectly well have been relaxed in fourth, or even cruising in fifth. Which reminds me how, in the 1970s, when my mother switched from the old Morris 1100 to a bigger Datsun, it was a year and more before she realised that the car *had* a fifth gear, and even then she wouldn't use it. I had been doing the same for thirty years.

But worse than all this, I had a habit, I discovered now, of *setting one part of my body against another*. Reading, legs crossed at the ankles, I would be pulling one ankle *against* the other. At my desk, I thrust my head back *against* linked hands that yanked it forward. Or I pushed my forehead forward *against* fingers that forced it back. Going to sleep on one side, the hand on the upper arm would form a fist *against* the lower arm and shove. The two sides of my body were forever fighting each other. Quite possibly I was sleeping all night in a state of constant tension.

And this is only the briefest summary of my chronically maladjusted state. Everything I did, I did with more effort than was required. It was a relief to find an activity that did require the effort I was putting into it: paddling my kayak upstream, for example, or forcing my body to run up the long hill from our house to the Pilotòn. These were really the only exertions that brought energy use and accomplishment into some kind of balance. Even then, when one of the kayak instructors was about, I was always told to take fewer paddle strokes. 'Plant them in the water more carefully. Don't hurry it. Don't fight the water.' 'Parks, you're too frenetic!' This was what the games teacher always used to tell me when we played football. 'Take it easy, Parks, or somebody'll get hurt.'

If there was one consolation in this painful process of self-recognition to which my relaxation exercises had unexpectedly brought me, forcing me to be still and feel the tension that was burning in there, it was that many of those around me were not much better off. Not many people, I began to notice, were genuinely at ease. At least I didn't wolf down food that I didn't need, as Carlo was still doing, despite his diabetes. At least I didn't bite my fingernails like my daughters, or tug at the skin round them like my wife. I didn't smoke.

At least I was waking up to the situation.

So, leaving aside residual worries about the nagging pains that had taken over my life, the question uppermost in my mind now became: would it be possible to change *profoundly*, in myself? Would it be possible, at fifty-one years old, to unlearn this tense and somehow, I felt, *language-driven* behaviour?

If so, how?

And I knew this question was the same as asking: could my father, Harold James Parks, whose nerves and anxieties frequently caused him to vomit of a morning, have learned to peel an orange *calmly*, without sinking his fingers into the pulp and tearing it to shreds? Would that have been possible? I also sensed that if I ever did achieve a transformation of this magnitude, if I ever did learn to stand up straight and hold a glass of water with the same serene stillness as the waterseller of Seville, then the pains that had set off this whole process would be a distant memory.

This link between posture and pain was no longer just a whimsical notion. *A Headache in the Pelvis* included, as was natural, a long section about the therapeutic massage they offered in their California clinic, together with guided courses in paradoxical relaxation. They had identified, Dr Wise claimed, a number of muscles which, in sufferers of my variety, tended to hide so-called trigger points. That is, as the muscle atrophied with little or improper use, a part of it would become taut; then within that taut band certain areas would grow particularly knotted and sensitive. Press on these 'contraction knots' and the patient's customary pains would immediately be triggered or intensified, often in organs or areas remote from the muscle in question, this thanks to the way nerves passed between layers of muscle. Identify the trigger points and massage them gently over a period of weeks, returning the muscles to something like health, and the pains would subside.

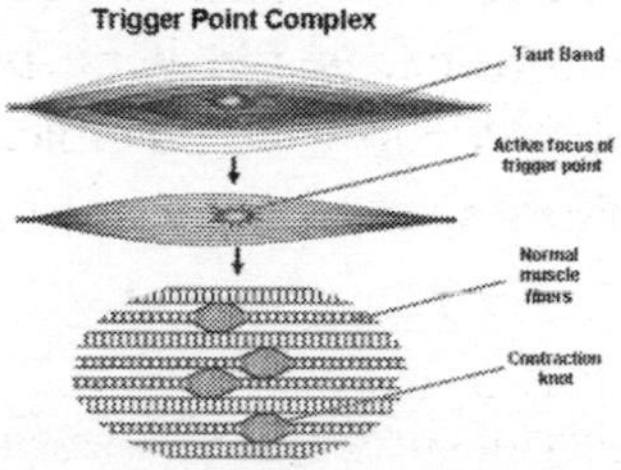

Thus spake Dr Wise.

The muscles involved were primarily those of the pelvic floor, above all the marvellously named levator ani, and the book included disquieting images, as if from inside the body looking downward, of a finger poking up through the anus to explore and massage these muscles. Each diagram explained where the muscle in question tended to 'refer pain'.

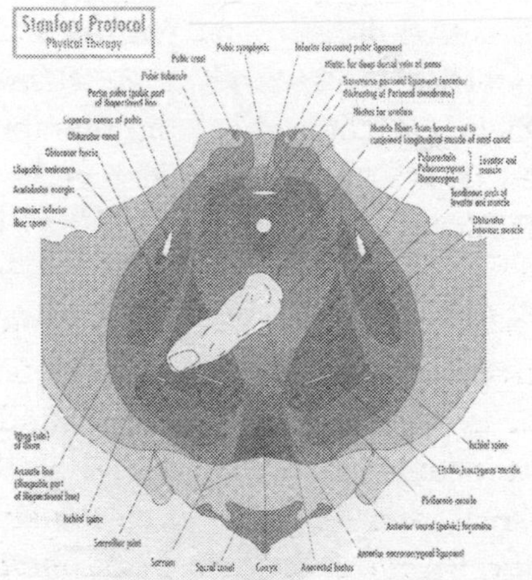

Once the trigger points had been identified and palpitated by expert massagers in the Stanford clinic, patients would be provided with a special stick or 'wand' (the Aneros perhaps) so that they could massage these points themselves. At home.

I wondered if I would ever rise, or sink, to such a do-it-yourself treatment. On my back, knees raised, a fairy wand up my bum. Or on all fours . . .

Best not to think about it.

Some of the offending muscles, however, were more easily and modestly accessible from the outside, in the thighs, around the groin, in and just above the buttocks. One of those that most referred pain to the bladder, my preferred hot spot, was the quadratus lumborum, the muscle that, at each side, attaches the pelvis to the spine. Checking the quadratus lumborum on Wikipedia, I found a detailed description of its susceptibility to deterioration as a result of constant contraction during prolonged periods of sitting, particularly sitting at desks, most particularly sitting at computers. The Wiki contributor then added the following reflection:

> *This chain of events can be and often is accelerated by kyphosis [a hunched spine] which is invariably accompanied by 'rounded shoulders', both of which place greater stress on the QLs [quadratus lumborum muscles] by shifting body weight forward, forcing the erector spinae, QLs, multifidi, and especially the levator scapulae to work harder in both seated and standing positions to maintain an erect torso and neck.*

In short, by not standing or sitting straight but rather peering forward from bent shoulders, I was stressing, among others, a muscle which, in its deteriorated state *was known to refer pain to the bladder*. Was this, I wondered, why the hunched Leopardi, his youth wasted, as he beautifully lamented, hunched over his '*sudate carte*' (sweated pages), had had his peeing problems and bellyache so young? With advanced scoliosis at eighteen he'd already screwed up his quadratus lumborum. And how uncanny that an idea that had suddenly come to me as I walked along the street one day – if only you walked tall, Tim, you would be better – an idea I quickly dismissed as foolish fancy, might actually have been a genuine insight.

As if my body knew things that I didn't! Or I knew things my mind didn't.

But how can you learn to stand up straight in your fifties?

Day after day, I lay on my back, eyes closed, breathing, concentrating on tension where I found it. At worst it was dull, disheartening, unconvincing. My attention slipped from its object like a man climbing an ice wall in ballet shoes. To latch on to things, I needed words. But words can only *describe* sensation, not experience it. Here, words actually loosened my grip, the ice wall fractured under their pressure, little avalanches running off with my attention. Without words I needed some purpose, some activity: concentrate on this muscle in order to contract it, to move it. But to relax I was supposed to focus *without making any effort to move or change anything*, remaining absolutely still.

I couldn't do it. I grew frustrated. I cursed Dr Wise for withholding those mysterious audio-tapes which might perhaps have helped. Some days I gave up.

But when by some miracle I did find a foothold in the ice, when my mind held and clung, even if only for a few moments, without trying to push or pull, just hung there, attentive and wordless, then the session would be positive, transporting; then, if I was lucky, the warm wave would eventually sweep over me, gentler now than the first times, friendlier, as if the landscape had already adapted to its passage. And I would suddenly find that my hands had sunk into my abdomen. The flooding water had allowed them to wriggle down into the seabed of my belly, like eels in sand. My hands were deep in my entrails, glowing. Sometimes they swapped sides. The left hand was on the right. To what end, I have no idea. I would be agog. Tension intensified and dissolved, heated and melted. In my thighs, calves, shoulders. On two or three occasions my body appeared to detach itself from the bed, to float. I was floating, head back, in warm salt water. On those days the pain receded dramatically, like rocks submerged by spring tide. Then I might get two or three hours quite free of pain. I might begin to hope it would never come back.

But the tide ebbed and the soreness raised its gritty edges.

Never celebrate when you have a good day, Wise warned.

Never despair when you have a bad day.

All the same, it was coming time to look for something else beside these relaxation sessions. I wanted more than to fight off the pain. I needed to look beyond.

I had no idea how or where.

Then, one morning, I woke very abruptly, sat up in bed, and pronounced the words, *You are two different people.* It was disconcerting. There was no dream to blame. No narrative. Just this sudden waking in the small hours, these words given as though in revelation. Two different people, Tim.

I went to the bathroom.

OK, so who?

A Strainer

It was July and time to go boating. Months before I had booked three days with a kayak guide in Austria. More than once I had thought of cancelling. I would be in too much pain. But it had been part of my strategy of denial never to cancel anything.

With life improving, I decided to go. These few days were a rare moment of escape from work and family. It was the first time I had booked a guide all for myself: a learning experience and a luxury. I dug out my white-water kayaking equipment, packed the car and drove north.

Two separate people. How strange to wake with words on my lips, with a message for myself.

My selves.

Or from one self to the other.

Not Physician, know thyself, then, but, Parks, know thyselves!

Probably dangerous to take stuff like this seriously.

I decided to leave early and make a small detour into the South Tyrol to run a river with my friend Roland. A warm-up. He's a dark, wiry little guy whose native tongue is the local German dialect; it must be funny for Italians to hear us speaking their language, he with his Tyrolese accent, me with my English. Yet we are both, to all intents and purposes, Italians, Roland thanks to the border-drawing folly of Versailles, me of my own free will. We met at the autostrada exit for Brixen, drove up the Eisack, left my car at the get-out and strapped the kayaks on his van to go up to the launch.

'What's the water like?' I asked.

He shrugged, rolling a cigarette as he drove along tight, winding roads, past Weinstubes and crucifixes.

'Fast, slow, safe, dangerous?'

A faint smile curled his unshaven lip. Far from Aryan, Roland has a pockmarked, gypsy look to him. Straggly hair under a sweatband, necklaces, tattoos. All I know of his past is that he once got himself a job with Italian public TV in Milan, so he must have trained at something. Six months later he was back in his remote village home in the Ahrntal. Perhaps he was afraid of a wound opening up between two selves: the Italian city man and the Tyrolese country boy. Now he teaches kayak and takes tourists rafting. He seems wonderfully at ease with himself.

'So, is it difficult or not?'

He laughed, blowing out smoke. Roland always makes fun of my pre-river nerves.

Eventually, he asked me what I'd been up to this year.

I'd just published a novel set right here in the South Tyrol, I told him.

He raised an eyebrow.

'About a big-time media man, London TV celebrity, who kind of escapes here to empty his mind. Deliberately chooses a place where he can't speak a word of the language, and high up in the mountains where there's no one to speak to anyway. Above Luttach,' I added.

Luttach was Roland's village. He smiled again. All around us steep pine slopes rose to dizzying peaks of blue and grey.

Then, just as we turned down a track to the river bank, I articulated something that had never come to me quite so clearly while writing *Cleaver*. 'It's a sort of death wish really.

He'd like to look so hard at the rocks and trees that he becomes one of them.'

This time Roland nodded. 'TV will do that to you,' he said.

About an hour later I nearly got the end Cleaver desired. It was a shock. The Eisack is a bouncy torrent tumbling through the boulders of a deep gorge, crossed here and there, high above, by the autostrada to the Brenner. It's strange with icy water on your hands, spray on your face, splashings and gurglings in your ears, to think of those vehicles a hundred feet above, droning across the landscape as if it wasn't really there. I suppose I go paddling to reconnect with the world, I thought. A moment later I went under.

I had made the mistake, even more unforgivable on the river than during Dr Wise's paradoxical relaxation, of drifting off into my thoughts: not connecting with the world, then, but reflecting on connecting. Close to the right bank, Roland paddled over the top of a little weir and thumped down onto rocks below. Not concentrating, I assumed this was an error and moved left into the main stream. Roland was yelling now but I couldn't hear what. Then I saw that while about a quarter of the river's flow did go over the weir in the centre, the main current was dragging me irresistibly towards a grey iron barrier on the left. Below it, I understood at once, would be a grille for catching debris. A strainer. To be avoided at all costs. But it was too late. In an instant I was against the barrier, side on, and tipping with the pressure of the water.

Life happens quickly. This would not be a warm wave that swept the mind clean and left it in complete ease. It was a trap. The moment I went below, I would be thrust against the grille in the conduit beneath and that would be that. Not two selves, but none.

Squeezed between current and barrier, the kayak began to flip. Ignoring Roland's shouts, lost in the watery roar, I yanked off the spray-deck and launched myself out of the boat in a frenzied freestyle towards the weir beyond the barrier. For a moment I stayed uncannily still in the grip of two equal tensions, the downward pull to the grille and the sideways rush to the weir. Then I was released, weir-bound. I suspect my buoyancy aid saved me.

The accident made Roland talkative. Again and again he apologised. He should have warned me. He hadn't thought. He marvelled at the lightness of my injuries. 'Move your wrists, OK? There's a cut on your hand. Your neck? Roll your head.' I had fallen three metres over the weir onto rocks taking only a bang on the knee and a fierce smack on my helmet. Freed from my weight the kayak had floated after me. 'I'm so sorry,' he repeated. He hugged me. 'Rest now. You're shivering. Cover up.'

Half an hour later I needed to pee. Once, twice, three times. In the car, my pains welled. But I felt euphoric. Got away with it! And optimistic too. The peeing and pain must be in response to the million-volt tension, the adrenalin. This reaction proved it. And however much I might need to change my life, I felt intensely that I did love it; I loved my body, loved Roland, loved the boats, the mountains, the smells of moss and resin, and above all the water, I loved the crazy, crashing, dangerous water. No death wish for Timmy, I thought. And when we stopped for a sandwich and I needed a *fourth* pee, I simply told Roland what my problem was. It was the first time I had talked about my health odyssey to anyone but wife and doctors. It was a release. And I knew it had been made possible by the breathing exercises, by my new state of mind and now this sudden swelling of emotion. I wasn't embarrassed at all. 'Yeah, I have this peeing problem.' The accident had become part of getting better.

People with pelvic pain syndrome, Dr Wise said, tend to swing dramatically from catastrophic thinking to the opposite: an excess of excited optimism.

What to do but enjoy the ups?

I kept the story brief. When I'd finished, Roland told me he had a groin hernia that needed operating. For the third time. It was very painful. He grinned. His wife taught yoga, he said. He knew all about breathing. Lighting a cigarette, he shook his head. 'So glad nothing happened to you.'

When we'd said goodbye, I found a side road and an empty meadow and lay down with the roll of my sleeping bag under my knees. One feels more vulnerable doing this kind of thing outdoors. I closed my eyes, then opened them. No one was sneaking up. A cloud had crossed the sun. There was a slight breeze on my skin. The thick grass creaked faintly. The pain was steady and strong.

I couldn't empty my mind. Every time I tried to breathe deeply and concentrate on some tension, I was suddenly back there, trapped against the iron barrier, the kayak tipping, the current tugging. I saw my body sucked down into the strainer, my dead face pressed against the grille. I shivered and pushed the image away. It came back. It came back like the pain, I thought. Caught against the grille, it couldn't flow. Blocked *vata*. After five or ten minutes I realised there was no point in fighting. Go towards it then, as towards the pain. Go underwater.

For a while I studied my dead self against the grille in the dark of the conduit as the river plunged under the barrier. It wasn't so frightening. There would be a couple of minutes' choking panic, then the definitive calm. Paintings of drowned people, I thought, tended to show them serene. Millais's Ophelia is transformed into something more beautiful than she was alive. The weeds and pond water suit her. And now I remembered a recent nightmare in which I found my son drowned in the bath. Tell me it isn't true, I kept repeating. He was fully clothed, drowned in the tub. Please, it mustn't be true! It can't be! But at the same time I was thinking how beautiful he was, how calm and solemn, eyes wide and untroubled. Ophelia is beautiful because she has stopped tearing herself apart over Hamlet. We despair on seeing her, but she is free to become one with the natural world. Relaxed even. Phlebas the Phoenician forgot the profit and the loss. A current under sea picked his bones in whispers.

Still, I reflected more sensibly, how much better, if you could shed the torment without losing your breath for ever, if you could stop agonising over the prince of Denmark, or the consumer price index, without being dead. What my hero Cleaver had wanted, I clarified then, was not exactly to die, but to '*die to this world*', to the clamour in his head.

A religious expression.

Of course the more intensely one thinks about all this stuff, the less likely you are to chill out. I couldn't make the pains subside. They were lodged there. Dr Wise's paradoxical relaxation was not an emergency bandage. I needed another pee.

Back in the car, the only radio station I could pick up was a political phone-in. People were indignant about Guantanamo. There was also a question of whether the high court would allow a man on an iron lung the right to die. The presenter had various experts on the line, apparently selected for their vehemently contrasting points of view. A listener from Bari felt we should accept suffering as part of God's plan. He was belligerent. Everybody seemed agitated. But I too get agitated about the news. There are days when I am more concerned about the American elections than anything else, days when I'm constantly on line checking opinion polls. A listener phoned to say that rapists should be castrated. Rape seemed to be the main sport of Slav immigrants, he said.

Time to turn off.

My car, an old Vectra, must be one of the last models produced with a tape deck rather than a CD player. I always bring a few books on tape when I travel. *Moby-Dick* is an old favourite. I must have listened to it a dozen times. But before turning on I attempted a brief summary, thus:

You have problems peeing and related pains. You dream

about rivers and beaches where water has run out, leaving only melancholic mud. For sport you go where water is abundant, violent, dangerous. You find it compelling. And you are attracted to literature that describes water as carrying away the mind, thoughts drowning in eternity. You imagine similar experiences lying on your bed relaxing. But when *really* carried off by the water, your mind reacts like lightning to keep you alive. And thinking.

The curious thing about *Cleaver*, I decided then, was how the novel had foreseen various developments in my life a year and more before I had been aware of them. Supposing myself creative, I had merely been scribbling down a memoir in metaphor of the months to come. Once again, some part of me had possessed and even expressed a knowledge that remained inaccessible to the voice that speaks in the head and calls itself *I*. Perhaps the two selves that had been announced waking up that morning were the one writing about Cleaver's problems and the one denying my own. The first, literary self doesn't do much to help the second, the sufferer. The literary self likes finding forms and words to talk about things metaphorically, to make them more dramatic and intriguing than they are. He thinks of this as art and congratulates himself when someone pays him for what he does. Meantime the sufferer tries to ignore his pains. The two selves don't connect.

Call me Ishmael.

I spent the rest of the drive with Melville. It wasn't silence, but at least it was a rest from *my* thoughts. I was crossing the Brenner while Ishmael got into bed with Queequeg and the Europabrücke as he met Captain Peleg on the deck of the *Pequod*. With all its excitement, the narrative relaxed me. I began to feel better. And again it was strange to think of the dislocations of literature, the mind and the flesh: Melville writing in New York, the whalemen setting out from

Nantucket, me speeding across Austria, but far away in my head. Then an hour and more later, climbing the Inn valley towards Switzerland while the *Pequod* was becalmed on the Line, things came together. I stopped the tape and rewound to listen again. It was a passage about keeping watch on the masthead.

> There you stand, lost in the infinite series of the sea, with nothing ruffled but the waves. The tranced ship indolently rolls; the drowsy trade winds blow; everything resolves you into languor. For the most part, in this tropic whaling life, a sublime uneventfulness invests you; you hear no news; read no gazettes; extras with startling accounts of commonplaces never delude you into unnecessary excitements; you hear of no domestic afflictions; bankrupt securities; fall of stocks.

Unnecessary excitements! In 1850 Melville had already understood how the media can make a man tense and dumb. He goes on:

> Lulled into such an opium-like listlessness of vacant, unconscious reverie is this absent-minded youth by the blending cadence of waves with thoughts, that at last he loses his identity; takes the mystic ocean at his feet for the visible image of that deep, blue, bottomless soul, pervading mankind and nature; and every strange, half-seen, gliding, beautiful thing that eludes him; every dimly-discovered, uprising fin of some undiscernible form, seems to him the embodiment of those elusive thoughts that only people the soul by continually flitting through it. In this enchanted mood, thy spirit ebbs away to whence it came; becomes diffused through time and space; like Crammer's sprinkled Pantheistic ashes, forming at last a part of every shore the round globe over.

The blending cadence of waves and thoughts. It sounded so much like some of the sensations I had experienced. But in this trance the lookout misses the whale he had been watching for. The crew curse him. And I missed the turn-off for my campsite. I drove ten kilometres too far and had to turn back.

'What's that doing in the car?' was the first thing Andy said. My guide turned out to be a gangly Yorkshireman. I have a lazy habit of just folding down the back seat of the car and sliding in my kayak.

'Break hard and it'll go shooting through the windscreen, if it doesn't take your head off first,' he protested. 'Strap it on the roof!'

It seems I'm always thinking, but never paying attention.

The following morning, after we'd run our first river together, Andy told me, 'Well, I'm glad you can paddle. I was worried yesterday when you got out of the car and I saw that miserable stoop you have.'

The Scafell Syndrome

Patients with a pelvic pain condition, remarks Dr Wise, will also tend to suffer from irritable bowel syndrome. It was one of the observations in *A Headache in the Pelvis* that convinced me its authors knew a thing or two more than your average urologist whose thoughts never stray beyond the urinary tract. I had been afflicted by this bowel syndrome myself from time to time. But never more so than on kayaking trips. You get up around six, knowing you're going to be doing a serious river, and at once you need a dump. You need two dumps, three, even four. Not the runs, real dumps. Around seven thirty, satisfied that you can have no more to give, you laugh and joke as you strap the kayaks on the roof-rack, only to find, as the river comes into view, roaring over a steep rapid, that you absolutely must dump again!

This is a serious problem if you've already put your wet-suit on.

And your dry cag.

And your spray deck.

Andy keeps a small plastic beach spade in his van. 'Bury your business and burn the loo paper, mate,' he sniffs grimly, handing me a lighter as well. He is concerned that river approaches are becoming minefields of human shit. Germans are the worst, he assures me. 'They lay their cables right at the launch spot.' I adventure into the bushes and invariably find that others have been before me. Without the spade and lighter.

Is this fear pure and simple, this repeated urge to go? There are so many things I am genuinely afraid of: mountain climbing, sky diving, hang gliding, bungee jumping, anything to do with heights. Nor would you ever catch me potholing. But however many dumps I may need before a river run, I am always eager to be on the water. If I'm afraid of anything, it's that I'll make a fool of myself.

On the second day we headed up to Switzerland to do Scuol gorge, one of the higher sections of the Inn. It had been raining all night and the river would be swollen. I was curious to see whether, by waking early and fitting in an hour's paradoxical relaxation before the drive, I might overcome this bowel-syndrome embarrassment, which I now suspected was another manifestation of the whole tension/adrenalin problem.

The plan worked. After forty-eight hours away from family, university, newspapers, books, text messages and email, it was already easier to focus on physical sensation and keep words at bay. Waking at six, sorting myself out in the tent with a cylindrical kit bag under my knees, I found I was breathing deeply and steadily almost at once. The various tensions – face, forearms, thighs – rose like prompt pupils to the register. I ticked them off one by one, had my breakfast, made my normal bathroom trip, then ... nothing. There were the usual pains, of course, but in the background, subdued. I felt fine.

Until we saw the river.

More than any guide I'd been with, Andy was making sure we inspected each tough stretch of water from the bank before we started. He knew all the paths and tracks to vantage points whence you could see the river swirling in an S through walls and rocks, or plunging between boulders into a gorge. At the bottom of Scuol, just before the get-out, the river tilts and slides to the left, crashing against a high cliff, so that for twenty metres or so the only passage takes the form of a furious wave boiling back at you from the rock wall.

Something shifted in my intestines.

There are three tough rapids on Scuol. Naturally one inspects from the bottom up as one drives up river to the launch spot. The first rapid, which we thus inspected last, has to be faced just a couple of minutes into the run. Too soon. The river narrows from the left to pour over a step of about a metre while a spur of rock jutting from the cliff on the right adds a cushion wave that you have to miss. As you go down into the rough stuff beneath the step – and you must hit it at the exact spot – you have an undercut rock wall to your right that you don't want to be anywhere near. To make it trickier, just before you can get to the rapid you have to punch through two standing waves, rather like permanent sea breakers, with the result that, even if you've seen it properly, your chances of being on course for that sweet spot are not good.

No sooner were we in the water than I screwed up. My mind was super-concentrated, but my body seemed stiff, resentful almost of this excited preparation and hyperawareness. The arms were reluctant. Hips and thighs were on strike. As the roar of the rapid approached, I knew what was going to happen. The standing waves knocked me off course. The cushion wave flipped me. I was flushed through the rapid upside down, caught my head on Andy's boat as I tried to roll up – he was desperately trying to grab me – then took a nasty swim full of knocks and scrapes that tore chunks out of my knuckles. It was disappointing. I was breathing heavily.

'Let's do it again,' I said.

Andy advised against. I must be shaken up, he thought. The water was icy. It would be hard work carrying the boats back. Why not warm up on the next section, which was busy enough.

'I want to do it again.'

We tramped back through rocks and undergrowth, cumbersome boats on our shoulders, paddles in our hands. I hate walking any distance in a wetsuit. Its tight rubber chafes. As we passed the rapid, I asked for more exact instructions. As if that were the problem. We studied the standing waves blocking the approach, the sweet spot between the cushion wave and boulder. It looked clear enough from the bank, but I knew that once back on the water everything would be bigger, more violent, more complex, and, above all, tremendously fast.

There's no pause button before a rapid.

Andy insisted on a few stretching exercises, then we launched. Sure enough, I was disorientated. Waves rose, fell, surged, broke. There were stones invisible from the bank. The river accelerated with ruthless purpose, the noise swelled to a roar. Why do I always feel a temptation, at these moments, to relinquish control, to let the water have its way?

'Paddle!' Andy yelled. 'Fucking *paddle*!'

My body responded, but as if to Andy, not to my own will. My wrist planted a firm stroke in the second wave. My thigh kicked into it. Suddenly I was *present*. I'd arrived. I found the sweet spot, held the boat upright through the chaos and ploughed into the calm of the big eddy beyond.

'Did it!' I yelled. 'Did it!'

Andy shook his head. 'You tense up,' he said. 'You stopped paddling.'

For the rest of the morning I was tensing up for that corkscrew wave along the cliff at the bottom of the run. There is a wonderful spot at the deepest point of Scuol where, with vertical rock walls rising hundreds of feet on both sides, you can beach the boats in a sort of alcove and climb a stone stairway to a café on a terrace perched over the river. The place was very pretty that morning with a beam of sunlight among geraniums on white tablecloths and it felt odd to sit there in our damp kit. Andy, I realised, was trying to get something going with the waitress and found it difficult to pay attention to my questions about how to tackle that last rapid.

'Relax,' he complained. 'Check the scenery.'

Did he mean the mountain landscape, or the handsome curves of the blonde bending to serve? He told her in broad Yorkshire that she was looking very cheerful today. She smiled and said something about *das Wetter*. I asked at what angle I should approach the wall.

'You're so verbal,' Andy observed when the girl went to another table. 'Just look hard at the water and go.'

'Please, talk me through it.'

He sighed and arranged coffee cups, spoons and biscuits to show the various rocks upstream of the feature. I repeated everything carefully.

'You've got it,' he nodded. 'Still, we're not there now, are we, mate? We're here, in the café. Enjoy.'

Handing him change as we left, the waitress smiled a twinkling *aufwiedersehen*, but Andy still couldn't find the courage to ask for her phone number. I couldn't see his problem. It looked to me like she would have jumped at it.

To each his own anxieties.

Before the rapid, we got out and climbed through a scrub of boulders and beech trees to look again. Despite being extremely tense, as if before some crucial exam, I didn't need a pee, I didn't need a dump. I was beyond all that. 'Don't tell me anything. I'll just follow you down,' I told him.

The wave coming off the wall flipped me on impact. The underwater rush was astonishing. The whole river funnelled through a passage less than two metres wide. As soon as the worst had happened, I relaxed and rolled up easily, hit the wave again and flipped again, then rolled up safe and sound in a deep pool at the bottom.

'Head-ruddering,' was Andy's only comment, 'is always better than swimming.'

That night was miserable. I had a big plastic bottle with me in the tent to avoid walks through wet grass to the loos. Every half-hour I had to kneel to pee in it. It took concentration. I had hung a torch from the apex of the tent and knelt in its yellow glow. The bottle filled slowly. By four in the morning I had the full array of symptoms. After another day on the river, the last night was even worse.

This trip has set me back months, I realised, driving away from the campsite at the end of the holiday. So why do I do it? The link between excitement and pain was all too clear now; one way or another, writing or canoeing, I got tense during the day and paid for it at night.

On the other hand, despite the soreness, bruised knuckles and broken sleep, I did feel refreshed. All the little niggles of home life, the small battles and bureaucracy at the university, the labour and sometimes tedium of writing, had been swept away. On the last day, two tough rivers had been run without a swim. Or a dump! Even Andy had had words of congratulation.

But shouldn't I be able to get the benefits of this physical activity without the pains? Andy was at ease on the water. His body responded naturally to every fluid alteration. On one occasion he had paddled down a rapid *backwards* so he could watch me following. My body in contrast seemed only to be there, really *there*, intermittently. Sometimes the mental impression I had of the water was so strong that my physical faculties downed tools. Then it was as though the body was a marionette without a puppet-master. I was swept away.

Joining the autobahn near Innsbruck, I slotted in the *Moby-Dick* cassette but couldn't listen. The question demanded an answer: Why do I do this dangerous sport? I ejected the tape and repeated the question out loud. 'Why?'

'You're so verbal,' Andy had said. 'Just look and go.' On the last day, when I hit a hole that we had planned to avoid, he told me I should try contact lenses. 'You wear glasses, normally, don't you?' He had the impression I didn't really see the river properly. 'You have to *really* see it,' he said. 'You're not seeing. You just listen to me describing it.'

Was it an eyesight problem? When my body did click in, it was wonderful, like finding the accelerator on some powerful machine. About half an hour into a run my hips and back would suddenly be there, intensely present, moving with a sure, flexible, intuitive knowledge. They took command. The conscious mind gave way to a sensation of pure focus. Then I could do anything.

It wasn't an eyesight problem.

I drove in silence, up to the Brenner Pass, then down into Italy, the Dolomites elegantly lofty in the haze to my left. Looking at the high slopes, I began to feel the pressure of some fact, or idea, that was trying to join the debate. A few years ago, working with a thesis student who was translating nineteenth-century accounts of mountaineering, I had come across Samuel Taylor Coleridge's description of his bizarre descent of Scafell in the Lake District in 1802, supposedly the earliest written account of recreational rock climbing.

Coleridge, I remembered, had been my first really *literary* love when I was around fifteen, though of course our school-teachers had not told us about Scafell. The first literary essay I wrote, in an exercise book on lined paper, was about his poem 'Frost at Midnight'.

So why was this relevant? In the car, I tried to summon up the details. Coleridge, an intellectual, almost always in poor health, an overweight dreamer, 'indisposed to all bodily activity', boasted that when walking in the mountains he liked to do a climb or descent without bothering to follow a path. Up or down, he just went for it. On Scafell this got him into trouble.

I shook my head. If there was a reason why I was remembering this, I couldn't see it.

Back in Verona, I Googled the story. Coleridge had felt constricted at his cottage home with wife and child and went walking to get relief. He wrote about his adventures in a letter to the woman he was really in love with, Sara Hutchinson. He liked dangerous walks, he told her, by rivers and waterfalls, on stormy days under heavy rain. 'I have always found this *stretched and anxious* state of mind favourable,' he says, 'to depth of pleasurable impression.'

At school, of course, they had taught us about the sublime and the cult of feeling. But reading these intimate words, the grand categories didn't seem important. Rather one wondered, what exactly was the mental condition that Coleridge was eager to replace with this 'stretched and anxious' state of mind? Certainly I had been stretched to the anxious limit on Scuol gorge. But why did I need that?

Then he describes a river. I hadn't expected this. I had only remembered the climbing incident.

> it is a great torrent from the top of the mountain to the bottom ... the mad water rushes through its *sinuous* bed, or rather prison of rock, with such rapid curves, as if it turned the corners not from the mechanic force, but with foreknowledge, like a fierce & skilful driver. Great masses of water, one after the other, that in twilight one might have feelingly compared them to a vast crowd of huge white bears, rushing, one over the other, against the wind – their long white hair shattering abroad in the wind.

It's odd stuff. No river ever made *me* think of white bears, though I know very well that impression of waters tumbling over one another as they crowd into a narrowing space. And what a strange mix of references: the water is 'mad' and in 'prison' (a mental hospital?). It is personified as struggling to get away, like Coleridge from home, with foreknowledge, 'a fierce and skilful driver'. Of what in 1802? A horse and cart? Then these bears with their 'hair shattering abroad'. Do bears have long hair? Does hair shatter? Abroad? Had these three words ever been put together before? What was shattering here was standard usage, even common sense. I remembered when I had written my novel on kayaking, *Rapids*, the tremendous challenge of describing mountain rivers. Perhaps Coleridge came to places like this because they stretched to the limit his ability to put the world in words.

I hunted out my old school edition of his selected poems and discovered that 'Dejection: an Ode' had been written just a few months before this adventure. There he laments his dire psychological condition and the way his many 'afflictions' have prompted him to *separate thought and feeling, mind and body*, with the hope that 'abstruse research' might 'steal from my own nature all the natural man'. Insomniac, he looks forward to a storm so violent it will force him to move beyond his troubles. Here was a man full of blocked *vata* just waiting to be blown away.

Scafell did it for him.

> Now I came to a smooth perpendicular rock about 7 feet high – this was nothing – I put my hands on the ledge and dropped down – in a few yards came just such another – I *dropped* that too, and yet another, seemed not higher – I would not stand for a trifle so I dropped that too – but the stretching of the muscles of my hands and arms, and the jolt of the Fall on my Feet, put my whole Limbs in a *Tremble*, and I paused, and looking down, saw that I had little else to

> encounter but a succession of these little Precipices – it was in truth a Path that in a very hard Rain is, no doubt, the channel of a most splendid Waterfall.

So now Coleridge is where the water should be. On the stones of a waterfall. Very soon he's describing *himself* as mad, as the water was mad in the earlier description. He has reached a place from whence he can't climb back up, but where the next ledge below is so far away that:

> . . . if I dropt down upon it I must of necessity have fallen backwards and of course killed myself. My Limbs were all in a tremble – I lay upon my Back to rest myself, and was beginning according to my Custom to laugh at myself for a Madman, when the sight of the Crags above me on each side, and the impetuous Clouds just over them, posting so luridly and so rapidly northward, overawed me. I lay in a state of almost prophetic Trance and Delight – and blessed God aloud, for the powers of Reason and the Will, which remaining no Danger can overpower us!

I couldn't figure this. He's overawed, and apparently delighted to be so – he's got what he was after – but simultaneously blessing God for the power of Reason and Will. Because they will help him get out of his predicament? Or because they will enable him to write about it afterwards? He 'explains':

> I know not how to proceed, how to return, but I am calm and fearless and confident – if this Reality were a dream, if I were asleep, what agonies had I suffered! What screams! When the Reason and the Will are away, what remain to us but Darkness and Dimness and a bewildering Shame and

> Pain that is utterly Lord over us, or fantastic Pleasure, that draws the soul along swimming through the air in many shapes, even as a Flight of Starlings in a Wind.

It's confusing; without reason and will, we alternate, as in dreams, between horror and fantastic pleasure; but Coleridge describes the latter state so enthusiastically it seems to cancel out the former, and make the calm, fearless mind he's so pleased with uninteresting. In reason-free pleasure the soul swims and changes shape constantly. Ergo, has no identity? Like my Cleaver, the poet doesn't seem quite sure whether he wants to end up badly or not.

A rather dull paragraph then explains how Coleridge in fact got out of gaol by shinnying down a gulley he hadn't previously noticed.

For some days I let this story turn over in my mind, occasionally going back to the net to read snippets of the man's biography or a poem or two. In particular, I tried to find out about Coleridge's many illnesses. It's amazing – and this was also true when writing about Thomas Hardy – how many biographies will simply say, Coleridge was ill and so began to take laudanum, to which he became addicted. Without telling you what the illness was. As if one could know a man without knowing his illness. One website said he had a swollen knee. Another that he had rheumatic fever. Shooting in the dark, I Googled 'Coleridge urine' and came up with this:

> *What a beautiful Thing urine is, in a Pot, brown yellow, transpicuous, the Image, diamond shaped of the Candle in it.*

Transpicuous! Meaning 'clear', I presume. But the word itself is more conspicuous than transparent. Anyway, here was someone used to peeing at night, used to holding a candle over his chamber pot. I remembered the torch in the tent shining down on my plastic bottle.

Then I found an article admiring Coleridge for his lack of squeamishness in his diary. He spoke openly of 'bowel agony', of 'testicles twice the usual size'.

For twenty dollars I purchased a research paper from Johns Hopkins University press that promised to discuss Coleridge's long, writerly obsession with his health. His poor health. It was a chastening piece. Given the poet's interminable descriptions of his bowel complaints, the writer decides, Coleridge was probably 'one of the most ingrained hypochondriacs in history', a man whose mental state 'manifested itself in semantically rich self-diagnoses typically fraught with internal contradictions that raised more questions than they answered'. The author goes on:

> Of course, the relation in medical history of the troubled medical condition and label 'hypochondria' to the gut represents a vast swath of cultural history that we cannot even begin to allude to properly here, save to say that Coleridge was the type of sedentary, solitary, scholastic, symbol-making figure who surely lies close to its center.

This very much reminded me of the cover of Dr Wise's *A Headache in the Pelvis*. The sedentary, scholastic Zechariah. This is the kind of guy who bellyaches. I felt uncomfortable.

The Johns Hopkins professor was ruthless. Because the poet's pains did not have any consequences beyond frequent bowel movements he concludes that Coleridge's obsessive writing about the matter was without substance, autistic, and of no help to anyone intent on understanding bowel disorders.

> Medical categories, stable and unstable, existed in his imagination primarily as linguistic constructs; because all language was by degrees metaphoric, unstable categories lent themselves rather more feverishly than stable categories to aberrant images.

In short, elusive as a mountain waterfall, the pain inspired Coleridge to conjure up strange images. Since the writer's self-esteem largely depended on his ability to be creative with language, it was worth being in pain, or imagining he was, as it had been worth risking his life on Scafell, because it stimulated his writing.

> Coleridge seems to have taken an avid, indeed almost morbid, pleasure in teasing out the semantic ambiguities of medical categories.

This is aggressive criticism. And of course we can't *know*. We can't know if he was really in pain, or how much. I tried to summarise. Afraid, five years on from the 'Ancient Mariner' and 'Kubla Khan', that he had lost his creativity, his mind unhappily divided between a wife and mistress,

Coleridge seeks in nature experiences so intense as to overwhelm those preoccupations, and indeed the whole unbearable thought process that daily afflicts him. Then he is so excited by extreme experience that he tries to exploit it to recover his creativity, to show he can still produce remarkable images, still force language to the limit, shattering the white bear hair of tumbling waters. There is a conflict at the core: language is to be shaken off as part of the distressing thought process ('thoughts that tortured me' I found in a poem of 1803); but language is also to be exalted as the (only) means of conveying the exciting experience of escape from thought (and language).

In 'Hymn before Sunrise, in the Vale of Chamouni', written in 1802, I found these words, addressed to Mont Blanc:

> ... I gazed upon thee,
> Till thou, still present to the bodily sense,
> Didst vanish from my thought: entranced in prayer
> I worshipped the Invisible alone.

And elsewhere in a note, this:

> To think of a thing is different from to perceive it, as 'to walk' is from 'to feel the ground under you'.

Perceiving Mont Blanc, without thinking it (in words), Coleridge enters a state of trance, as he was almost in trance on Scafell. And it was in a kind of trance, as I recalled, that the Ancient Mariner redeemed himself by blessing the watersnakes. *Unaware*, is the word. I looked the verse up. 'He blessed them *unaware*.' It was when – after a 'lapse of stillness' perhaps – you entered into an immediate perception of the world, unmediated by language, that there was a chance of love and joy gushing from your heart. 'No tongue their beauty might declare,' the mariner says of the watersnakes. Ineffable.

When he didn't have Mont Blanc to look at, Coleridge tried to force himself into this immediate relationship with the world by tumbling down rocks in the Lake District. When he didn't have Scafell he took Laudanum, and brought back 'Kubla Khan' from his trance. The movement was always the same: away from pain/thought/words via extreme experience/the sublime/drugs; then back into words/thought/pain via sublime poetry. Hence escape actually fed the compulsion it was seeking to escape from.

> I pass, like night, from land to land;
> I have strange power of speech.

This is perverse, I decided. Coleridge was perverse. I am perverse trying to see his experiences in relation to mine. The only glimmer of analogy, perhaps, was that the sort of mental tension I lived in – notoriously a world of words – had encouraged me to develop a pastime, kayaking, which had the advantage of sweeping away thought and returning me to an immediate, urgent relation with my body and the world. In doing so, however, I raised my adrenalin levels to the roof and created an even higher level of tension, albeit of a different variety. I then exacerbated this by fretting about how to bring those experiences back into the world of words. Hence I oscillated between an obsessive super-verbal tension in my office and an intense physical tension on the water. Either way my gut paid the price.

As did Coleridge's.

Conclusion. It is a big mistake to imagine you can get back to a better relationship with your body simply by bullying it into extreme action. In my own case, it was time to find a way out of my predicament that didn't involve chasing out one form of tension by plunging into another.

Resolution. If ever I wrote about this 'illness', it would only be when I had recovered and it was no longer a 'complaint'. And then in the simplest of words. No white bears with shattering hair. No fancy literature at the expense of well-being.

Dreams of Rivers and Seas

Early in September I cancelled my season ticket at the stadium and made an appointment with a practitioner of shiatsu. What exactly was wrong with words, I'd been asking myself? The same thing that was right with them, presumably. Without words it's hard to refer to something that isn't here in front of us, now, it's hard to get conceptual or even tell a story. It's hard to plan. Hard to worry.

What a loss that would be.

With words, on the other hand, you range everywhere, over everything, you can go back to the past, forward to the future. Past worries, present worries, future worries: things you ought to say tomorrow, things you ought to have said yesterday. With words you can plan and change plans. You have dates to remember and numbers. You can build castles in the air. And demolish them. With words you can talk about things that don't exist, about times that never were, might-have-beens, eternity, grammatical constructs. If you want, or even if you don't want, you can live entirely in books and newspapers, chat rooms and radio talk, dimensions entirely detached from the here and now of your own existence. You can phone in and express opinions on AIDS in Africa, on the Oscars in LA. You can send the same email to three friends simultaneously, or read text messages while making love. It's an intensely *mental* process. Wasn't that, it occurred to me, what the second part of 'Kubla Khan' was about?

Could I revive within me
Her symphony and song,
To such a deep delight 'twould win me,
That with music loud and long,
I would build that dome in air,
That sunny dome! those caves of ice!
And all who heard should see them there,
And all should cry, Beware! Beware!

Words build domes that never were. In the air. Pure mental material. Beware indeed! For when can you ever say, with words, where the real starts and ends?

because all language is by degrees metaphoric

Language builds domes, then other domes over them, as the first dissolve. Because words are never still. The opening of a sentence projects you forwards; the end demands you have the beginning in mind. One paragraph leads to another and this page to the next. The eye is ahead of the lips. Reading, we turn the page while the last lines of the one before are still falling into place. Typing, my thoughts run ahead of my fingers. Driven on. Never now. Never grounded in this moment.

Reading, writing, talking, thinking, you move in a separate system. The map may be a real one, but it's not the territory. To think an object is not to perceive it. To text a girlfriend is not to be with her. You lose your grip on things as they are. But this second life is compulsive. You can't stop. A whirling word machine lifts off from the heavy surfaces of soil, cement and skin. Mind and body part company. You're more at home on the page now than the pavement, on the net than the street. Your mind is you. Your body is a vehicle.

An enabler. An ear to hear, a mouth to speak, eyes to read, fingers to write. Sometimes a fashion accessory. Or else an embarrassment. When some physical disturbance forces its way into your consciousness, into words, you feel disorientated, betrayed.

> This breathing House not built with hands,
> This body that does me grievous wrong,

Thus Coleridge.

Uneasy, you take drastic action (from time to time). You try to draw your body back into a relationship with yourself (every now and then). You compel it to run further than it wants (twice a week), to swim a hundred laps (on Saturday afternoons); that way it will transmit feel-good endomorphines. You force it to paddle dangerous torrents (twice a year), to leap from a plane with a parachute, or from a high bridge with an elasticated rope (on annual holidays), that way it will pump adrenalin and emotions: fear, excitement, exhilaration. You imagine that by doing this you are rediscovering your body, giving it an airing, putting it through its paces, keeping it *presentable*, as my parents always wanted our bodies to be presentable. You don't want to become obese. Or anorexic. Then you sit it down in front of the screen and write about your experiences. The whole thing was mental from start to finish. Even when it seemed most physical, it was mental. The mental life has triumphed over the physical, says Lawrence in *Lady Chatterley's Lover*. The modern gym with its machines and mirrors, the cosmetic surgeon with his enticing brochures, these are telling signs. Likewise pornography and the obsession with underwear. Men don't love women, Lawrence complained, they love their underwear. The mind fantasises the body, builds curves in air. Over caves of ice. 'While kindness is the glib order of the day, underneath … we find a coldness of heart … Every man is a menace to every other.' To be out of touch with your body is to be out of love with your neighbour.

And if you haven't the energy for the weights or the stomach for the knife, you can go to the stadium and *watch* the serious athletes perform. For ten years I had held a season ticket for Hellas Verona FC. Right in the *curva sud*. The stadium wired me into frantic focus on the here and now of the game, the back and forth of the ball, the immediacy of the moment in front of goal: Shoot now! Do it *now*! No replays, no second tries. No chance to rephrase, or translate. The drama of the moment. Time ticking away. Life running out.

In the stadium the words you use are locked into the present, they are exhortations, chants, mantras. *Hellas, Hellas, Hellas!* Attack, attack, attack! Go, go, go! It's a battle (with Hellas a relegation battle). The crowd shares in its team's struggle. But only at a psychological level, of course. I am not the player in front of goal. I don't have to do anything now. Anything physical. I'm agog, but with another's performance. I savour the terrible immediacy of life, his life (my disappointment), from a distance. Raised from the field of action to the vantage point of the terraces, I shout back down at the performers. I know they don't hear my imprecations. I'm shouting for myself. To excite myself.

At the beginning of a big game, my body shivers. I'm tense. I have to go to the bathroom. My body suffers the mind's excitement. Reading the programme, my hand trembles. Today we stay up or go down. Hellas are on the brink. Hellas are always on the brink. I can't watch while a penalty is taken.

Leaving the stadium, I'm emotionally drained, exhausted. Euphoric or depressed. On the car radio urgent voices have begun the post-match analysis. Waking in the night, I'm still furious we were denied a penalty. My belly is on fire. I can't pee, I have to pee.

Enough. This autumn I didn't renew my season ticket but went instead to lie down on a large futon, perhaps three metres by three, all but filling a small airless room overlooking the river in central Verona. Warm hands lifted my right foot.

'Let go,' a voice said softly. 'Let me take the weight.'

I tried to relinquish control. The hands took my foot, firmly but gently. Then, after some exploration, resting the heel on one palm, he enquired, 'Here?' and pressed a finger into the sole. A connection lit up. The pain shot from foot to bladder and *simultaneously* from bladder to foot. There was a live wire along the back of my leg.

'Ow! Yes!'

'The water meridian,' Ruggero said.

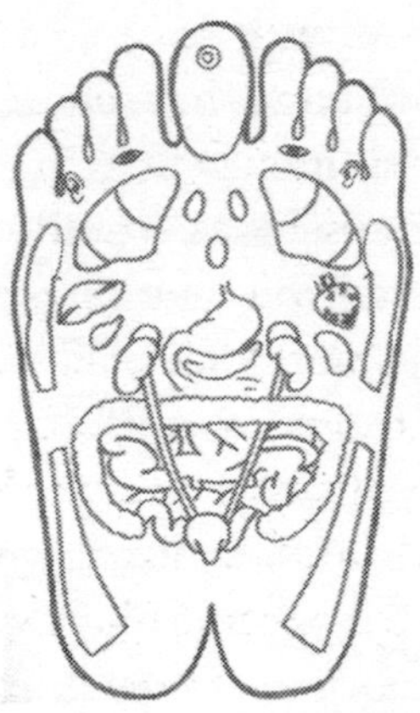

Beforehand I had been sceptical.

'If you can't go to California for the anal massage,' my wife laughed, 'why not try some shiatsu?'

Over two months the paradoxical relaxation had gradually subdued the pain. Wider and wider pools of comfort spread out around my sessions. But they were still shallow. There were setbacks. The nights had not improved. Then in my new-found optimism I became impatient. I wanted things to change *quickly*. Introduced to my body and its curious pulsations and connections, I wanted to know more, *now*.

All the same, I was sceptical.

'Ruggero's just a dressmaker,' I said. 'What can he do for me?'

We knew a man our own age, a local Veronese, who had become a shiatsu practitioner. Ten years ago, during a midlife crisis. He now taught shiatsu in Milan and Padua. Prior to that he had made dresses for the rich women of Verona. He was the father of one of my son's early school friends. The two families had once eaten a pizza together. Ruggero's wife was a court stenographer. They were hardly sophisticated folks.

'It can't do any harm,' Rita said.

I had a mental block about massage. Perhaps I associated it with laziness and self-indulgence, or with things oriental and threatening. Perhaps I was scared of being touched. I remember once, in my thirties, at the gym where I did furious abdominals and played volleyball with frantic intensity, the management decided to offer Christmas-time treats to the clients. Taking a small red parcel off the tree in the foyer, you might find inside a token giving three months' free membership, or ten visits to the swimming pool. Mine awarded me three massages. I was so upset I begged them to substitute the gift for something else. Anything. They gave me the visits to the swimming pool and I splashed back and forth to see if I could still swim as many laps as when I was eighteen.

'Shiatsu is not massage,' Ruggero corrected me. 'It's a form of therapy through touch and pressure.'

He wanted to know why I'd come. As briefly as possible, I described my situation. He made notes. He was careful to check that I had done all the relevant medical exams. He told me to strip to pants and T-shirt and lie down. Then, like someone plugging in a wire to check a circuit, he chose a point on the sole of my foot and pressed. The pain in my bladder was immediate and intense but disappeared the moment he eased off.

'What about dreams?' he asked.

'What about them?'

It would be the first of many embarrassing conversations. Ruggero talked about meridians and yin and yang as if they were as real as red and white blood cells, nerves and skin tissue, not just words, inventions, stories. I decided to humour him, but was unsettled. The opening gambit with my foot had been impressive.

'Dreams may tell us about our condition,' Ruggero said. 'I imagine you dream of water.'

I stared. I was presently finishing a book whose title would be *Dreams of Rivers and Seas*. But I wouldn't tell him.

'From time to time,' I said.

He wanted to know what kind of water I dreamed of, what other elements were present. I told him that most recently I had been looking down from a hilltop watching excavators shifting the course of a riverbed; one enormous boulder wouldn't budge. In another dream I had heard a voice calling and descended a staircase hundreds of feet beneath our house where I found a stream flowing steadily in pitch darkness through solid rock.

Ruggero pondered. He consulted charts that showed different coloured lines forming elaborate circuits in the body.

He is a small, softly paunchy man with a round friar's face and bushy beard. I was vaguely irritated, thinking that if I had come and was paying him to do the therapy, he should get on and do it.

He wasn't a doctor, he said. These problems had to do with elemental imbalances and blocked energy. Earth must contain water, for example, but not block it. Water must refresh earth but not sweep it away. He could work on those relationships, but if I wanted to recover fully there would very likely be things in my life I would have to change.

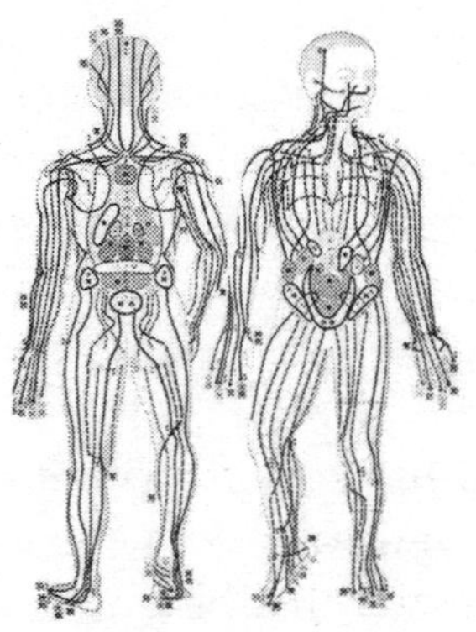

I let these bizarre notions pass in much the same way that I make no comment when my mother talks about the gifts of the Holy Spirit and the inevitability of Armageddon. A flaky, New Age mentality was beckoning. Often, Ruggero said, it was a question of the time of the year, the position of a planet. I recalled Dr Hazan and his birth charts, his theories about tussles in the mind. Each element, Ruggero explained – earth, air, fire, water and wood – had its stronger and weaker seasons. No doubt my troubles were worse in winter.

Ruggero loved to talk of these things, none of them

remotely demonstrable. But when he started to touch me all talking ended. Kneeling on the futon he seemed to fall into a trance of concentration, or even prayer. When he took hold of a leg, or arm, his hands immediately transmitted reassurance and knowledge. You were held, and he was knowing you, through touch. Sometimes he seemed to be waiting for your body to tell him something. He held a hand for some moments without moving. It was all new to me and I have to say beautiful, even moving. Emotions moved in me like mud stirred with a stick. 'Let go,' he murmured lifting my head. They were the only words he spoke. Or rather, in Italian, one word: '*Molla*', let go.

An odd relationship developed. Before and after the treatment, I let him talk for a while about reinforcing this or that meridian, or draining energy from the upper or lower body. It was mumbo-jumbo. At the same time I trusted his hands absolutely. I knew those hands knew things. It seemed better not to try and say exactly what. When I stood up at the end of the session I felt either pleasantly exhausted, or bursting with energy. On one occasion I walked up the hill to the car park with the springy step of a fifteen-year-old. I could fly. Other times my body temperature dropped drastically. I froze.

Never did Ruggero give me the same treatment twice. He asked how I was. I kept the talk brief; I was impatient to get going with the treatment, irritated by his time-wasting, already removing my shoes to hurry him. Then I would feel ashamed when, instead of giving me an hour, he went on for an hour and a half, even two hours. But always charged the same. 'Each treatment is a response to your condition as I find it that day,' he said. So obviously it changed from time to time. If, in the interim, I had dreamed of water, or any of the other elements, I would tell him the dream in one line. Once he remarked that more than any other patient I had convinced him that the shiatsu masters were right about dreams. I laughed and told him I didn't believe a word of it. It was his hands. Just his hands. Then on impulse I asked him: 'Make me stand up straight, Ruggero. Please. Help me walk with my head up.'

The Tangled Wisteria

For the most part Dr Wise is careful to back up the claims in *A Headache in the Pelvis* with references to respectable research papers. The concept of paradoxical relaxation, for example, is presented as a development of work done by Dr Edmund Jacobson in the 1920s and '30s. In general, the implication is that if this isn't mainstream medicine just now, it soon will be.

But as I suggested earlier there is also a more mystical side to Dr Wise. At one point he cites the Four Zen Horses as an analogy for four levels of readiness for therapy and towards the end of the book he allows himself to mention the 'ancient wisdom of the Buddha' as if this positive assessment were something we were all agreed on, rather than a claim that would prompt my mother to throw up her arms in disgust. Attempting to describe the proper 'attitude of acceptance' for those embarking on paradoxical relaxation, he quotes, of all things, a Japanese haiku.

Crisp autumn leaves
Rustle softly
Then blow away.

Written without embellishment, judgement or interpretation, Wise remarks, this description shows the poet simply accepting things as they are, a state of mind pelvic pain sufferers should emulate. As I see it, there is a great deal of embellishment in these brief lines; what is helpful, perhaps, for the person seeking to relax is the image of something disappearing, naturally and rightly, without resistance, as autumn leaves must, the poet's voice falling silent exactly as the object he describes is swept away. Reading the haiku, you are encouraged to imagine that its eight rustling words have blown off with the leaves, naturally and inevitably, and the mind can now repose in their absence. Dr Jacobson had noticed, Wise explains, that *any thinking, however silent*, always tensed the various muscles that control speech. To relax deeply one must be rid of thought.

When I mentioned this relaxation technique to Ruggero he suggested it dated back rather further than the 1920s: I was actually practising an ancient form of meditation, he told me. If I wanted to get more out of it, he knew an organisation that arranged retreats.

I resisted 'meditation'. Without having ever really understood what the word meant, I felt that it smacked of the mystical, the oriental. My mindset was not compatible with such practices (whatever they were). To accept that I was engaged in *meditation*, rather than a therapeutic relaxation exercise developed by medical experts with Ph.D.s, would mean surrendering the tough, realistic side of my identity that had been adopted with a certain urgency when I abandoned my parents' religious faith.

And the word 'retreat', needless to say, couldn't help but remind me of times the Christ Church Youth Club took us away for a week at Easter to preach and pray us into born-again imbecility. No amount of pain would drag me back to such foolishness.

Lying on the futon in Ruggero's tiny study, I tried to get into the relaxed, non-thinking Dr-Wise state, the better to concentrate on what the shiatsu man was doing to my body. There seemed to be greater benefits if the mind focused wordlessly on the sensations he provoked, perhaps because the more focused you were the more deeply you could relax the muscles he was kneading.

Suddenly the radio went on very loud right outside the door.

This was infuriating. Ruggero rented his one room from a dietician who owned the small apartment and used the other room to see her patients. Often there would be two or three anxious, overweight women sitting in the small passageway, reading *Gioia* or *Gente*. Sometimes there was an angular mother with her anorexic daughter. To prevent those in the passageway from hearing the secrets confided in her office, the dietician, a busy lady in her fifties with a loud, confident voice, had placed a large radio on a shelf and insisted that it stay on for as long as she was 'receiving'. The channel she chose was RAI 2, the most inane of Italy's public stations: between pop songs and publicity spots, two facile middle-aged men joke with each other and various guests and callers in the most wearisome way imaginable.

The moment this radio disturbed the silence, the efficacy of the shiatsu was in jeopardy. I felt it, and the more I felt it, the more distracted I became and the more the treatment was in jeopardy. I just could not *not* hear and hate the two grating voices with their dumb banter. I couldn't not listen to their jokes and opinions; on the contrary I found myself listening carefully precisely to confirm how idiotic and poisonous they were. This is costing me fifty euros, I thought. With the radio blaring, it was money thrown away. Not to mention the time.

My muscles tensed, I couldn't relax. I needed silence.

Ruggero sensed what was happening. He had tried, he assured me, to talk to the woman and get her to use some more soothing form of music, but she had refused. He sat quietly, holding my foot, as if to let me know that he was aware of the rise in tension. A few moments later, he said: 'By the way, hyper-sensitivity to noise is one of the things associated with imbalance in the water meridian.'

Ruggero would pronounce these truths, or myths, with such confidence that there was little I could say in response, unless perhaps an unconvinced, 'How fascinating.' I wasn't going to start reading up on shiatsu theory.

I began to bring my earplugs. At the same time, I noticed that if I managed to get into Dr Wise's relaxation mode *before* the noise began, then it would hardly affect me. I heard it, but it didn't matter. This was curious. On the one hand I resisted Ruggero's meridian mysteries, on the other, things were indeed related in unexpected ways.

'The fact is,' Ruggero said, 'that if you want to stand up straight, a meditation retreat would be useful.'

This seemed mad. Presumably one spends ninety per cent of a meditation retreat sitting cross-legged with one's brain in one's navel. What I needed were some serious back exercises. Perhaps a physiotherapist.

Meantime, Ruggero's treatments had become progressively more violent. No, 'violent' is the wrong word. 'Aggressive' is also wrong. I can't think of a word that properly describes what Ruggero's treatments were becoming. Let's say that he did everything with more strength and force and pressure. 'You'd have been in hospital, if I'd tried this the first day,' he chuckled, forcing fingers under my shoulder blade. Many of the moves resembled wrestling grips. Legs, hips, back and neck were stretched this way and that. His fist sank into my stomach. Yet I never perceived it as violent. If there was pain it was always combined with a pleasurable sensation of release. He pushed the ball of his hand deep into the muscle at the top inside of the leg, and if I hadn't decided never to talk during the session itself, I would have asked him to do it again.

'Next you'll be making love,' my wife commented.

'I'm afraid I'm not his type. He says my muscles are woefully stiff.'

No homo-erotic thoughts crossed my mind, but I did wonder how Ruggero managed with the young woman sometimes waiting in the corridor when I left: early twenties, long legs, bright nervous smile.

'Oh, I'm very shy,' he laughed.

He wasn't.

I'd been seeing Ruggero for about three months when something new occurred. In the night, the thigh muscles immediately above my knees were suddenly seething with tension. I woke and couldn't sleep. My thighs would burst. I had to get up. It went on for weeks.

Did I have varicose veins? I wondered. My wife thought I should go for a check-up.

'Drainage,' Ruggero said.

Ruggero never has any problem fitting unexpected developments into his vision of things, his narrative. In this he is like my mother who ascribes everything positive to God and everything negative to the devil. The work he was doing, Ruggero explained, was aimed at draining trapped energy (*vata*?) downwards from my belly through my legs and out through my feet. Evidently, it had now descended to my thighs. Like sludge in a blocked pipe.

If nothing else, I decided, this was an innocuous and optimistic version of events and certainly better than the one that saw me winding up on the operating table. It was also true that I was now ninety per cent free of the pains higher up that had made life so miserable for a year and more. Apart from the frequent night-time trips to the bathroom, I was cured.

'So at some point I can expect the action to move down from thighs to calves?'

'That's right.' He was confident.

'Then ankles and toes?'

'Ankles, soles and away.' Ruggero smiled. 'The meridians terminate beneath the foot.'

'And why would meditation help me to stand up straight?'

After he had finished and I had got dressed, Ruggero sat down at a tiny wooden table and made notes of all the things he had done to me. He was meticulous in this regard. Everything was written down and filed. He might have been a doctor.

'At the moment you're just trying to lift your head and force your back straight.'

This was true: when I went running in particular I made a huge effort to fix my eyes high, on distant trees and hedges; but as soon as my concentration wavered and I started to think of something else, I was looking at the stony ground again. All my life, mind elsewhere, I have looked at the ground.

Grinning, Ruggero got to his feet and mimicked a man bent double but with face thrust up, a hunchback hoping for the moon.

'Like that.'

'Hard to see what else I can do,' I said despondently.

The truth is, I had no idea what sort of process it would be, learning to stand up straight. I had supposed Ruggero would free things up a bit, muscle- and bone-wise – perhaps there would be a dramatic, liberating crack at some point – and then I would finish the job with a superhuman, largely masochistic effort of will, pushing out my stomach and yanking back my shoulders, as if in thrall to some bulldog sergeant major.

'It won't work.' Ruggero shook his head.

I did everything in my power to prove him wrong. Constantly pulling my head up, I got a stiff neck, which Ruggero then relieved, but without any advantage to my posture. A summer passed, and a winter. If I did an hour a day on my back, following Dr Wise's rigmarole, the stomach pains stayed away. But I knew they hadn't gone far. They prowled the borders of the small haven of comfort I'd staked out, predators waiting for me to tire, wolfish shadows beyond the firelight.

And I *was* tiring. The relaxation sessions were getting boring. Occasional waves of relaxation no longer impressed me. I didn't know where to take them or what else there was to achieve. I began to skip. After all, I still had so much work to do. It was getting more and more difficult to find sufficient time for the university, and my writing, and my translating, and my family, and, of course, the need to keep fit.

So, gradually, the excitement of having 'cured myself' gave way to disappointment. A revolution had been left incomplete. It hadn't delivered. I hadn't changed. Life is so much longer than any of our enthusiasms, I thought. To every wave its undertow. I dreamed I was on a balcony with wife and friends and we were trying to unravel a wisteria that had grown in and out of the railings to the point that the two seemed inseparable. It was an ancient thing and I knew it was important to detach every tangled inch of it intact, otherwise it would never flower again. Everybody was helpful and handling the plant, which was *my* plant, with immense care – but the wisteria did seem so knotted, so stiff, so very old and unbending that sooner or later, I was sure, we would just have to hack the trunk down.

Catastrophic thinking.

Eventually, in April 2008, I boarded a train to the small village of Maroggia in the Valtellina, north of Milan, whence I was picked up and driven to a haphazardly renovated farmhouse high up on the Alpine mountainside. As the gate was closed behind us, I saw a card with the notice:

PARTICIPANTS AT THE RETREAT MUST NOT LEAVE THE GROUNDS FOR THE DURATION OF THEIR STAY.

The Gong

Paradoxical relaxation is done lying down, knees raised over a cushion to flatten the back. Vipassana meditation is done sitting cross-legged like a Buddha. Before confirming my booking, I phoned the meditation centre to warn them that I had never been able to sit cross-legged; I wasn't a flexible guy. They reassured me I could always use a chair. Lying down, however, was not permitted. The back must be upright.

I was anxious.

'The position is not the problem,' a man with a haggard, monkish face announced.

On arrival, I was surprised to find people talking. I had assumed the whole retreat took place in silence. Sitting on the front doorstep of the farmhouse, looking out over an Alpine panorama of peaks and stone and misty cloud, a girl in her mid-twenties had been expressing her concern (and mine) about spending ten to twelve hours a day with her butt on a low cushion.

'The position is not the problem,' this gloomy, handsome man repeated. From the way he spoke it appeared that there was a problem, perhaps a very considerable one, just that it wasn't 'the position'.

What then?

Before departing I had looked up 'Vipassana meditation' on the net:

> ***Vipassana*** *means seeing things as they really are. It is the process of self-purification by self-observation. It is a universal remedy for universal problems.*

'Universal' and 'remedy', I thought, are two words that when put together can only epitomise wishful thinking, unless we are talking about a bullet in the brain. Purification, on the other hand, was a concept I couldn't begin to understand and hence a goal I could hardly desire. As for seeing things as they are, I knew that meditation was done with the eyes closed.

'Vipassana helps you to start feeling your body,' Ruggero said. Lots of shiatsu practitioners did it; it enabled them to explore the meridians. He suggested I look on the retreat as a *merely physical therapy*.

What could that mean from a man who didn't believe in the separation of mind and body?

In the early evening we gathered in the meditation room and were invited to take a vow of silence. Seventeen of us. From now on we wouldn't be able to compare notes. Since the centre advertised itself as a lay Buddhist, non-religious organisation, I was surprised by the liturgical solemnity of the language and the moral seriousness of some of the avowals. For the space of our stay: we mustn't speak or communicate in any way; we mustn't kill, or harm any living creature; we mustn't steal or use what was not ours; we mustn't ingest intoxicants or any mind-altering medicines; we mustn't indulge in any sexual activity; we mustn't disturb those around us; we mustn't read or write; we mustn't engage in any other religious or meditative practice; we mustn't leave the grounds; we mustn't wear shoes in the meeting room; we mustn't lie down in the meeting room; we mustn't sit with our feet pointing towards the teacher.

I had no problem with any of this.

There was one positive instruction: we must ask the teacher, a certain Edoardo Parisi, to teach us Vipassana. He was not proselytising. We must seek him out.

Repeating a formula that was read out to us, we asked. We wanted to be taught.

There was then a 'guided meditation'.

The meeting room was a modern wood-and-glass extension built onto the side of the renovated farmhouse, itself perched on the steep slope of the mountain. Outside, rain fell steadily through the darkness. Inside, the only light came from burning logs behind the glass door of a stove and a dim lamp on the floor. The participants, men to one side, women to the other, sat cross-legged on cushions facing the teacher who was slightly raised on a low dais. Just one elderly lady had chosen a chair. Was it vanity, then, made me choose to sit cross-legged? Looking around as we removed our shoes and entered the room, I had simply copied the others. Against the wall there was a stack of cushions, hard and soft. I put two under my butt and pillows each side of my feet to support the knees. My ankles had to be yanked into position.

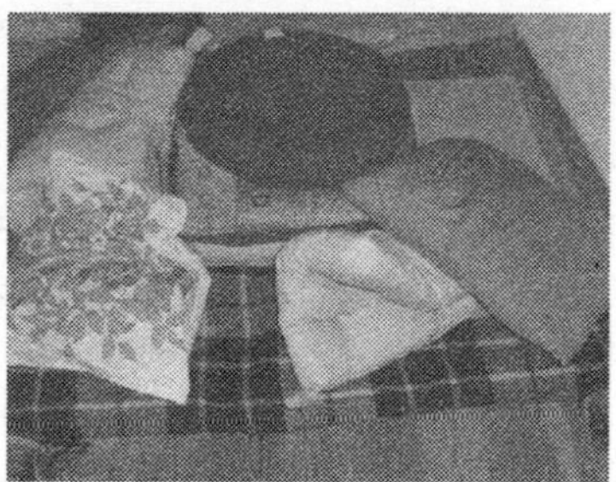

There was a long silence. The outside of the feet pressing against the mat would be the first to complain, I thought.

'May all beings live in peace,' the meditation began.

'May all beings be free from all attachment and all sorrow.

'May all beings be happy and enlightened.'

'Sadhu Sadhu Sadhu,' the more experienced meditators replied.

I was taken aback by the religious feel of this – the mumbo-jumbo 'sadhu' in particular – but accepted that it was a rigmarole that must be gone through if I was to enjoy the benefits of the days ahead. There was no assent in my mind. The idea that all beings might ever be free from sorrow was impossible and hence it was impossible for me to wish it. I remembered Emil Cioran dismissing utopian ideas that 'do honour to the heart and disqualify the intellect' and simultaneously warned myself that if I had come to pit my 'superior' intelligence against ancient formulas I might as well have stayed at home.

After another long silence we were invited to concentrate on the sensation of the breath crossing the upper lip as it enters and leaves the nostrils. Already the pressure of my left ankle bearing down on my right was painful. Already the straight back I had forced myself to assume was collapsing into a hunch. How could I concentrate on something so nebulous as breath on the lip in this state of discomfort? Lying down, I might have done it. Lying down I had learned to dispel the tension in my body. Thanks to Dr Wise. Cross-legged, tension was intensifying rapidly. Everything went rigid.

I wriggled. Perhaps I had got the position of the cushions wrong. They should have been tipped forward a bit.

I tried to adjust them, tried to sit still. This was hard work.

'If thoughts should arise,' the teacher at last intoned, 'don't worry, it doesn't matter, just say to yourself: thoughts, fantasies, not *my* thoughts, not *my* fantasies, and bring your attention gently back to the breath crossing the lip beneath the nose. The in-breath crossing the lip' – pause – 'the out-breath crossing the lip.'

The voice was soft and reassuring and I tried to follow its instructions. At the same time it was now evident that I had made a mistake coming here. I would never sit through an hour in this position. It had definitely been a big mistake not putting a third cushion under my butt, plus something to ease the pressure where my crossed legs touched. 'Not *my* thoughts,' I repeated, disbelieving. When, for a moment, I felt a light breath on my lip, I clutched at it as a man falling into a fiery pit might clutch at a thread. It snapped. The fiery pit was my legs where pins and needles were advancing rapidly. Amid a turmoil of angry reflections, I remembered something I had translated once from a book on pre-Vedic philosophy: 'So as not to be hurt, before coming near the fire, the wise man wraps himself in the meters.' The arcane instruction had impressed, I remembered it, and I had a vague idea it might now be appropriate in some way, but it also sounded like something from Indiana Jones.

'Thoughts, fantasies,' I repeated determinedly and went looking for my breath again. It eluded me.

'If pains should arise,' came the teacher's quiet voice, 'don't worry, it doesn't matter, just say to yourself: aches, pains, not *my* aches, not *my* pains, and bring your attention gently back to the air crossing the lip beneath the nose. The in-breath crossing the lip' – pause – 'the out-breath crossing the lip.'

Saying 'pain, not *my* pain' worked even less than saying 'thoughts, not my thoughts'. Whose pain, if not mine? After twenty minutes the pins and needles had crept up from my crushed ankles to my cramped calves. My thighs were simultaneously burning and numb. My curved shoulders were a rigid block. There would be no warm wave of relaxation tonight. Angrily, I hung on. When the hour mercifully ended, I couldn't stand up.

So why did you come? I demanded of myself in bed. Surely you didn't really believe this experiment would help you stand up straight. Who cared about standing up straight, anyway? Why had I chosen to give the business of posture such symbolic force?

Oddly, it now appeared that there was a gap between my actually being here, in this remote valley, sharing a room with two younger men (one snoring steadily), and some moment in the past when, presumably, I had had my good reasons for signing up to five days of Vipassana meditation.

Had I thought of it as penitence?

No. Since age fifteen I have refused to think of myself as a sinner.

I stayed awake for some time, got up to go to the bathroom, returned, listened to the man snoring, put in my earplugs, turned to the wall.

'You were looking for a showdown with yourself,' I muttered. That was it. A showdown with this tangled self, these tussling selves. You decided that without that showdown the pains would soon be back. Or other pains.

What form would the showdown take? I had no idea. But I had been told that, sitting in silence for days, people do come to a new knowledge of themselves. That was the goal. Knowledge, confrontation. To plumb the source of my tensions and defuse them once and for all. Settle *once and for all* that 'tussle in the mind'.

Of course, I had no more believed I would be successful in this project than a knight setting out to find the Holy Grail supposes he will be the one chosen to recover it. At some deep level, I wasn't even surprised to have spent a miserable hour merely verifying the fact that my hips, legs and thighs were too stiff for me to sit cross-legged. What else had I expected? Yet the following morning, after a tedious night taking care not to wake my room-mates as I padded back and forth to the bathroom, I went once more to the cushions, not to a chair. And I went *without hesitation*. I went cheerfully, *expectantly*.

In the end, I no longer believe that it is given to us to understand why we behave as we do. I should stop trying.

I say 'the following morning'. In fact the gong sounded at four a.m. Dead of night. It was a rather beautiful gong, a sort of auditory moonlight rippling through the deep silence of the house, promising calm and clarity. I was already awake and went downstairs at once. In the kitchen were flasks of herb tea. I poured something minty and went outside to drink it under the eaves of the house looking out into cloud and fog. A woman about my own age came and lit a cigarette beside me. It wasn't unpleasant, standing silently there together, listening to trees and gutter as they dripped, smelling her cigarette smoke in the damp air. I remember she shifted from one foot to the other. The not-talking actually made us more aware of each other's presence.

At four thirty the gong sounded again and the meditation began. Unguided, two hours. Seventeen people breathing, sniffling, coughing. Some wore hoods or swathed head and shoulders in blankets against the chill, which gave the scene a monkish feel. I had built my seat a little higher and brought a T-shirt to fold between my ankles. I did not expect these small expedients would bring comfort, nor did they. After half an hour toes, feet, ankles, knees, thighs and hips welded together in a scorching pyre from which my curved trunk rose like the torso of some broken martyr. Round this carnage, thoughts flitted and circled like bats in smoke. It would be impossible to convey how many thoughts arose, or how ferociously they blocked all attempts to focus on my breath. There had been nothing of comparable intensity when I had begun the paradoxical relaxation at home with Dr Wise. If, for three seconds, I did focus wordlessly on the sensation of breathing, immediately a yell of self-congratulation was raised, followed by a pertinent reflection on the inappropriateness of such a yell, then another reflection, equally pertinent, that this verbalised statement of inappropriateness only compounded the problem, then another reflection that such pertinent reflections were stealing away the experience that I had come for, the experience of wordlessness. Reflection comes at the expense of being, I told myself. Perhaps especially when pertinent. I was pleased that I had framed the idea so succinctly. And ironically. Would I be able to remember these words at the end of the session? How could I make myself remember, without pen and paper? Oh, but what is the point, Tim, of trying to meditate if you are only interested in describing the perversity of everything that prevents you from doing so?

So it went on. A mental seething. A stampede of cows, flies buzzing round shit, rats at a corpse. By some cruel stroke of irony, our farmhouse was situated in a valley with at least three churches whose mixture of clocks chiming the hours and bells summoning the faithful kept one constantly aware of time passing, and thus hopeful of an end, but also constantly confused as to how much time had passed, and thus despairing when no end came. If I opened my eyes and turned a little I could see the watch which the companion to my left had placed on the floor beside him. But what was the sense of checking the time? What was the point of being here if I was merely yearning for the two hours to be over, my mind projected into the future when I was supposed to be savouring the present – 'the present where there is no conflict' the teacher had said in yesterday's guided session? What did that mean? On the other hand, how savour the present when the present was pain, pain that I knew would dissolve the moment I made up my mind to move? But when I did move, swaying my trunk back and forth, for example, or, more radically, uncrossing and re-crossing my legs, then, after a moment's relief, the hot pain returned stronger still. It was worse.

Accepting defeat, I opened my eyes. There was no sign of dawn. The dark windows were a glossy mirror. The fire glowed red. Raised on a low platform, the teacher, in his early sixties, balding, blond, with a fine, pointed nose, sat in perfect stillness, swathed in a thin white blanket. Around me, others too sat perfectly still. One young man in particular had a wonderfully straight back, a marvellously smooth face. The woman to my right sat in a half lotus, unflinching, motionless, her breast rising and falling very slowly and gently. I envied them. And I held on *because* of them. Something about that young man, at once virile and serene, focused and silent, seemed to rebut my sophisticated objections. Closing my eyes again, I struggled once more to find this elusive point where breath and skin met. Perhaps for a whole minute then, I had the impression that the air coming in and out of my nostrils was a silver thread passing through transparent water. All around me was dark still transparent water, not unlike that in the waterseller's glass, and this delicate, mercurial thread of air ran gleaming across it connecting me to some distant point beyond my ken.

Had I left the retreat after lunch on day three, I would never have 'meditated' again. On the evening of the second day two young men disappeared. I heard angry voices from the garden during the afternoon break and at the evening session they were gone. If I had left with them, I could have read a book, or gone running, or canoeing, or for a walk with Rita and the dog. Halfway through the third morning, another place was empty. The maestro spoke calmly of 'right effort, right concentration, right awareness'. 'If you experience pleasure in your meditation,' he said, 'do not attach to it with yearning. If you experience pain, do not attach to it with aversion.'

Attachment with aversion was a new idea to me. But I sensed at once what he meant. It was like when I read an author I despised *because* I despised him, because I enjoyed thinking what a scandal it was that this man was a celebrity. Or when I kept complaining about a colleague at the university because my identity was intensified by my opposition to him. Or when I listened to the radio outside Ruggero's study *in order* to loathe it. Did I attach to pain in the same way? Scratching sores. Was it possible that this grand showdown with myself that I had planned and been denied actually had to do with the pain I was now experiencing? The showdown was taking place without my realising it *was* the showdown. Why else would I continue to sit cross-legged, without a break, when others had chosen to remove to chairs from time to time?

This form of meditation where you concentrate entirely on the breath was called Anapana, we were told, and merely preparatory to Vipassana, which was something quite different and more challenging. Only when the mind had been tamed and tied down to the breath crossing the lip, like a dog to a chain, could we progress. That would be the fourth day. I knew I wouldn't be ready. But on the third evening, towards the end of the last session, something happened. In the midst of the usual fierce pains, with a strange naturalness and inevitability, my consciousness at last fused with my upper lip: the breath, the lip, the mind, these apparently incompatible entities did, in fact, fit together, flow together, were one. I was my lip bathed in soft breath. At once the breathing that had been irregular and forced subsided to a light caress passing back and forth across the skin, a soft rising and falling breathed, not by me it seemed, but by my whole body, by the air outside my body, by everything around me. Then, as if at the touch of a switch, the scalding rigidity tensing thighs and hips dissolved. In a moment, the lower body sank into suppleness. Where there had been formless pain, I became aware of thighs, knees, calves, ankles, feet. A strange heat was being forced downward through them. My bare feet were cold but a hot pain was passing out pleasantly through the soles.

The experience could not have been more unexpected. Or more welcome. I was immediately anxious it must end at once, anxious that some malignant thought would rise up to cancel it out. Don't think, Tim. Do *not* think! Do not give yourself commands not to think! Silence! I focused on that breath that now seemed so strangely detached from me, or rather that I was just a small part of, as if the boundaries that routinely separated me from the world that was not me had blurred. And after perhaps a minute – but there is no measuring time in these circumstances – like a prisoner released from a yoke, my back, which had been cramped and bent, rose gently upright and was straight. As it did so, I was aware of each of the muscles that quietly lifted it. I felt how natural the erect position was. I felt blessed.

A few moments later and things were back to normal: the pain, the frustration, the waiting for the gong that would bring release.

Surprise Party

On the fourth day, I wept. It is more embarrassing to talk about this than about my urinary troubles, but to miss it out would be to lose a turning point.

I had got through the two-hour early-morning session. There had been no repeat of the previous evening's brief beatitude, but a corner had been turned nevertheless, for I discovered that the more I let go, without worrying when each session would end or what I was thinking or feeling, then the less the pain of sitting like this bothered me. Rather, it was now as if this cross-legged pain were helping me to discover a movement of the mind that I had never really made before: unquestioning acceptance, letting go. It had been hard work getting to this point and it was not until I discovered that movement, or rather until it simply happened to me, that I even appreciated it was possible. Words can describe a mental experience, after the event, but had the same words been spoken to me a thousand times before the experience, I would no more have understood them than a child born in the tropics would understand sleet and snow. That gloomy man had been right: the position was not the problem. The problem was in my head.

So I sat, still in some pain but no longer angry. And the less I was angry the less I was in pain. At times the position began to feel comfortable, even beautiful, the way it invited stillness: the legs locked, the back anchored, the hands quietly joined, and the mind too seemed to have been quietened *by the position.* Everything came from having accepted that one really was here for the whole five days, from truly *not* wishing for the time to hurry by, truly *not* wanting to be back at one's computer writing it all down.

How right they had been to forbid us pens and paper!

After the morning session, at six thirty, we went to breakfast. We picked up plates, queued at a small table stacked with food, then sat together in silence. I had not expected what a pleasure this would be. The long hours spent wrestling, eyes closed, with wayward thoughts seemed to have heightened our sense of taste. Everybody ate slowly and with relish. A piece of fresh white bread seemed as good as any cake. And each face took on a calm and dignity that made one feel unusually happy to be part of the human race. There was no competition for attention, no flirting or coteries, no exhibitionism, no privileged partnerships. In short, nothing for a story. If you needed milk or water or tea, people understood and offered at once, with a faint smile. Afterwards, each person went to the sink and washed his plate and cup. No wonder they called it the Noble Silence.

But this morning I didn't make it to the food. Leaving the meditation room, you stepped into the small garden, whence it was a few yards to the door into the house and the dining room. On the threshold, I felt a sob rising from chest to throat.

The novelty of the experience was that I was not feeling unhappy in any way. Rather the contrary. Also unusual was my immediate appreciation that what was happening was beyond the usual social controls. My body had decided to sob, the way when it's ill, it decides to vomit.

I stepped aside to let the others pass and, to hide my face, turned to look out over the low garden parapet across the broad valley with its shreds of cloud and shafts of sunlight, its villages and churches, and then, beyond the valley, the great chain of mountain peaks: woods, scree, snow.

The weeping burst on me like a storm. I shook.

This crisis lasted half an hour. On two occasions I tried to go in to eat – I was hungry – but each time the emotion surged up with renewed force. My throat ached. So I sat on a stone table under a pergola and continued to gaze through my tears across the valley which seemed intensely part of the experience, as if, again, there were nothing separating self and outside – I was truly *in* this huge panorama, mind and body, weeping.

Then, as though a voice were calling a class register, name after name was announced to my mind, people I knew or had known; and together with the names came faces, bodies, vivid expressions and gestures. One after another, faster and faster, these folk were crowding into consciousness. It was as if, at some carefully engineered surprise party, a door had been thrown open and I was confronted with everyone who ever mattered to me: my wife principally and throughout – we had been together thirty years – then my son, my daughters, my mother and my father, my brother and sister, my friends, lovers, everybody precious, but colleagues too, old acquaintances, neighbours even, they were all here beside me on the terrace under the pergola looking out over the valley, not summoned by myself, not expecting to see me, but glad nevertheless to be here at this impromptu gathering – and solemn too, solemnly aware of our shared mortality, aware that some had already passed on, while others of us were well on our way through life's journey. Then I saw that the long valley we were gazing over *was* the journey. I was one with the group, the living and the dead, and we were one with the landscape. And slowly, between fits of bewildered tears, it dawned on me, at long last, that the roads to health and to death were one: to recover my health, fully, I must accept death as I had accepted the pain sitting cross-legged in the meditation room. I couldn't do that. I just couldn't. But I knew that if I did, this was what they meant by purification.

I have never wept so deeply. Like most people, I have sometimes been very unhappy, and sometimes very happy. But there had never been this outpouring, nor this feeling simply of being present, a mere witness, while something necessary unfolded. Had I wanted to resist, I could not have done so.

Finally, when it really was over and I could go to the bathroom to wash my face, I was struck, glancing in the mirror, by this obvious thought: that the two selves that had shouted their separateness on waking that morning almost a year ago were my daily life on the one hand and the ambitions that had always taken precedence over that life on the other. I had always made a very sharp distinction between the business of being here in the flesh, and the project of achieving something, becoming someone, writing books, winning prizes, accruing respect. The second had always taken precedence over the first. How else can one ever get anywhere in life? That was why I had been so challenged when Dr Wise warned me that I must put my painful and embarrassing condition at the centre of my 'project'. What he had meant, I saw now, was that the real project was always mortality.

A black cat had climbed on board.

The next meditation session was not till eight a.m., and, retiring to my bed in the meantime, I called up a thousand bookish references to get a fix on what had just happened to me, to turn it, as always, into words. 'Life presents itself first and foremost as a task. We take no pleasure in it except when we are striving after something.' I remembered reading that, but couldn't remember where. It had sounded a warning, I had made a mental note. But over the years I had read a hundred warnings and made a thousand mental notes and none had carried the conviction of the ugly bellyache that had stopped me sitting at my computer.

'We go to novels for life,' I had read those words, or words to that effect, quite recently, in James Wood's book *How Fiction Works*. But they might easily have been spoken by D. H. Lawrence or F. R. Leavis. And I understood now with absolute certainty that this claim was a false and self-regarding piety. Life is *not* in novels. The novels that most compellingly keep us away from life are those that most accurately, intensely and wonderfully imagine it and replace it for us, the novels of Dostoevsky and, yes, of Lawrence, of the truly great writers. But the novels themselves are *not* life and we don't go to them for life. If it's life we want, we put the book down. There were some dumb lines from O-level Browning:

> And you, great sculptor – so, you gave
> A score of years to Art, her slave,
> And that's your Venus, whence we turn
> To yonder girl that fords the burn!

'Yonder', 'fords' and 'burn' were awful, I thought. Why had such poor poetry stuck in my head?

Or there was Poe's story about the painter who so obsessively has his young wife sit for her portrait, that only when the absolutely life-like painting is finished does he notice the girl is dead. Art at life's expense.

Then I remembered – the weeping experience had set my brain racing – Robert Walser and the Benjamenta Institute of his novel *Jakob von Gunten*. Yes. Jakob, the narrator, is sent to a school where he must 'learn to think of nothing', something he at first finds absurd, but that eventually wins him over. 'One must go courageously into the inevitable,' was a line I remembered.

But why seek to tie down the intensity of what had happened to me with all these literary references? First the emotion, then the excited reflection on emotion, attempting to divert it from its initial function, to enrol it in my career project, to turn it into smartness and writing. First the illness to warn you away from monomania and back to life and then the reflection on that process, moving you away from life and back to monomania, back to writing and books. Coleridge again. Or even Wordsworth. 'Emotion recollected in tranquillity.' The formula sounded so innocuous, but the next logical step was to seek the emotion *in order* to recall it in tranquillity, to care more about the recollection than the emotion, because it was the sophisticated recollection that brought recognition and celebrity and self-esteem. 'Who can ever feel at ease when he cares about the world's praise and admiration?' *Jakob von Gunten* again. I had remembered that line too. More warnings. Jakob comes to appreciate the school's curriculum of thinking about nothing because he is disturbed by the power and ugliness of the instinct to achieve. I remembered an anecdote about Walser. One day his admirer, Carl Seelig, went to visit him in the mental home where he lived. You know, Robert, Seelig told him, you are perhaps the greatest writer in the German language at this time. Walser was upset. If you ever say such a thing again, he told Seelig, I will never speak to you.

I lay on my bed, leafing through the pages of my literary memory. As I did so I knew that it was foolish. The thing to do was to get back to the silence. Go to the meditation room now, I told myself, even *before* the next session. Go and sit in silence. At once a quotation rose to possess even this decision.

> The important thing is not to learn, but to undergo an emotion, and to be in a certain state.

That was Aristotle. I laughed and discovered something that has served me well since: the more we threaten thought and language with silence, or simply seek to demote them in our lives from the ludicrous pedestal on which our culture and background have placed them, then the more fertile, in their need to justify and assert themselves, they become. Reflection is never more exciting than when reflecting on the damage reflection does, language never more seductive than when acknowledging its unreality.

This is the territory of Beckett, I thought. 'Of it goes on!' *The Unnameable*. The mind's mindless chatter. Beckett too had spoken of being brought to an awareness of his sick psychological state by an array of inexplicable pains.

I stopped myself and went downstairs for the first session of Vipassana.

Anicca

Wordless wakefulness, lively stillness, meditation resists description. When, at the beginning, words and images fizz in resistance to our attempt to put them aside, the writer can have fun. But when thought at last relents, when eyes close behind closed eyes and the mind sinks silent into the flesh, then it's hard to describe that strange state of alertness, oneness, quiet. Moreover, the meditator loses all desire to do so.

To what end?

Vipassana, however, does offer a few fireworks on the way to composure which all practitioners recognise. Something can be told, though the experience lies beyond any verification. Above all, you can't see it. There is nothing you can copy, the way we might all copy the movements of a tennis player, or the way Eugen Herrigel copied his Zen master of archery.

'Now,' our teacher says, 'take your concentration away from the breath crossing the lip, and raise it to the top centre of the head, a small area, about the size of a coin, corresponding, in an infant, to the fontanel. Focus your attention there. Take note of any sensations that arise, without seeking to induce sensations where there are none, without resisting or altering sensations when they occur.'

So, at each of the retreats I have been to, whether of five days or ten, of twenty people or of sixty, on the fourth morning, it begins. Never, at first attempt, do I find any sensation in this neglected area of my anatomy: the bald spot. I can't even locate it. What does happen is that a headache flares as the mind detaches from the breath and moves out to explore the body. The tension swells into the skull for a few seconds, then fades.

Superficially, the Vipassana process is not unlike the autogenous training that I failed at so abjectly in my early thirties, or indeed Dr Wise's paradoxical relaxation. One is to contemplate sensation as it flows and ebbs throughout the body. The difference lies in the intensity and thoroughness of the exploration and the attitude with which it is undertaken. One renounces any objective beyond the contemplation itself. You are not here *in order* to relax, or to overcome pain, or to resolve a health problem – the experience is not subordinated to a higher goal – you are here to be here, side by side with the infinitely nuanced flux of sensation in the body.

First the fontanel, then the forehead, then the temples (left and right), the back of the head, the ears (left and right), the eyes (left and right), the nose, the nostrils (left and right), the cheeks (left and right), the lips (upper and lower), the gums (all), the teeth (every one), the tongue (above and below), the pallet, the jowls (left and right), the throat, the jaw, the neck.

And we have only just begun. The body is a universe. It has many parts. It is made up of many materials. The skin, the muscle, the nerves, the tendons, the blood, the bone ...

But what does it mean that the mind, or the attention, *moves* around the body? The body is absolutely still (you are not flexing muscles to feel, as you did in the early days of paradoxical relaxation), yet, within the three-dimensional stillness of limbs, head, trunk, you have the impression of the mind shifting, exploring, travelling up and down, left and right, as if, with the body parts that are usually in movement now firmly anchored, the usually anchored mind can move at will. And this is not the movement of the schoolboy's eye over diagrams of anatomy. It is not the movement of looking. Rather it is like a man wandering through the rooms of a house, in the dark, knocking on this door and that, perhaps after a long absence, checking if anyone is home, if anyone wants to talk, or gripe, or rejoice, or simply turn on a light for him.

For a while, perhaps, there will be no response. The doors are closed, perhaps locked. You must be patient. Nobody has passed this way for some time and it would be impolite of you to start rattling the handles. This is not a police raid.

The forehead doesn't respond.

The ears don't respond.

The nape of the neck never responds.

In another part of the house, on a lower floor perhaps, a noisy melodrama demands your attention. A fierce cramp is shouting in the calves. An ache hammers at the back. These people want an argument. They are protesting. But those are not the doors you are knocking on now. Their turn will come. For the moment you tap politely at the nose. You listen politely to the skin at the bridge of the nose.

No response.

But you have time! Hours of time. You are not in a hurry. There are many doors to try.

Attention attends, unrequited.

Then, all at once, the temples!

I remember distinctly, my first session of Vipassana, it was in my temples that it began. First one, then the other: singing, buzzing, dancing. Had I wished to induce a sensation in this part of the body, I would never have imagined such mayhem, as though insect eggs had hatched, or breath on ashes found a nest of live embers. Yet it wasn't creepy. And it wasn't hot. It was the lively sparkle of freshly poured soda water.

In my temples.

At this point you realise that focusing the mind – eyes closed – on a part of the body is quite different from focusing on something outside yourself, a ball, say, or a bottle, or a boat. In that case the object remains an object, however long we look at it. But like light through a lens, or through a glass of still water perhaps, the mind sets the body alight, or the body the mind. It is hard to say which; the skin glows in the mind and the mind fizzes in the skin. Together, neither flesh nor fleshless, or both flesh *and* fleshless, they burn.

This is the beginning of Vipassana.

The inclination now is to enjoy this novel sensation. It's such a relief, after twenty minutes perhaps, to get a response from the body at last, to understand at long last what the teacher was leading you to. So relax now and enjoy. As you relaxed with Dr Wise. This song in the temples, this temple song, is such a pleasurable sensation.

But the teacher is moving on. We must not attach to pleasures as we must not attach to pain.

Nose now.

Lips now.

Tongue now.

The encouraging thing is that once one part of the body has answered your polite enquiry, others too seem more willing to respond: here a band of heat, there a patch of coldness, here a dull throb, now a tingling current. The whole house is waking up and as you pass from door to door each occupant acknowledges your presence by turning something on: now a blue light, now a red, here a coffee grinder, there a TV. The tower block starts to hum.

These varied sensations, our teacher now tells us, are manifestations of *anicca*, which is to say, the constant instability of all things. He invites us to contemplate *anicca*. To know *anicca*, the eternal flux, in our hands, our chests. To recognise that nothing is fixed. Ego, identity, they have no permanence.

Immediately, my thinking mind rebels. My determined self resists. Who needs this mumbo-jumbo – I'm angry – these mystifying foreign words? *Anicca!* Who needs this *theory*? The body may indeed be subject to constant change, but it is also true that it remains largely the same for many years. I recognise my friends year in year out. In childhood photographs, my face is already essentially me, *Tim Parks*.

As I think these thoughts, the temple dance fades, the lights dim, the pain mongers on the lower floors increase their clamour.

Damn and damn.

I choose to forget the debate and concentrate on sensation. I remember Ruggero: treat it as an entirely physical thing.

The thud of the beating heart, the rise and fall of the diaphragm, a burning hoop around the waist, a warm tremor in the belly – very slowly, part by ageing part, the body was put together. The book I had translated on early Indian philosophy, Roberto Calasso's *Ka*, told the story of the so-called altar of fire. Blessed with longevity, but nevertheless mortal, the lesser gods sought out the first god, Prajapati, whose broken body was dispersed throughout the world, *was* the world, to ask if there was any way they might be 'saved'. 'You must reconstruct my lost wholeness,' Prajapati told them. 'How?' 'Take three hundred and sixty boundary stones and ten thousand eight hundred bricks…' The numbers corresponded to the days and hours of the Vedic year. Every brick was an 'intense concentration'.

The altar was built from the outside inward, focusing the mind. Its shape was that of the eagle, bird of eternal wakefulness. If ever you managed to complete the construction, a fire would kindle and the eagle would take flight to the paradise of immortality.

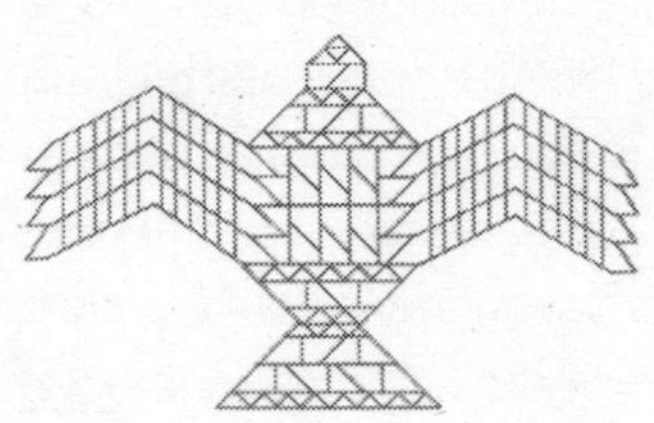

Well, there comes a moment in Vipassana, if you are lucky, if you stay focused, patient, if you learn not to want such a moment, when the entire body links up and ignites. Once, I remember, it began in my wrists. Pulsing waves accelerated into whirling orbits of bright electrons, pure energy, without substance. Contemplating this marvel, it did seem the ego was bleeding away into the hectic flow. If they wanted to call it *anicca*, let them.

But more often, for me at least, it begins when contemplating pain. It is hard to sit with pain in stillness, allowing it to be there, uncomplaining. A knife blade thrust between the vertebrae, for example. But if you do, then, perhaps, just perhaps, for one can never command these things, a sudden intensification will invade the spine, a rush of fierce heat flushes through the chest and dissolves away through arms and legs. The pain is gone. The hunched back straightens, the lungs fill, and the body is one, as if all the doors in a house had been taken away allowing free movement throughout. You are feeling *everything*, simultaneously, or rather, you *are* everything, from toes to fingertips to the hairs on your head. You dance through the rooms, you who never learned to dance.

The first time this happened to me, on the last session of that first retreat, the experience came together with three warm showers. Implausible as science fiction, that small area at the top centre of the head had begun to buzz, to glow, then overflowed in three drenching floods of warmth. A baptism. When the hour ended I jumped to my feet.

In the car to the station at Maroggia the young man driving was furious. The whole five days had been an utter waste of time. The teacher was a charlatan, a fool. We had been taken for a ride. *Anicca, Anicca, Anicca!* The Buddha was rubbish. Nirvana was rubbish. Reincarnation was rubbish. There is no way anyone can feel the breath crossing his lip. Bullshit. He had been through the pains of hell trying to sit in that dumb cross-legged position when he could have been skiing. He could have been playing tennis.

I believed in nothing, I said, least of all reincarnation, but it had been an important experience for me.

The other man in the car was the gloomy, handsomely haggard fellow who had told us the position was not the problem. Session after session he had sat two places to my left on a cylindrical cushion in granitic stillness. He did not respond to the angry boy who dropped us at the station, but on the train to Milan he told me he ran a very busy car insurance agency. He had been to a dozen such retreats. These were the only days in the year that were truly his own. It was a rule of his, he said, never to speak of his experiences during meditation. However, one aspect of

Vipassana still bothered him, indeed had come to bother him more and more, to the point where he was now ready to stop meditating. 'What does it mean,' he asked, 'when they say the thoughts are not *my* thoughts? What can that mean? How can the thoughts not be *my* thoughts?'

The Booker Speech

No longer much interested in standing up straight, I found my back pulling upright by itself. It happened over the spring. Taking my familiar run across the hills, I was surprised to find myself aware of muscles at the base of the spine. How odd. Days later I could feel my shoulders. A slight warm presence. Finally my neck. It was as if skeletal spaces had been very lightly pencilled in. Becoming aware of the muscles turned out to be one with straightening them. Or letting them straighten me. I didn't do anything. I just had to pay attention. The only difficult thing was getting used to seeing the world from a different angle.

'*Complimenti*,' Ruggero grinned. He insisted I looked ten centimetres taller.

No longer interested in prostates, pelvic floors and plumbing problems, I found my pains were gone. Truly gone. Even the wolves had departed. I had stopped watching out for them and they had slouched off. The ease and lightness in my stomach and back made walking a pleasure that was at once a powerful sense of nowness and a memory of childhood. I walked very slowly, savouring my body walking. On my way to the café in the morning I nodded at the moustachioed man in the white cowboy hat. He nodded back, with new respect, I hoped. It became genuinely hard to believe the state I'd been in two years ago. Had I really written those desperate notes in my diary? Had it been *that* painful?

Only the night-time trips to the bathroom remained, three or four. Irreducible to any pathology, they had stayed, I decided, to prevent me from growing too pleased with myself, or to keep the night present. My kayaking turns also had not improved.

With varying results, I continued the meditation at home. Paradoxical relaxation was behind me. It had been directly addressed to the symptom and the symptom was gone. I fixed up a mat and a few cushions in a corner of the bedroom and tried to meditate an hour a day. It was at once more comfortable than at the retreat, and less intense. The warm showers did not return. Nor the fierce pains. It was liturgy after revelation.

Knowing that I had scarcely scratched the surface, I signed up to a ten-day retreat in August. This time there would be a famous teacher, an ageing American, John Coleman. I made no attempt to find out about the man or to look up the philosophy that underpinned Vipassana. The last thing I needed was to turn Buddhist. I just wanted the quiet sitting, the increased perception of the body, the Noble Silence. I went confident that there would be no pain this time. I had sorted that out at home. I knew how to sit cross-legged. At times I even experimented with the Burmese position. It's so hard not to feel pleased with oneself.

Since there were sixty participants, the retreat was in an ex-monastery, in the Tuscan hills. Less chic than you would imagine. On arrival, in the fervour of conversation that precedes the vow of silence, all the talk was of Coleman and what a fantastic teacher he was. '*My* teacher,' someone said. '*Il* mio *maestro*.' 'I switched to Coleman from Goenka,' said another. There was a general rush to place one's mat and cushion towards the front of the meditation room, near the charismatic guru. May all beings be free from all attachment, I remembered, but, not wanting to be left out, I hurried along with them. I got a good place.

Coleman was on his last legs, shuffling, pushing eighty, fat, sometimes fatuous. He spoke slowly in a sonorous voice between heavy sighs, sprawled in a deep armchair, wearing loose jeans and sloppy sweater. A bland smile suggested he too was pleased with himself. Sitting on a table beside him, a young man with only one leg translated his words into Italian in a grating, high-pitched voice. At once this translation business irritated me. It hadn't occurred to me that language would be an issue. Much of the translation was inaccurate and all of it expressionless. There were occasions when it was hard not to shout out better solutions.

Coleman talked about the three refuges, the four truths, the five precepts, the seven stages of purification, the eightfold path to enlightenment, the ten perfections, the Buddha, the Dhamma, the Sangha, karma, anicca, anatta, samsara, dukkha, suffering, the root of all suffering, the remedy for all suffering, the bodhi tree.

What drivel this was, I thought. And why do all faiths – because this clearly wasn't science – share this mad appetite for numeration? The Trinity, the seven sacraments, the ten commandments. It wasn't *worth* translating properly. On the other hand, I always tell my students that translating accurately is a pleasure *in itself* regardless of the inanity of the original. Certainly I was suffering more for the poor translation than the mystical content.

Every few minutes the man behind me – and he was very

close behind me – sniffed three times in rapid succession, then cleared his throat, then coughed. To my dismay, when the meditation proper began, fat old Coleman had someone fetch a large kitchen clock and place it at his feet. It was the kind of clock I could have heard ticking about ten miles away. Immediately I thought of all the guestrooms, classrooms, university offices and rented apartments, where the first thing I'd done on arrival was remove the battery from a ticking clock. What a satisfaction that is, killing the sound that constantly returns you to the passing moment, that stops you being elsewhere in your head. Here I was helpless. This will be hell, I decided.

And I hadn't conquered the pain at all. Twenty minutes into the first session I was in agony.

Nor had I learned to sit up straight. My back collapsed, doubled even. My nose was at my feet (my aching feet). Why? This was *worse* than Maroggia. I should never have come.

The meditation room was narrow and very long and I was about four rows from the front in ripple and cross-ripple of fidgeting and buttock shifting. Every time I thought I might at last be getting a hold on my breathing, every time the pain began to ease up as the mind focused on the skin of the lip, from behind, came, Sniff, sniff, sniff, er er hemmmm! At once the clock ticked more loudly. Sniff, sniff, sniff, er er *hemmmm*! Tick tick *TOCK* **TOCK**! The volcano that was my haunches threatened to erupt.

'If there are feelings of pain,' the would-be hypnotic Coleman crooned for the nth time, 'just make an objective note, pain pain ...'

So what would a subjective note be, Mr Coleman? Or a note that was neither subjective nor objective, for that matter? Why pretend there is anything *reasonable* about all this?

For the nth time the one-legged man on the table translated – *fare una nota obiettiva* (does anyone say, '***fare*** *una nota*?') – his voice as bored and mechanical as Coleman's was sonorous and rhythmic.

I now felt homicidal.

From the corridor came the din of someone wheeling a trolley full of plates and cutlery along the monastery's uneven, unending, stone-flagged corridor. First you heard it approach for a minute or more. At the crescendo, it stopped, right outside the meditation-room door. Now I was waiting for it to start again. Was it going to go away or wasn't it? It was teasing us. I couldn't meditate until it moved off, or until I knew it was staying. Then just when you thought it was staying, off it went with a long drawn-out squeal followed by a great clatter of plates, knives, spoons and pans, like a goods train at dead of night, the rattle, bang and boom sustained for another minute and more before the din began to fade at what I judged must be the turn of the corridor. How many clock ticks before it is gone completely, I wondered? Twenty? I counted. Tick tock. Tick tock. No, ten ticks more. Still the clatter echoed faintly off the stone surfaces. And the rattle. Fainter and fainter, but still faintly there. Tick ... tick ... tick. The guy was *deliberately* going slowly! And a jingle of teaspoons. Tick tick tick. Still ever so faintly. Perhaps he was taking a step back for every two steps forward. He was *deliberately* choosing the uneven flagstones, he was rattling the cutlery trays!

Gone, it was suddenly gone. But now the clock's ticking had got into my skin and was stitching my lips together, each tick was a stitch, up and down, through my lips. How could I feel my breath with a needle sewing up my lips? I imagined the first major massacre at a meditation retreat. 'The assailant was a man in his fifties known to be searching for inner peace. It is not clear why he came to the monastery armed with a Kalashnikov.'

At the same time I recognised this package of feelings all too well. This is me, I thought, me of old. Unredeemed TP. Old resentments, dramatisations, would-be black comedy. You are getting off on being angry now. You're enjoying it, imagining yourself *imaginatively* angry. À la Geoff Dyer who himself wanted to be à la D.H. Lawrence. Gritting my teeth, I hung on to the end of the session and stumbled over a fizz of pins and needles to collapse on the lawn in the garden.

The monastery was supposedly in a secluded area, high on a steep hot hill and surrounded by an impressive stone wall, but the village immediately beneath the hill had arranged its summer fête for this week. At eight in the evening rock music began, as poorly played as Coleman's meditations were poorly translated. The summer air filtered out most of the treble leaving only a dull beat of drum and bass and the lament of a direly strained voice.

Added to which the Olympics were now under way. From the windows of the convent located directly across the courtyard from our meditation room came the sound of nuns cheering on Italian athletes. In China. If there is one thing I loathe it's the Olympic Games, festival of empty pieties, crass patriotism and sophisticated performance drugs. It was extraordinary how excited and patriotic those old nuns were. Apparently it did not occur to them they might be disturbing us. What a terrible, terrible farce all this was. Ten days of my precious and very busy life wasted!

Still I hung on. I had no idea why. My diligence was a mystery to me. One day I wondered if they had deliberately arranged for us to be assailed by these noises to test our meditative stamina.

The routine at these retreats is that you eat breakfast at six thirty, after the wonderfully quiet early session, lunch at eleven, then just a piece of fruit late afternoon and nothing till the following morning. 'A little hunger in the evening will do no harm,' fat Coleman smiled. The food, all strictly vegetarian, was not as good as the homemade fare at the smaller retreat in Maroggia. Brought in from outside, the pimply caterers grinned at us as if we were picturesque eccentrics. They seemed to take special pleasure in banging down the knives and forks when they laid the table and then shaking them vigorously in their metal trays when they collected them again, as if panning for gold. The fruit in the evening was chiefly kiwis. I'm not fond of kiwis. How can you peel a kiwi without getting sticky fingers? Fifty people queued around two kettles for tea. I had the distinct impression that old Coleman was enjoying little natters with the prettiest woman on the course. I had caught them three times at the turn of the staircase. Talking.

Where was the Noble Silence?

Every other afternoon, for an hour, there was a so-called 'check-up'. In alphabetical order people were invited, four by four, to bring their cushions to the front, sit before the teacher and report on their progress. On the second day, almost everyone spoke of their pain with the sitting position, their difficulty eliminating their thoughts; many complained of a film playing out before their closed eyes, some old drama rehearsed a thousand times with no solution, as when a ghost appears again and again in the same place in the same clothes – an ex-husband, a dead sister – makes the same gestures and is gone, then back. Never there, never not there.

'I'm in a loop,' one man said. He found it distressing.

'I have a big decision to take when I get home, I just can't get it out of my mind, I see the conversation over and over.'

People couldn't identify the place on their lips where breath met skin. When they did identify it, they couldn't focus their attention there, they lost it. 'It must be my moustache,' one man thought. He would shave it. Perhaps they felt the breath going out, but not the breath coming in. Or they could feel it in their nose, but not on their lip. Why was it so important to feel the breath on the upper lip?

'I have a pain in my shoulder, from an accident a few years ago.'

'I keep getting this fierce headache right behind my eyes, it won't go away.'

'My feet are on fire.'

'I've got period cramps.'

To all these people, sitting cross-legged on their cushions before him, Coleman, enthroned in his armchair, gave the same advice. 'You must say, doesn't matter, pain, pain, not *my* pain. You must say thoughts, thoughts, doesn't matter, not *my* thoughts.'

He smiled and settled his bulk.

I felt rage.

Given my place in the alphabet, I knew I wouldn't be invited to present myself to the grand old man until the third day. Try as I might to eliminate the mental chatter from my mind, I began to go over and over what I planned to say. I would mention my surprise that while I had no problem meditating at home, here I was experiencing all kinds of pains. Why? I sat up straight at home, here my back collapsed. Did he have any advice beyond, pain, pain, not *my* pain?

I thought of all kinds of attractive ways of phrasing this little speech, ways that would make it clear that I was neither an absolute beginner nor a practised meditator. I would say something different from the others. And of course I would speak in English, rather than going through the translator, the lousy translator. Perhaps I could take the opportunity to offer my own translation services.

Then I was angry with myself. What was this, a theatre? A TV show? I remembered how, on being told I was on the Booker Prize shortlist, I had been unable to stop a modest acceptance speech from playing itself over and over in my mind for weeks before the event. Literally for weeks this acceptance speech had driven me crazy. From the moment of the phone call telling me I was on the list to the moment of the announcement that someone else had won, my acceptance speech refused to stop accepting the prize in my head. Each time with some tiny addition, some precious new flourish. The experience was simultaneously infuriating and immensely gratifying. It really was such a clever, ironic, modest speech. People would not be impressed immediately, I thought. They would just think what a nice ordinary guy I was. Only later would they see what a clever speech it had been. Then they would think me doubly clever, and doubly modest for not having wished to impose my full cleverness on them immediately, but with delayed effect, like those fertiliser sticks you put in the ground that dissolve slowly for months.

On and on this speech performed itself for me, on and on and on. And now I was doing the same thing *for Coleman*. At every new pain and ache and itch that arose, every sound that irritated and interrupted, I revised my little speech. I polished my speech, shortened my speech, lengthened my speech. Which was insane. At least for the Booker there was an audience. Would have been an audience. T.V.! If I'd won. Here there were just sixty people living in silence, trying in silence to achieve some better relationship with themselves, with existence. *What could it possibly matter how I came across to them*? They didn't care about me. I didn't care about them. And then, how can it *ever* truly matter how one comes across? What on earth could anyone care about a Booker acceptance speech? For Christ's sake! And then, I had known from the beginning that I couldn't win the Booker with the novel I had written. My chances were not six to one but six million to one. It was a miracle they had put me on the list with such an angry book that had sentences more than two pages long. They'd never let it win. So preparing my acceptance speech was doubly ridiculous. At least here I was bound to get a hearing. From sixty people. The speech would happen.

Or maybe not. Because now it occurred to me that what I must do was ask to be excused from saying anything. That was the solution. Then I could stop playing the speech over and over in my mind. I might simply announce: 'Please, Mr Coleman, I would rather say nothing.' Or, 'Teacher, I wish to take refuge in the Noble Silence.' That was good. Then people would know that I *did not want* to draw attention to myself. Perhaps I would speak in Italian, so they weren't obliged to marvel at my being English. Except there was my accent, of course. There is always something that gives you away. Then they would be obliged to marvel how well I spoke Italian. Despite the slight accent. And of course I would immediately translate what I had said into English so that Coleman wouldn't have to hear my carefully chosen words from this incompetent one-legged wonder who disturbed us all from time to time by dragging himself in and out of the room on his crutches. Presumably to go to the bathroom.

'I would rather say nothing, if that's allowed,' I would say, in Italian. Or even better, I could approach Coleman in the corridor before tomorrow and, murmuring softly, ask if he could avoid calling me out to the front. Certainly people could hardly say I was looking for attention if I stayed sitting when the others went up to talk.

Or could they?

It was simply maddening how insistently this meaningless chatter ground away in my head those first three days of the retreat. Perhaps I should confess, I thought, when I was called out to the front, that I had wasted hours and hours of this precious meditation time with self-regarding thoughts about what I should say when called out to the front, thoughts entirely directed to the effect of my performance on the audience rather than an honest comment on the way my meditation was going. Badly, needless to say. Should I be confessional? Or would that have even more *effect*?

Of course I then imagined *writing* about this meaningless chatter and how brilliantly I could deconstruct myself, or someone like me (very like me), in a novel perhaps. I could very cleverly show how useless I was. Should I write a novel or should I make it non-fiction? Which would seem more *necessary*? And if I wrote non-fiction, should I perhaps use a third person, as Coetzee had in *Boyhood* and *Youth*, or accept the slithery candour of the first person like everyone else? Those are strange books that Coetzee wrote. They make you feel uneasy.

It went on and on. I hated it. I couldn't find a way out. After the first retreat I had read Coetzee's essay on Robert Walser and been astonished by a curious fact and by Coetzee's response to it, a fact that now came back to my mind as being extremely pertinent to this speech madness. In his mid-thirties Walser suddenly found that he could no longer hold a pen. His hand became painfully cramped every time he picked one up. He couldn't write. But of course he had to write, otherwise who was he, where were his old ambitions? So he fell to writing with a pencil. And his handwriting changed drastically. Instead of the generously rounded calligraphy of the well-educated young man from the provinces, he now wrote in a script so minuscule that to the naked eye it looked like some indecipherable code. Even experts, Coetzee remarked, cannot be sure they have got it right.

Why could Walser work with a pencil but not a pen? I wondered now, partly as an antidote to playing this idiotic speech over and over in my head and partly because I suspected that, however self-aggrandising it might seem, Walser's problem and my own were not unrelated. And why, in particular, did he talk about his 'pencil method'? Here comes Coetzee's bizarre interpretation. Like an artist using charcoal, the Nobel winner claimed, Walser needed 'to get a steady rhythmic hand movement going before he could slip into the frame of mind in which reverie, composition, and the flow of the writing tool became the same thing'. That is, he needed the rhythmic movement of the pencil to overcome some obstacle which Coetzee wasn't eager to identify.

But why is a pencil more rhythmic than a pen? Is the charcoal analogy pertinent? Painters do not try to execute miniatures in charcoal, do they? Surely if Walser's script had now shrunk to the indecipherably microscopic, the hand movements would have been *more cramped* and not free and rhythmic at all. Isn't it more likely that Walser's problem lay with the egotism and exhibitionism inherent in writing and publication? That was what was cramping his hand. 'Writers do not know what they lost when they sacrificed anonymity,'

Walser had written somewhere. Words to that effect. His novels were all glaringly autobiographical, with an alter ego at the centre of each story. Was it possible that the switch to pencil, which, unlike ink, can be erased, gave him a feeling that what he was doing was provisional, could be reversed? And that writing in such a tiny script he was in a way *hiding* his work from others? He was doing it and not doing it. For a while Walser would copy out his pencil manuscripts in a fair hand for the publishers, using a pen. Detached from the moment of creation, or self-revelation, self-affirmation, the pen was mysteriously useable again. But later he left his work in pencil without trying to publish it, and later still he *stopped writing altogether*.

I kept thinking about Walser in relation to this conundrum of self-presentation, of simultaneously wanting to take the stage and truly not wanting to take it, above all not wanting to want to take it, or not wanting to be seen to want to take it. And wasn't there something of the same conundrum in Coetzee's disquieting decision to write his autobiography in the third person? As if he wasn't writing about himself, but someone else. And no one is harder on that someone else than Coetzee in *Boyhood* and *Youth*, that person responsible for his committing the unforgivable indiscretion of writing these books. He was hard on himself because he was writing books about himself. And everyone knew it. Even though he pretended it wasn't himself. That was what he hated. Writing about himself, he wrote against himself. Himself being a writer writing himself. 'Not I,' Beckett proclaimed. Or had a mouth proclaim. A mouth without a face. Without an I, without an eye. 'Shall I never be able to lie upon any subject other than myself?' wonders Malone, or Beckett, in *Malone Dies*. A rhetorical question. No. Pain, pain, not *my* pain. Please. And when Deirdre Bair went to interview Beckett for the biography the first thing he said was, 'So you've come to demonstrate that it was all, after all, autobiographical.'

And it was!

And I was in deep trouble. I couldn't go on. For long periods, as the hours ticked by, I felt I was swaying from side to side and must sooner or later crash to the floor. I began to look forward to it. Or fall on my nose. I was so hunched. It would be such a relief when I crashed on my nose and everyone would see how much I was suffering and then I could stop and take a rest, take a walk, go to bed, go home perhaps. There was now a stabbing pain right between the shoulders. It was ferocious. Stab, stab, stab. Bizarre lights and burning heat radiated out from it. How could I be in so much pain when I knew there was nothing at all wrong with me? What was I learning from all this, I wondered? Nothing. Nothing except that *every single thought* that rose to my mind was in some way *self-regarding*. No, in *every* way self-regarding. Every thought. My analysis of Walser's problem was no doubt accurate, I complimented myself, and fitted in with many other elements in Walser's biography. My sense that Coetzee actually needed to miss the point was in line with his own obvious conflict when it came to presenting himself. But what is there to present, in writing, if not oneself? Even if I wrote about the man on the moon it would be self-presentation. *Especially* if I wrote about the man on the moon. What I must say when I am finally called to the front, I decided, is that these three days of meditation have revealed to me that every thought I think is, in one way or another, an ugly, fatuous form of self-congratulation. Even what appears to be the most searing self-criticism is in fact self-congratulation. A man capable of seeing his worst side, you congratulate yourself. Coetzee is pleased to have been so hard on himself. Nice observation, Tim. Was there no way out of this? How could I stop it, really stop it, *forever*? Without blowing my brains out.

'Gently return your attention to the breath crossing the point on the upper lip. The in breath crossing the point, the out breath crossing the point. Nama and Rupa, mind and material. Everything in the world, mind and material. Without identity.'

Tom Pax was called to the front with three other names.

So much for identity. The translator was misreading from his list of names. Pax I'm used to, but I hate it when I'm called Tom.

Knowing that Coleman always proceeded from left to right, I put down my cushion on the far right.

The first man admitted to panic attacks.

Coleman was silent. 'Just concentrate on the breath,' he told him eventually. 'And make an objective note of the fear.'

The second man confessed he kept falling asleep then waking himself up as his body slipped and slumped.

Like the disciples at Gethsemane, I thought, and thinking this was simultaneous with congratulating myself for the pertinent allusion, then wearily ticking myself off for another manifestation of self-regard.

'One does tend to get sleepy the first three days,' Coleman told him. 'It will stop as we go on. Don't be angry with yourself. Make an objective mental note – sleepiness – then return your concentration to the breath on your lips.'

In a late change of plan I decided I would simply say I was having a lot of pain and was finding it hard to concentrate. Nothing else. The most bland summary of what everyone else had said. I hoped that wouldn't sound provocative. I hoped it wouldn't sound anything at all.

I would say it in Italian. Speak in Italian, as if you were one of them.

What was the 'as if' about?

Then the third man confessed that his main difficulty these last two days had been that he had kept thinking about what he would say, now, when he was called to the front. And Coleman laughed. Coleman laughed deep in his fat belly, a really hearty, rumbly, fat laugh, and said he had been wondering when somebody was going to own up to that. He was evidently much amused.

We had been set up.

'And now I'm saying something completely different from what I planned to say,' my companion lamented.

Coleman smiled. 'So you lost the present for a future moment that didn't even happen.'

That was my Booker story exactly.

'We never say what we plan to say, do we?' Coleman added kindly. 'So why not just leave the words till the moment itself? Nothing is at stake here. You're not being interviewed for a job.'

My turn next. Stay to plan, I decided. The new plan, that is. There is nothing worse than the penalty taker who decides at the last second to go for the other corner.

The fat man turned to me. There was a charisma about him. There was a merriment in his heavy features. Sunk in the flesh, the eyes were bright and young.

'Well, Tom Pax?'

I opened my mouth and nothing came out. It's an experience I've had a thousand times in dreams, but never till now in life. I was voiceless. I was supposed to speak and I couldn't say a word. Three or four times I tried. Nothing but air and pain in my throat.

Shaking his head, Coleman looked down on me from his armchair throne with a mixture of condescension and sympathy.

'I don't know what's happening,' I finally croaked. The words were barely audible.

He leaned slightly towards me. 'Why don't you go back to your place?' he said.

Personally Of Course I Regret Everything

Over the next four days I decided I must stop writing. I had just gathered some concentration, tuned my mind to the breathing, allowed the ticking clock to enter my unresisting pulse, to run across my cheeks and lips and up and down my arms, dissolve in my chest and belly, just got myself settled, in short, into the sitting position, into the meditation room, into the company of my fellow meditators, when the time came to switch from Anapana to Vipassana, from breathing to exploration. Then it was like stepping from a darkened bedroom into a burning house. Or coming out of anaesthetic after surgery. First a prolonged explosion deep in the skull, then, one after another, in the dark landscape behind closed eyes, not so much fires as burning rocks, great boulders of obstruction and pain.

After the first hour of this I hurried outside into the afternoon sunshine, overwhelmed by déjà vu. Had I been writing these experiences as a novel, I thought, then the crisis on the mountain terrace that rainy dawn in Maroggia would have been the obvious place for the story to end, with a life-changing breakthrough. But it had not been life-changing. Here I was five months later, back at square one, back with my old self, back with a sense of something that would never budge, with a body that seemed to resist me, didn't want my company.

Back with my bent back.

I watched the others bringing tea and kiwis out into the garden. On day one, day two, day three, people had walked vigorously up and down, or lain on the grass to do sit-ups and stretching exercises. It was a flat, symmetrical renaissance-style garden, a lawn split by a cross of paths. Now on day four everybody was moving in slow motion. People would take a few steps then stop, standing absolutely motionless for five minutes, even ten, transfixed. They sipped their tea slowly, peeled their kiwis as if it didn't matter whether they ever actually ate the fruit or not. Nobody was exercising. I too had lost any desire to exercise. And I had the impression that I wasn't the only one to have been caught out by the Vipassana. There was a shell-shocked look to the young man passing back and forth in front of me, placing one foot in front of another, heel to toe, as if walking a tightrope over an abyss.

Then it seemed to me that the only way to force an irreversible change in my life would be to dump the project that had been driving me, goading me, making me ill, I decided, for as long as I could remember: the *WORD PROJECT*. If illness is a sign of election in an author, I thought – where had I read that? – then renouncing writing might be a necessary step to being well. Not that I was actually *ill* any more.

But I certainly wasn't *healed* either. Otherwise, what was I doing in this crazy place?

Pulling my ankles into place for the next cross-legged hour, I remembered it had been V.S. Naipaul who had said that to me. We were eating lunch together at a conference many years ago. 'A writer must undergo a serious illness,' Naipaul had confided solemnly. This was some years before his Nobel. 'To awaken his conscience.' Which of course was only Naipaul's way of saying that *he* had undergone a serious illness and *he* was one of the elect. The man was nothing if not vain. How could I have fallen for such nonsense? Because he had indeed written some great novels, of course. Then I recalled that moment in *The Information* when one literary author wonders why a rival literary author bothers to keep on writing. And you know at once that the question is really Amis's question. He calculates the man's earnings. Less per hour than a taxi driver makes. Why does he do it? *To avoid facing up to naked, unmitigated, unmediated reality*, the author (and no doubt Amis) decides. Perhaps it was time, then, for me to face up to that: the simply being here, instead of taking refuge in writing about being here. I must go speechless. The moment of aphony at the check-up had shown me the way.

Guru Coleman, I felt, was trying to tell us something similar in his evening talks. The most immediate reality, the *only* reality to which we had access at every moment of our lives, the fat man said, was the breath, this breath, this instant, crossing our upper lip as it went in and out of our lungs. *The* breath, not *our* breath. Everything else was empty imagining.

These evening talks – from six p.m. to seven – were remarkable for their combination of blandness and pessimism. Sprawled in his chair, vapid smile on slack cheeks, ham hands on chubby knees, Coleman lurched into the sort of wet, preacherly parables my father would not have stooped to with a Sunday School class. 'So you want to have a red Ferrari?' Coleman almost crooned to the Italian crowd. He paused at every rest point. 'All your life you have dreamed of a red Ferrari' – pause – 'you *have* to have that red Ferrari' – pause, smile – 'and when you get it?' – pause, deep sigh – 'When you *get* it?'

He didn't bother to say, what then?

Please, I thought, while the translator trundled through his deadpan approximation for the benefit of the very few Italians who hadn't already grasped the idea, please, do me the favour of finding an object of desire that it would be genuinely hard to relinquish.

I must have a certain woman.

I must win the Nobel Prize.

It irritated me immensely that he drivelled on about this red Ferrari. People on meditation retreats are hardly of a kind to sell their souls for a sports car.

I supposed.

Sometimes Coleman felt too tired to talk and had his translator read us something directly in Italian, while he looked on with the same bland smile on his face.

'There are ten levels of awareness in Vipassana meditation,' the translator read swinging his one leg from the table top.

Sammasana, theoretical recognition of *Anicca*, *Dukkha* and *Anatta* (change, dissatisfaction, emptiness), through observation and analysis;
Udayabbaya, awareness of the appearance and dissolution of *Nama* and *Rupa*, mind and material, through observation and analysis;
Bangha, awareness of the rapid change of *Nama* and *Rupa*, like a swift current or a flow of energy; intense awareness of things dissolving;
Bhaya, awareness that this existence is terrible;
Adinava, awareness that this existence is full of misery;
Nibbida, awareness that this existence is disgusting;
Muncitukamyata, awareness of the urgent need and desire to flee this existence;
Patisankha, awareness that the time has come to work for complete liberation, through *Anicca*;
Sankarupekkha, awareness that the time has come to detach ourselves from all contingent phenomena (*sankhara*) and to break with our ego-centred lives;
Anuloma, awareness that speeds up our attempt to achieve liberation.

When he reached *Adinava* I began to smile and by *Munci*-whatever-it-was I was laughing. I couldn't help it. It was so *Beckett*, so like Arsene's great speech in *Watt* that I always use with my second-year students, and that always sets me chuckling:

> Personally of course I regret everything. Not a word, not a deed, not a thought, not a need, not a grief, not a joy, not a girl, not a boy, not a doubt, not a trust, not a scorn, not a lust, not a hope, not a fear, not a smile, not a tear, not a name, not a face, no time, no place, that I do not regret, exceedingly. An ordure from beginning to end.

And it goes on:

> The Tuesday scowls, the Wednesday growls, the Thursday curses, the Friday howls, the Saturday snores, the Sunday yawns, the Monday mourns, the Monday morns. The whacks, the moans, the cracks, the groans, the welts, the squeaks, the belts, the shrieks, the pricks, the prayers, the kicks, the tears, the skelps, and the yelps …

But why did these lines of Beckett make me laugh, I wondered, the way I was laughing now at *Bhaya, Adinava, Nibbida* – this existence terrible, this existence full of misery, this existence disgusting? Because they were so over the top, I suppose, because the trite rhythms and rhymes showed how misleading language can be, making everything sound hunky-dory while in fact what we were talking about was deep despair, as if I'd recounted my own months of pain as a nursery rhyme.

But it was more than that. I had been laughing at Beckett, I realised, ever since I was an adolescent, because these ideas were *forbidden*. My Anglican parents would never have countenanced such a vision of life. The blandness of the Anglican sermon always ended in optimism: the risen Christ, redemption, renewed commitment, the promise of glory. All my life I had associated blandness with Christian conformity, socialist optimism, complacency; and hence, vice versa, pessimism with non-conformity, intellectual acuity, liberation from coercive fairy tale into unpleasant truth.

My parents hated Beckett, hated it when I started reading Beckett. 'You've been led astray by your brother!' they yelled. They hated Beckett's *nihilism*, his defeatism. 'And if I could begin it all over again,' Arsene goes on,

> knowing what I know now, the result would be the same. And if I could begin again a third time, knowing what I would know then, the result would be the same. And if I could begin it all over again a hundred times, knowing each time a little more than the time before, the result would always be the same, and the hundredth life as the first, and the hundred lives as one. A cat's flux.

A hundred lives as one. A cat's flux! I loved that. And now I discovered that it was the essence of Buddhism, and that I was supposed to be arriving at an awareness of this awfulness while meditating. So many people see reincarnation as reassuring, even wishful thinking – you don't die, you get another shot at it – but Beckett, like Buddha, knew better. Every existence plumps you right back on the rollercoaster of desire and disappointment, scratching yourself out of one itch into another. Best out of it! And too bad that suicide only thrusts you deeper into the *samsara* shit.

Nihilism was evil, my parents insisted. Just the way my mother said 'nihilism' gave it a dangerous foreign sound, like an Italian stiletto. Or like Nietzsche. Foreign names, evil foreign words. Nothing sensible and Anglo-Saxon about nihilism. Nihilism was of the devil, it was the beginning of all criminal behaviour. Who would ever behave if life was meaningless? Even worse, nihilism was the beginning of *not trying*, not making a wholesome Anglican effort to improve the world. God had created us in his image, life was good; if the Fall had left the world less than perfect, that was our fault and it was up to us to make it better. Not to bellyache. Nor to bail out like a wimp. Buddhist fatalism was evil and led people to corruption and despondency which was why millions were dying of hunger and disease in Asia. 'We know because we've been there,' my parents would say, referring to missionary trips to Malaysia, India, Pakistan.

All this when I was sixteen, seventeen.

Now, listening to the complacent, pessimistic Coleman, it occurred to me that Buddhism framed things differently. To perceive the emptiness at the heart of existence, you must *first* achieve purity. Far from being a plunge into criminal behaviour, such a vision was – how odd! – the *reward* for good behaviour, and a key in the first door that would get you out of gaol. It was impurities and ignorance that prevented you from seeing things as they really were (awful) and hence prompted you to grow attached to life and suffer. The person who perceives deeply that life is empty, must be morally admirable otherwise he could never have arrived at the concentration required to grasp this. Certainly, I thought, I had always had an impression of Beckett as somehow saintly, or at least hermit-like in his pessimism, hardly a man plagued by the desire for this world's goods.

On the other hand, and this was where it all grew complicated, there was no way I personally thought of life as a veil of misery. No way could I accept Coleman's vision. Or Beckett's, for that matter. Precisely the problem for me is that life is *so beautiful.* I am very attached to it. My misery when I was ill was only in part the pain. More important was losing beauty, being unable to enjoy. But I have never imagined joy was impossible.

Thus my confused reflections in the old monastery garden after that evening's talk, with the air now silvering to twilight and that grating music striking up in the valley below. It was beautiful being here, I decided, in this balmy air beneath the cypresses high on the Tuscan hills. The fairground noise had ceased to bother me. It was beautiful watching my fellow meditators cloaked in their thoughts at dusk, noble in their silence. There was a young woman, I remember, six or seven months' pregnant, standing at the low parapet gazing down into the valley. Her fingers, just meeting on her belly, were relaxed and slender, and from time to time she turned her head this way and that, twisting her long neck, as if to relieve some stiffness there. Life is *too* beautiful, I decided. Not disgusting at all. There was a shadow of a smile on her lips. And the act of meditation was making it *more* beautiful, causing me to experience it more calmly. Simply eating had become an intense, slow pleasure, feeling a rough crust of bread on the roof of your mouth, a crisp carrot between your teeth, a forkful of rice melting in saliva on the tongue, slithering down the throat, then the cool cleanness of the water that washed it all away, the quiet sense of repletion. Sitting silently at table with the others was also an intense pleasure, watching their silent faces as they ate, watching their concentration. Breathing the evening air was beautiful.

I should definitely stop writing, I decided. How could I possess this deep calm day by day if I went on writing, hoping, fighting? I remembered Emil Cioran saying of Beckett that, if, over dinner, someone started discussing the relative merits of contemporary writers, Beckett would be furious and turn his chair to the wall in mute disgust. He refused to be part of such conversations. Wasn't all Beckett's later writing, it occurred to me, like Walser's tiny pencil script, an attempt to stop writing while still going on writing? First the switch to French – language, language, not *my* language – then the pieces getting shorter and shorter, with each sentence appearing to cancel out the one before, the whole thing more and more resistant to the reader, more and more concentrated on simple physical movements, walking, shifting the eyes, breathing. 'All writing is a sin against speechlessness,' Beckett had said. He would have stopped, I thought, if he could.

Again I recalled the evening I was at the Booker dinner. My acceptance speech churning in my head, I nevertheless prepared myself to clap when Arundhati Roy won. I think all of us on the shortlist knew that Arundhati Roy would win: the book was charming, it was already a bestseller, it was from India, it was about poor children who suffer abuse but make good, the author was beautiful without being too young, sophisticated without being a member of the English upper classes. How could she not win? I prepared myself to clap, and I *did* clap, damn it! And Arundhati Roy went to the podium and stood there smiling, beautifully – she was wearing a beautiful dress – and said she was lost for words, quite lost, because she had *never imagined* she could win, she hadn't prepared anything to say. And I knew this was false because I had been to lunch with her the day before and she seemed more than prepared to win. If nothing else, the bookmakers were giving her as odds-on favourite. So this speech, like the one I never delivered, had been carefully prepared, I realised, and prepared, like mine, to seem modest and unprepared, hence doubly false.

Then Salman Rushdie walked over to me and frowned and said if it was him he would be furious; he would be throwing chairs round and complaining that he should have won. I smiled and said I *was* furious, but not in this particular moment, just generally. Generally in a fury. If I threw chairs around all the time there would be nowhere for anyone to sit.

How can one lead such a life without running into an ulcer or two?

Stop.

I suppose it has taken me an hour and more to write down these last few reflections, but it only takes a second or two for them to flash through the mind as you try to focus on the breathing on your lips. How many times did these ideas race through my head in the following days, in the long silent dawns, in the guided sessions as Guru Coleman invited us to explore our bodies, in the twilight hour with the cackling nuns and the clashing music and the strong cries of children playing outside the monastery walls? Stop writing, I told myself. Enough. Enough.

Uncalled for, unwanted, the thoughts flew across my mental space, back and forth, hither and thither, like birds in the evening sky, chasing and losing and finding each other, racing, wheeling, dispersing, gathering, gliding a while then flapping in hard flight, always moving, through each other and across each other, at different altitudes, different speeds, as the light fails and the breeze comes up and the rain spatters on rustling leaves. Then one by one, at last, they begin to settle, they drop from view. With a last flutter, a thought settles on its perch and is quiet. On a rooftop perhaps, or

in your wrist, in your throat. Another joins the first, and another. Thoughts fluffing their feathers before falling still. Perhaps one last squawk – *Rushdie was right! I should have hurled a chair!* – then silence. Until, huddled together on their wire, between your ears, they lose definition, merge into each other, become a single pool of feathery shadow, deep shadow in the darkness, one layer beneath another, beneath others, as eyes close behind closed eyelids, watched by still deeper eyes, and the mind at last discovers itself transparent; the mind is finally still and clear as clear water, and from top to toe the body brims with transparent wordless mind the way a glass held between steady hands in the porticoed chiaroscuro of a sizzling afternoon in Seville might brim with transparent water around the dark secret of the black fig.

It was on the sixth or seventh evening that I came to myself in the meditation room and found I was alone: the others had gone. I was late for bed.

Coleman

Itch by itch, ache by ache, pulse by pulse, the body was explored. There was the first time I felt the roots of my teeth, a deep vibration in the gums, the first time the tongue throbbed and twitched and was truly present in my mouth, the first time a ball of fire rose slowly from stomach to chest. Pains flared, burned, petered out. Then returned.

Meantime one's personality was being stripped apart. It was a complicated demolition job where work had to proceed in a certain order: first this certainty came down, then that, then the one on the floor beneath. Not a sudden collapse but a steady dismantling. Or perhaps it was simply that without the people each side of you who make you who you are – wife, family, colleagues, friends – without work, TV, radio, without newspapers and books, phone and email, without a keyboard or paper to write on, the construct that was me was falling apart, rather as though a ship held together by the water it sailed in had been lifted into dry dock. Bits fell off. There was a day of tears, a day of confusion, a day of panic, a day of optimism.

'May all beings be free from all attachment,' Coleman intoned and he explained the pains we were experiencing thus: the body was an asbestos-clad stove full of burning coals. The coals were the smouldering accumulation of our past thoughts and actions. If we felt no heat in the ordinary way it was because the constant stimulation of our senses, the interminable churning of our mental activity, were powerful insulators: always moving, thinking, doing, we didn't notice. But by taking the five precepts and practising Anapana we had stripped off the asbestos and cracked open the stove. Then we felt our karma's painful heat. Now, day by day, with Vipassana, we would go into every corner of the stove, we would turn the coals so that they glowed and scorched. It was hard, he said. But slowly, surely, they would burn themselves out and all would be calm. Our minds would be pure and empty.

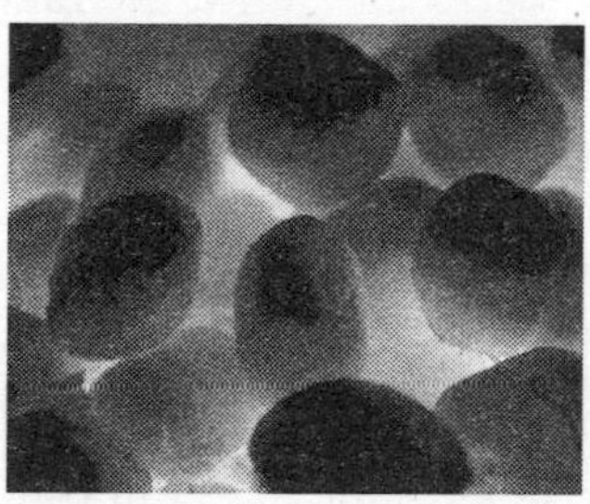

I thought: So they wait until the seventh day to tell you that the whole thing is based on pain, experiencing pain, accepting pain, something that, had you been informed beforehand, would most likely have deterred you from coming.

'Attachment to self,' Coleman said, 'is so strong that we will never be rid of it unless the suffering we feel within is stronger.' I remembered Beckett's *Endgame*. 'You must learn to suffer better than that, Clov, if you want them to weary of punishing you – one day.'

I had developed a curious state of mind during these evening talks. I believed nothing. I found the ideas ridiculous and contradictory: if life was utterly empty, how could you ascribe a value to purity, how could there be rules governing reincarnation based on your behaviour? etc, etc. At the same time I listened attentively, I enjoyed listening, and I saw that there were indeed ways in which Coleman's words could be applied to my experiences. I felt I knew what he meant when he spoke of everything flowing, mind and material dissolving into energy. Nor was it unthinkable that the strange pains I had been feeling had in some way to do with all those years sitting tensely, racking my brains over sheets of empty paper, building up hopes, rejoicing over some small achievement, over-reacting to setbacks and disappointments. And it was true that if you placed yourself, or your attention, as it were *beside* these pains, if you just sat together with them and let them be, not reacting or wishing them away, they did in the end subside. Likewise the thoughts: if you let them bubble up without judging them, or engaging them in any way, they gradually fizzled out. What's more, you felt that a certain serenity had been acquired in this process, an understanding that much of the pain we feel comes from our reaction to pain, much of our agitation from our excitement with agitation.

Above all, and more generally, I did sense the first hints of that famous equanimity Coleman was constantly speaking of. I had learned to put up with the lazy translation. I forgave our one-legged interpreter. In the end the guy seemed extremely pleasant, and now I was getting some perspective, not at all as incompetent as I had supposed. Some remarks he made in answer to people's questions were extremely helpful. I even forgave *myself* when, from time to time, I still grew irritated with him. Of the two, forgiving myself was harder. It came to me now that I'd always risen to the bait of yelling at myself, I'd always been determined to savour just how humiliating failure can be, and to make an exhibition of it. So this was progress, of a kind; paradoxically, letting go, you actually gained control, albeit of a different kind from the control you'd spent your life seeking. Distance, rather than grip. All you have to do now is stop writing, I decided, and you'll have clinched it. You'll have changed for ever.

But if I stopped writing, what would I do for a living? It was a false question. I had my teaching. I would be a teacher, a sort of servant. Robert Walser had been obsessed by the idea of service, of burying the ego in service. He dreamed of being a butler and actually worked as one for a while. I knew that this was a bridge too far for me. But teaching is an honest job. I enjoy teaching. With the writing behind me, the tussle in the mind would be over, likewise the gap between experience and fabricating a written account of experience, plus the foolish yearning for praise and success. All over. My health could only improve.

On the eighth morning I had an appointment to see Coleman. The afternoon check-ups had been suspended from day four. I wondered if this was because they were concerned that some of the more negative, aggressive participants might start a rebellion (one woman had used the word gulag when complaining about the rule against leaving the grounds); or because, with sixty people, they felt it was too much of a waste of time, too distracting to have everyone listen to everyone else. If you needed advice, they said, you could sign up for a fifteen-minute appointment with Coleman during the unguided meditation sessions on the seventh, eighth and ninth days.

My first thought was not to sign up. I had nothing to ask Coleman, or to tell him. If I wanted to know more about Buddhism, I could read about it, though I couldn't really see the point of pursuing notions so whimsical that I would never be able to accept them; those born in a rich, beautiful, peaceful country like Italy, Coleman had told us, could congratulate themselves on having scored highly in their previous lives. Ergo, those born in the Sudan had behaved badly. Nor did I imagine the guru would be interested in my views or reflections. Why should he be? Why should I want him to be? No, the only reason for my going to see Coleman would be curiosity, meaning, in my case, the possibility of collecting an interesting conversation to put in a book at some later date. Or in an article. I could write to the *New York Review* and ask them if they would be interested in an article on Vipassana meditation. Or to the *Guardian*.

But if you don't want to go on writing, what is the point of collecting things to write? Don't do it.

On the other hand, I *was* curious about Coleman. He was a type I'd never encountered before, a strange mix of blandness, serenity and shrewdness. He had spoken of an earlier life, in the 1950s and '60s, working for the CIA in Thailand before his search for a more tranquil state of mind led him to Burma, Buddhism and Vipassana. The anecdotes in his evening talks were infantile, deliberately so I had begun to sense, and delivered with a childish take-it-or-leave-it enthusiasm. He was deliberately insulting the intelligence, attempting to put that pesky faculty in its place. On the plus side, he had none of the sanctimoniousness that fatally attaches itself to every Christian clergyman. Nor did he wear any item of clothing that smacked of robe or ritual, or New Age vogue, for that matter. It was always: old slippers, shapeless pants, a colourless T-shirt. 'I had to have these pants made for me,' he announced apropos of nothing. 'Because I'm so fat.'

My immediate impression, then, was that the man was harmless. He wouldn't harm a fly, which was just as well, being a Buddhist. But once we shifted from the monotony of Anapana, to the more taxing adventure of Vipassana, I began to sense how powerful Coleman's charisma could be.

He would wait until we were all settled in the meditation room before making his entrance. We would take off our shoes at the door, go to our places, reorganise our cushions, drag our ankles into place, arrange our hands in laps or on knees, close our eyes and settle. Only when we had been there for some minutes would we pick up the sound of slippers shuffling along the corridor. Outside, the guru would pause, as if he hadn't quite made up his mind whether to come in. Then the door clicked, creaked open, swung to and clicked shut again. Again he paused, standing at the threshold, and I remember having the impression that he liked to hold onto things for support, the door handle, the table where the translator sat. Or perhaps just to touch them. He liked to touch things. We listened to his footsteps, teasingly slow, as he made his way to his shabby armchair. He sighed heavily, slumped into the upholstery and was silent.

Behind our closed eyes, his presence filled the room, his laboured breathing became our breathing. The clock ticked. Sometimes, in the far distance, you might hear a train hooting, or, on one afternoon, very faintly, an ambulance. More often dogs barked, a chained dog barking at others passing by, I thought. Thoughts, thoughts. I made my objective note. The minutes passed. Coleman was silent. There was no hurry. At the same time a fine tension began to creep around the room, a collective waiting for his voice; when at last it did ring out, we started. It seemed to speak from inside us.

'May all beings live in peace.'

Guiding the meditations, Coleman had a deeper, more measured, sonorous voice than the one he used in his talks. 'May all beings be free from all attachment and all sorrow. May all beings be filled with happiness and sympathetic joy.'

'Sadhu Sadhu Sadhu.'

I didn't say the words myself, but I assented.

He began tamely. He had us focus on the breath for some minutes, the breath crossing the lip. When he didn't speak for a while, you wondered if he mightn't have fallen asleep. Then the voice boomed out again. No doubt because our eyes were closed and because we were sitting so still for so long, sounds became physical things. The clock ticked in fingers and toes. The gong that began and ended each session tingled in my cheeks. A door slamming was a slap. Coleman's voice clanged a bell in your chest. Your body rang.

'Now we will take our attention away from the breath,' he said calmly, 'and move it upwards to the top of the skull.' He began to lead us through our bodies, and when Coleman named a part of the body it really was easier for you to get in contact with it, easier than if you were meditating alone. Naming a part of the body, his voice touched it, but without using any mystical formulas. 'Now move your attention to your cheeks. To the left cheek. To the right cheek. To both cheeks. Pay attention. Take note of any sensation that arises in this part of the body.'

His timing was impressive. He would have you concentrate on a wrist, thigh, or shoulder to the point that it became an agony to be so focused. I had never imagined that this combination of emptying the mind of thought and concentrating it on physical sensation could be such hard work. 'Feel how the sensation changes, in your hands, the back of the hands, the fingers, the fingertips, constantly changes, infinitely nuanced, infinitely delicate; *anicca*, know *anicca*.'

Then after a long pause, just when it seemed you couldn't maintain this focus a moment longer, he would say: 'And now, let go. Not holding on to the sensation if it's pleasurable. Not fighting the sensation if it's painful. Just … let … go.'

And I did. It was as if Coleman, Coleman's voice, were able to command those waves of release I had come across so unexpectedly in paradoxical relaxation. He commanded and I let go; a strange fluid rushed in, rigidity dissolved.

'Deeper,' Coleman insisted. 'Deeper and deeper, into the muscle, into the bone. Feel the sensation in the very bone. Feel that even the bone is subject to change. *Anicca.*'

We were concentrating on the arms, the elbows, and now it seemed I really was feeling the two bones in my right forearm. The ulna and the radius were present to me, their shape and consistency. It was the first time Coleman had invited us to go into the bone and, sceptical as I always am, I wondered if this was hypnotism. Was I the object of some clever hypnotic suggestion? But if it was hypnotism, would I be able to wonder if it was hypnotism?

'Let go,' Coleman said softly, 'just let go,' and another barrier went. I began to look forward to him saying the words. I was disappointed when he didn't. I realised that in the future, meditating alone at home, I would say this formula to myself – let go – imagining Coleman saying it, imagining his voice and the particular cadence he used, and I would feel how much more effective the words would have been if he were there in person to say them.

I decided I would, after all, make an appointment to see Coleman and signed myself in on the morning of the eighth day. Standing outside his door, I felt unexpectedly emotional. I had made a considerable effort over the last day or so not to plan a speech, or imagine the conversation, or even make a list of things to say. All the same, the meeting had begun to loom in my mind as something special. Outside his door I felt agitated. Something important was at stake. The feeling irritated me. I was an adult, canny, experienced and illusion-free. Why on earth was I going to talk to a guru?

With impressive punctuality, the woman before me came out of the room together with the translator and I went in and sat down. Coleman smiled and asked me if I had got my voice back and I said, 'Now we'll see.'

'Bravo!' he laughed.

It was a small sitting room with two armchairs arranged face to face and the shutters half closed against the August sun. I asked him how come he was limping so badly and he explained that they had been moving him around a conference complex in Malaysia on an open golf buggy when the driver braked hard and he had fallen out of the buggy and broken his hip.

Coleman spent some minutes describing the accident and the hospital. He seemed oddly enthusiastic about it all. 'The Malaysian nurses were wonderful!' Then he asked, 'But how are you getting on?'

I told him the retreat had stirred up a lot of emotions and reflections.

He waited.

I looked at him. He smiled at me. Not inviting, just waiting. The problem was, I said, that I didn't see how one could go on living the same way one always had and incorporate Vipassana into that. I felt this discipline was demanding pride of place, demanding that my whole life change.

Even as I said these portentous things I appreciated that had someone like myself made this kind of declaration, this admission of weakness, to my mother and father in their evangelical heyday, they would have had him on his knees giving his heart to Jesus in no time at all. There would have been tears and prayers and rivers of emotion. Coleman raised a bushy eyebrow. After a long pause he said: 'A lot of people get that idea into their heads.'

I was a little thrown. I waited but nothing more was forthcoming.

'Well,' I eventually said, 'I'm being asked to look on life as an affliction, a source of suffering, and to learn not to want it, whereas, the truth is I find the whole thing very beautiful. Living. These hills, the people here. I'm very attached to it all. Perhaps that's why I don't see how Vipassana is compatible. With the way I live, I mean. I keep feeling I'm being asked to say goodbye to life.'

Coleman was attentive, pleasant, distant. Again, after a pause, he said, 'Concentrate on *anicca*, get to know *anicca*.'

This did begin to sound like, 'Get to know our Lord Jesus.' I felt annoyed. I could play mute as well as anyone, I decided. I wouldn't say anything else till he started taking the interview seriously.

We watched each other. He seemed to understand my decision and instead of prolonging the silence asked, 'What do you do for a living?'

'I teach translation. And write books.'

'How interesting. What kind of books?'

'Novels, essays.'

He sat smiling at me. I waited. Then I realised he was smiling because he knew I was waiting for him to ask another question about my books, so that I could talk about them. And he wasn't going to.

'I mean,' I said hurriedly, 'I wonder how one can square writing, desiring success, with Vipassana. I've been wondering if I should stop.'

'Vipassana?'

'No, writing.'

'Oh.' He frowned and sighed. 'You know, lots of people come to these retreats and get it into their heads they should retire to a monastery or something. I can't see why.'

I was beginning to find the encounter galling. 'Well, monks don't write books, do they? The two things are evidently incompatible.'

Again the slow smile. 'Monks don't do lots of things. Who said you have to be a monk?'

'The fact is, more than anything else, words seem to take me away from the present moment. I'm never really here. Always word-mongering. I feel a lot of what's wrong with my life comes from words.'

He always waited a while before replying.

'We're speaking now,' he eventually said. 'We're using words now. It's quite pleasant, isn't it? Maybe useful.'

'It's different with books.'

The way he watched made you feel that despite his eighty and more years, he was focused on you, he cared. Then the answers were offhand.

'But books are wonderful things.' He chuckled. 'I even wrote one myself way back.'

'*The Tranquil Mind.*'

'That's right.'

I had seen a copy on the table outside the meditation room.

'It's not a very good book, I don't think, but an effective way of communicating a lot of information to a large number of people.'

Realising I would get nowhere, I said abruptly, 'Mr Coleman, perhaps you could help me with a smaller thing. I have trouble sitting up straight when I'm meditating. Especially here. At home I seem to manage. Here my back just collapses. I keep feeling I'm going to keel over.'

Coleman reflected, or appeared to. Perhaps it was the merest performance.

'I used to have a lot of problems sitting up straight,' he said.

'But what can I do?'

He breathed deeply. 'I wonder why you want to sit up straight.'

'Well, because it would be more comfortable, for a start, better for my back. I'd breathe better.'

He seemed unconvinced. 'I wouldn't do anything about it.'

'It does seem a fair thing to want, though.'

He looked out of the window. Perhaps he was going senile. He was losing touch.

'Sure.' He turned back to me. 'Everybody would prefer to sit up straight, yes.' He waited. 'You know, sometimes, when things don't happen for us, it's because we want them too much.'

I was silent.

'*Anicca*,' he said. 'Concentrate on *anicca*.' He leaned forward and offered me his hand. 'It would be interesting to go on talking, but I only have fifteen minutes per person.'

So that was it! I shook his hand, smiled daggers and went to the door in a fury. I had demeaned myself coming to talk to a guru and he had barely acknowledged my existence. So much for acquiring wisdom. As I left, an elderly man was waiting to come in. Coleman was running to schedule.

I stood in the stone corridor. It had recently been renovated and whitewashed but the Gothic arches round the doorways still kept their antique feel. The window at the far end was a square of brilliant light around the dark candle of a cypress outside. I went to look. The hills were ablaze with dusty sunshine. Down on the lawn, smoking and sunning herself on a deckchair, was the pretty young woman I'd caught Coleman talking to the first days of the retreat. She was taking time out. Join her, I decided. The hell with it.

Downstairs, approaching the main entrance, I stopped. The old bastard had called my bluff. He had seen through me. I was that simple. I shook my head, hesitated, and turned back down the corridor.

I had never entered the meditation room in the middle of a session. I closed the door as quietly as I could, and even so, as it clicked, a tremor ran through the bodies around me. The door was at the back of the room where three or four people sat on chairs. I passed them and padded barefoot up the narrow space between the men, two by two on mats to the left, and the women, two by two to the right. The four windows along the right-hand wall were open and a soft summeriness drifted in. Nevertheless I was aware of an intense, still calm, a hum almost. There was a collective mental energy around me that seemed tangible, as though I were wading through a warm sea of mind.

Having reached my place, I stood still to take a last look. Rows and rows of seated and kneeling figures. A fat man on a mountain of cushions. A gaunt Arab-looking boy who used nothing more than a low block of wood for a seat. Some sat straight-backed, some bowed. There were smooth, untroubled faces, frowning faces, faces smiling faintly. Some had all the gear, the oriental shawls, the cushions with esoteric symbols; some wore washed-out shorts, shapeless T-shirts. The pregnant woman was serene in a half lotus. One man rested his hands on his knees, the palms turned up, forefinger and thumb just touching. Another let his arms drop in his lap. Then I saw that the elderly woman to my right had a fly on her cheek. A black blowfly. It was walking up from her neck to her cheek. She didn't flinch. The clock ticked. The fly followed her hairline above an ear. She had greying hair tied in a bun. Was she aware of the creature or not?

I sat down. I was glad I had come back. I felt privileged to have seen the room when everyone was so still and concentrated. I settled down as quietly as I could and closed my eyes. My anger with Coleman had abated. He had been right to suspect my reasons for wanting to sit up straight. I wanted to prove I could do it, to myself and others. Exhibitionism. Perhaps he was right about the writing too. Maybe the real change would be to stop trying to impress myself with all this talk of drastic changes. 'A lot of people get that idea into their heads,' he had said. And: 'I used to have problems sitting up straight myself.' You and I are alike and like the others too, he was saying. Don't look for some special relationship with me because you're a tortured writer. He'd been very polite, I thought. He wasn't proselytising, he wasn't out to recruit disciples. I closed my eyes and waited for the breath to declare itself on my upper lip.

Charity

Things as they are. This bowl. The table. White yoghurt. At the last breakfast I was overwhelmed by the sheer presence of it all. This bread, this square of butter. Things as they are. My hand. The blemished skin, a scarred knuckle, a dirty fingernail. Everything was intensely itself, source at once of fascination and indifference. Scattered crumbs, splashed milk. I gazed at them. As in a Cézanne, each object had been set free from the mesh of human interpretation. A cup beside a slice of melon. Absolutely themselves. I say the words now – cup, melon – but my mind at the time was wordless. The cup, the melon, were things without words, not in relation, not part of a sentence or a story. And there was no distance between us. I was in the cup, I was sticky with melon. Raising my eyes, I looked at the young man across the table, cheeks freshly shaven, a red T-shirt, a tattoo on his middle finger. The tattoo mimicked a ring, etched into his skin. I watched. He was holding a biscuit, using a knife to smear it with pink jam. It was too intense. The jam was too pink. The strong fingers too present. I was touching them. The fingers were touching me. Watching was touching. Words protect us perhaps. Words keep the world at bay. I say that now. The thought didn't occur to me then. I was tongue-tied, there, in the middle of it all. I really was right there.

In slow motion we went to the meditation room. The man behind me took his place, eyes closed, lips pressed together. I hadn't heard him cough for days. The man in front was a sack of coal, bulk settling into bulk. The woman to my right perched electrically still; she was a bird, a parrot. She could fly off at any moment.

I closed my eyes and waited. Sure enough, other eyes opened in the dark. I was in the pitch dark putting out to sea. Mine was a frail craft, an oarless skiff. I wasn't concerned. I had put out to sea before without coming back. It wasn't a problem. The keel grated on the stones and bobbed free, free as the breath floating on my lip.

How quickly I'd got going!

Time passed. Despite sitting still, my body was twisting; my face had detached itself from my head, it was drifting away: lips, nose and eyes stretched and skewed like a gargoyle's. It didn't matter. The sea has its tides and currents. Looking across the space between skull and skin, I saw coils of grey smoke under my nostrils. I watched the smoke turn. It seemed extraordinarily delicate. The coils were very tight and fluffy among the hairs poking from my nostrils.

'May all beings,' Coleman's voice boomed out, 'be free from all attachment.' A tremor stiffened my back. I hadn't heard him come in. He sighed heavily and said, 'Today, our last day, the Metta bhavana. Today, the sharing of merits.' Raising his voice to its most vatic and hypnotic, Coleman began to read:

> Though I speak with the tongues of men and of angels, and have not charity, I am become as sounding brass, or a tinkling cymbal.

Damn. The wave that swept across me now was the exact opposite of a wave of relaxation. Nothing could have jerked me more sharply out of my tranced focus on the present moment than these words, nothing could have thrust me more forcibly back into history and narrative. I Corinthians 13 was Dad's favourite passage from St Paul. For a moment my father's voice and Coleman's were one. My little boat sank like a stone.

> And though I have the gift of prophecy, and understand all mysteries, and all knowledge; and though I have all faith, so that I could remove mountains, and have not charity, I am nothing.

Charity! My mind raced. Why was Coleman reading *this*? Did he know my past? I saw my father in the pulpit, robes gleaming in the sunlight that fell through the rose window on summer mornings, bald head gleaming. These were the words, he believed, that more than any other established Christianity's superiority. St Paul's great hymn to charity. Being read by a Buddhist.

> And though I bestow all my goods to feed the poor, and though I give my body to be burned, and have not charity, it profiteth me nothing.

As Coleman read each verse so the one-legged translator read the Italian version. Knowing both languages, each blow struck twice.

> *Se distribuissi anche tutti i miei beni ai poveri, e dessi il mio corpo ad essere bruciato, se non ho la carità, tutto questo non mi giova nulla.*

What did it mean 'though I give my body to be burned'? Why would anyone do that? I was right back in the world of words and angry questions, the world of my young self pitted against my dad's preaching, against every form of proselytising and coercion and mystery-mongering.

> Charity suffereth long, and is kind; charity envieth not; charity vaunteth not itself, is not puffed up.

It was odd. I was furious with Coleman for reading this passage, for bringing back my father, my embattled adolescence, furious with him for ruining what I had supposed would be another long, peaceful emptying of the mind into the spell of the present. At the same time, how could I not assent to these words? How could I not see that they were in line with all I had been thinking? Charity vaunteth not itself. It is not forever preparing prize acceptance speeches. Ergo, self-regard is uncharitable. How right that was! And though I sell a billion copies of my next novel, though I win the Nobel twice over and join the holy canon of literary greats, and have not charity, I am nothing.

> Charity doth not behave itself unseemly, seeketh not her own, is not easily provoked, thinketh no evil; rejoiceth not in iniquity, but rejoiceth in the truth; beareth all things, believeth all things, hopeth all things, endureth all things.

This was mad. How can you believe all things, hope all things? For some reason I was on the brink of tears. I tried to remember a sermon where my father had explained the different words for love in the Bible, told his congregation why the word here had been translated as charity rather than love. I couldn't. I couldn't recall it. I must swallow down these emotions. The storm had blown up so quickly. There had been no warning.

> Charity never faileth: but whether there be prophecies, they shall fail; whether there be tongues, they shall cease; whether there be knowledge, it shall vanish away.

Right, all this was so right! Whether there be novels, they shall disappear from the shelves. Only a month after publication most likely. And essays and articles and newspapers and websites and even the most beautiful poems. Though your book last a thousand years, though it last a hundred thousand, it will vanish. You are nothing.

But wouldn't charity vanish too? a cool voice remarked. What did it mean, charity never faileth? That was empty piety.

> For we know in part, and we prophesy in part. But when that which is perfect is come, then that which is in part shall be done away.

Listening to Coleman's deep voice, listening to the translator's lame echo, I realised I had never really taken in this passage before. It had always been one of those irritating parts of the Bible that obliged you to acknowledge that Christianity wasn't all silly, that St Paul wasn't just an anal retentive. Here we know 'in part'. That was exactly the problem. Knowledge comes in parts. The urologist, the neurologist, the psychologist. And the mathematician, the linguist, the climatologist. Even in daily conversation, every word divides the world in parts. But when that which is perfect is come …

What? What is perfect? And when?

I opened my eyes and watched Coleman read. Like my father, he knew the text so well he barely needed to look at it.

> When I was a child, I spake as a child, I understood as a child, I thought as a child: but when I became a man, I put away childish things. For now we see through a glass, darkly; but then face to face: now I know in part; but then shall I know even as also I am known.

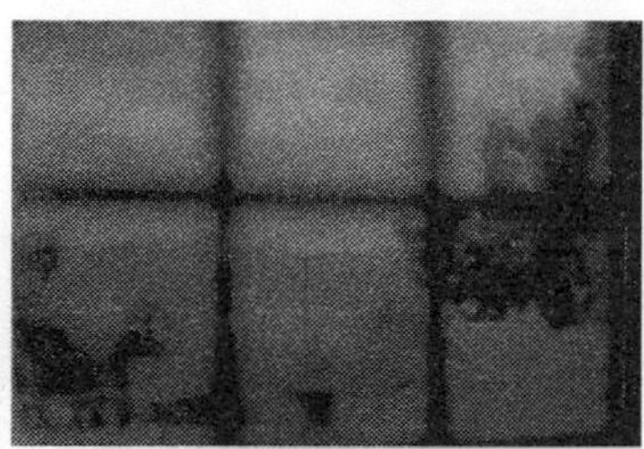

Did I ever become a man? I wondered. And what would it mean, to know as one was known? Who really knows me anyway? Nobody. Despite all your novels and half confessions, nobody knows you. There was something very fine about the words 'through a glass darkly', so fine that you hardly wanted to know things any other way. Through a glass darkly was OK by me. Or through a glass brightly, like the waterseller and the young boy.

Coleman paused and launched into the last great verse:

> For now abideth faith, hope, charity, these three; but the greatest of these is charity.

Why, I demanded – my head shaking slowly from side to side – why why why wasn't it possible for me to have the benefits I had no doubt obtained from this retreat, from this meditative practice, the mindful breathing, the exploration of the body, the growing awareness and equanimity, without bringing in these religious imponderables that always shake me up so badly? Why couldn't Coleman have done one last session of Vipassana and sent us off happily home?

The guru was talking now. By the end of our ten-day retreat, he was saying, we should have reached the stage known as *sotapanna*, 'he who has entered the stream', sometimes also called *sotapatti*, 'stream-winner'. He smiled blandly. He hoped it would be clear how these words related to the discipline we had been following. We had been learning to enter the stream. *Anicca.* But we hadn't done this exclusively for our own benefit. We weren't here to gaze at our navels. The very hard work we had done, he said, had accumulated for each of us a large number of merits. Every moment's escape from the confines of our narrow egos was transformed into a wealth of merits. Now, if we shared these merits with others, we could help them, we could improve the world.

How beautiful St Paul was, I thought. At least in that one passage on charity. At least in the King James version. And what drivel Coleman was talking.

There followed one of those strange half-hours where the intellect is hopelessly at war with the emotions. Our guru rambled on about merits and how, by sharing them with others, they actually multiplied for you too, so the more you shared your merits the more merits you had to share. We would embark now, he said, on the Metta bhavana, or meditation of loving kindness, which involved thinking intensely first of those closest to us, wishing them well, then the wider family, then, gradually, those we knew less well, those we didn't know at all, those who suffered in every corner of the globe, and those who killed and tortured and raped, even those who pushed destruction's buttons in the Pentagon, the Kremlin. We would share our merits with them and improve their lives and ours.

Crap. If one could save the world thinking good thoughts, it would have been done time ago.

While Coleman spoke, people fidgeted, nodding their heads, or shaking them, swaying from side to side, shifting their weight here and there. It was interesting that the moment you lost the concentration of Anapana and Vipassana it became impossible to maintain the meditation position. You had to move. I wondered if the others felt as embarrassed as I did by all this.

Coleman invited us to think of our parents. We were to close our eyes again, to concentrate on our parents, to recall their faces, to recall all they had done for us, to share our merits with our father and mother, to wish them well. 'May they be free from all attachment. May their lives be full of happiness and sympathetic joy. I gladly share all my merits with them.'

I thought of my dead father, my ageing, sick, but still sprightly mother. Naturally I couldn't wish my father well, because he was dead.

Could I?

Or could I?

I mean logically I couldn't, but what if I did wish him well anyway? What harm could it do for me to wish my father well? It was meaningless because Dad was beyond harm and beyond being well. He was beyond being. On the other hand, it couldn't harm, could it, for Christ's sake? Is it such a problem to do something meaningless?

Why was this bothering me so much?

I wished my mother well.

Wish your father well, a voice said. I resisted. It makes no fucking sense to wish my father well. He's dead. I won't have anything to do with this mumbo-jumbo and he wouldn't want me to, or rather, wouldn't have wanted me to. In fact, he would have been the first person to tell me to get up and walk out of this pagan bullshit right away. I smiled. Anglican through and through, Dad loathed the Catholic practice of praying for the dead. 'Paganism!' he would shake his head. 'Sheer, unadulterated paganism!' If I couldn't remember his face clearly, I had his voice spot on.

I wish my mother well because I always wish my mother well. I won't share my merits with her because I can't possibly believe in the claptrap of metaphysical accountancy. Next we'll be selling indulgences. Next we'll be lighting candles by photos of the dear departed.

Jesus!

I was stuck. Why? Why was all this emotional stuff happening? Why couldn't I just have sorted out my bellyaches and peeing problems and got right back to work?

I wish my father well, I thought.

How strange it seemed to say those words in my head! Dad has been dead so long. We argued before he died. I wish him well. We argued because I would not say, standing beside his bed, his deathbed, I would not say that I believed in God, that I was a Christian, to please him. 'I'm sure you do believe, Timothy,' he said. His face was grey, spectral. 'Tell me you do.' His lips barely moved. It was two days before he died. He stank. 'No.' I stood my ground. I wouldn't say the words for him because they weren't true. I wasn't a Christian. 'You shouldn't ask me to say such things.' I had been furious. It was the most underhand coercion.

Dad, I wish you well.

Then I sensed a stirring of the mind, a deep well-wishing in the mind, in the belly, in the bowels, that wasn't the words I was rehearsing, but that had been awakened or revealed by those words. Light had fallen on a dark place. I really did wish my father well, *enormously*. I was *bursting* with well-wishing for my father. There was a rolling ocean of well-wishing in me. Where had it come from?

'Maybe we have issues with those close to us. They have made us suffer. How we have suffered for the way they have behaved! And we have made them suffer. No doubt they too have suffered a great deal.' Coleman paused and sighed. 'All the same, I willingly share my merits with them. I share my merits with them gladly. May their lives be full of happiness and sympathetic joy.'

It was really too bad I couldn't believe in this merits clap-trap. There was such a deep ring of sincerity in Coleman's voice. I began to have a little respect for him, even though it was intellectually disqualifying to hold such nutty points of view. I fell to thinking of my wife. How we had made each other suffer!

Don't go there.

Our children. Our three children. My brother. My sister.

Faces appeared. I remembered those moments on the terrace at Maroggia. It was the same story, more controlled now, but the same. Something in this business of sitting still, emptying the mind of self-regard, settling into your flesh and blood, something in the soft breathing and the long hours just being there, just accepting that you really were here, here today and gone tomorrow that is; at some point it opened your heart.

There. I have used words that normally make me cringe. It opened your heart to the people around you. Suddenly you wished them well. Even people you really did not wish well. Now you did. However briefly. It brought down barriers and blurred boundaries. In your muscles, first, and your mind. Inside you. Rigidities, routines. They broke down. The mind melted in the flesh. The gap between you and the breakfast utensils shrank, between you and the landscape, between you and the people sitting beside you. We were all on a level. On the eighth or ninth day I had found myself sitting on a bench in the garden, a cup of herb tea in my hand, when the man who had talked about shaving his moustache to feel the breath on his lip came and sat down beside me. It was the only bench in the shade. He was a big athletic man in his early forties, I suppose. The sun was hot. We were sitting a foot or two apart, on the bench, and did not look at each other. We observed the Noble Silence. Yet at once there was an uncanny communion between us. I felt it instantly, intensely, and I knew he was feeling it too. We both knew, without having looked for it or wanted it, that the other was feeling a deep sympathy, a knowledge, but devoid of content. A knowledge of each other. We were both surprised and knew we were surprised. We were both glad, quietly. It must have lasted some minutes. I didn't know him from Adam. But, crazy as it will seem, I do believe that if some old man had poured us a glass of water from an earthenware pot, with a fig in the bottom of course, and offered it to us, we would both have put a hand on that glass, myself and the man who hadn't shaved his moustache, and held it there, on the shady bench in the sunny garden, held it perfectly still, without looking at the water, without looking at each other.

Was this charity?

How can you, I wondered, as Coleman shared his merits now with American generals and Iraqi suicide bombers, how can you pretend to escape from the compartmentalisation of Western medicine and then complain when people go the whole hog and talk spirituality and aura and reincarnation?

How can you? Where draw the line?

Believeth all things. Hopeth all things.

Perhaps it's impossible to integrate mind and body without integrating both with everything.

Would it have been charity to tell my father I believed in God, even if I didn't? I don't.

Suffereth long, and is kind.

I wish you well, Dad.

I couldn't listen to Coleman. 'How they must suffer for their crimes,' he was saying of Bush and Blair and Putin and bin Laden. 'I gladly share all my merits with them.' Coleman was mad. I went back to St Paul, to Dad's first love. If I have all those wonderful skills, he says, which are just a part, or parts, and have not charity, then I am nothing. It profiteth nothing. Because incomplete, transitory. The part is nothing. Charity is beyond parts, beyond boundaries, beyond time. Hence beyond words. Defined by negatives. It vaunteth not. It faileth not. Or by the absence of exclusions.

Beareth believeth hopeth endureth all things. Perhaps it was charity, then, that I had been learning through Vipassana. The knowledge that you are one with the whole. Perhaps the day will come, I thought, when the water snakes rise beside my little boat and I will bless them with all my heart.

'Your vow of silence is lifted,' Coleman said. 'You may talk.'

At once there was movement in the meditation room, there was noise, commotion. I was astonished how eager everyone was to speak, to know each other, how loudly they cried out their names. People jumped from their mats and were shaking hands, saying hello, introducing themselves. Shrill voices, deep voices. Eye contact, gestures, multiplicity. A camera flashed.

In a daze I had just reached the door when a young woman danced up to me, barefoot, beaming.

'Are you, by any chance,' this pretty woman asked, 'Tim Parks, the writer?'

Cathedral

'The air conditioning is out.'

'Damn!'

The caretaker shrugs: 'I've opened everything I can.'

On the fourth floor the students are already in the classroom. A wall of windows faces south-east over a small park in the industrial suburbs of Milan. Rising through a polluted haze, the sun sends girders of glare through the open window. Forty desktop computers add to the heat.

Emanuela tells me she's afraid she'll faint. She has blood pressure problems. I sit her near the door. Maybe there'll be a nice draught. I apologise profusely for the situation. 'The only way out would be to move to the main building where the air conditioning is working, but that will mean doing the exam on paper. No computers.'

Without exception the students opt for the computers. 'I barely know how to write by hand,' Silvia giggles. One of three Silvias. She's nervous.

Everyone is sitting next to his or her best friend. The back row is packed. I rearrange them. It's an old-fashioned, rather English obsession of mine that exams must be rigorously fair: absolutely no talking, no exchanging notes, no glancing at one another's work. The students resist this. A certain assumption of authority is required. I break up the gang of four and send them to the four corners of the room. The others laugh. I split the twins. I don't call them by name since it's impossible to tell them apart. Leaving one space between every two students there are exactly the right number of seats. Then Francesco arrives. Francesco is always late, always polite, vague, as if surprised to find himself here. The only thing to do is to put him on the teacher's computer behind the big desk. This leaves me with the one chair that isn't screwed to the floor and no writing surface to sit at.

I distribute photocopies and repeat instructions. 'Remember to save regularly on your pen-drives. It's nine ten. You have until twelve ten. Let's go.'

Understandably, some of them gripe. It's already stifling in the room. It's humid. Since we need the door open for air, there's noise when people walk down the corridor, chatting, laughing. A teacher yells in a distant classroom. Everything echoes. These are not great conditions for a final exam. All the same, the moment I give the order to start, the students get their heads down. As though some powerful appliance had been turned on, there is a tension in the room. If it were audible, it would be a steady hum; twenty-three kids thinking as hard as they can; and me watching, protecting, on guard.

They have three tasks. Translation of an article by Christopher Hitchens. Translation of a passage from Beckett. Critical analysis of the published translation of a paragraph from Woolf. Barely ten minutes have passed when a strimmer begins to whine in the park across the road.

I suffer for them. A couple of years ago, I would have been in a frenzy of irritation. I remember one afternoon exam during which a rock band started playing in the forecourt, warming up for the university's end-of-year party. In my head I had composed an outraged letter to the rector. Throughout the exam I was editing this letter and recomposing it and correcting it and composing it all over. Even as I did so, I knew there was no point in sending it.

I walk over to the window. In green overalls a man is trimming the borders and the grass round the tree trunks. The motor revs and strains. Why did he have to choose this morning?

Bowed over their papers, the students don't seem to have noticed. Maddalena has twisted her thick hair round her fingers and is holding it up over the nape of her neck. Michele has a pencil in his mouth and a thumb pressed to a temple. Someone's knee is jerking. I'm struck by how similar this is to the scene in the meditation room, almost a year ago now, and how different. There is the same immersion in mental activity. Without the serenity. You can feel the students winding up their bodies to have the mind work harder and faster, reading words, understanding words, substituting them with other words. Comes the first clatter of a keyboard. Francesco has started to write. In the second row Teresa raises her head. She is anxious. She's not finished reading yet.

The strimmer stops. In the stairwell someone is shouting into a mobile. Now it starts again. It roars, settles, drones. I hate the sound. But I can do nothing about it. 'Always ask yourselves,' guru Coleman said to us during one of his evening talks, 'in what way am I contributing to my own suffering?'

If you can do nothing about it, don't torment yourself.

I sit down and read through the tasks I've set them. Hitchens is difficult, but he is one of the journalists *Corriere della Sera* often translates and that's the level we're aiming at. In fact, because this material is translated already I've had to block the computers from using the net. Otherwise the students could just search and download. As a result, they can't use online dictionaries. They've brought paper. Some of them have come with three or four big tomes, wheeling them in suitcases. They put them on the desks that are empty and flick fast through the pages, switching urgently from the bilingual to the monolingual and back. Sitting at the end of a row, Paola has had to put her books on the floor. She tries to balance a Zanichelli on top of her Oxford on top of her suitcase. As she turns to type, both dictionaries clatter to the floor. The noise prompts a deep inhaling of breath throughout the room, then renewed activity. A dozen keyboards are at work.

'Fidel gets Religion,' the article is headlined. Then a subtitle: 'Why on earth did Castro build a Russian Orthodox cathedral in Havana?'

I have sometimes envied Christopher Hitchens. Always on the move, in the public eye, provocative, admired, presumably well paid. The article begins:

> In January of 2009 – on New Year's Day, to be precise – it will have been half a century since the brave and bearded ones entered Havana and chased Fulgenzio Batista and his cronies (carrying much of the Cuban treasury with them) off the island. Now the chief of the bearded ones is a doddering and trembling figure, who one assumes can only be hanging on in order to be physically present for the 50th birthday of his 'revolution'. It's of some interest to notice that one of the ways in which he whiles away the time is the self-indulgence of religion, most especially the improbable religion of Russian Orthodoxy.

On the other hand, would I want to write this sort of thing? Does Hitchens really care about Cuba? Or Cuba about Hitchens? Or the reader about either? '... who one assumes can only be hanging on in order to be physically present' is horrible.

I try to imagine how the students will translate the piece. Clumsy prose is hard. 'It's of some interest to notice that one of the ways in which he whiles away the time is the self-indulgence of religion ...' I wonder how much time Hitchens whiles away polishing his self-indulgent sarcasm. Not enough. Russian Orthodoxy is not a religion. Why is 'revolution' in inverted commas? Will any of the students be smart enough to eliminate that superfluous 'physically'?

The piece is so difficult that I have only given them two paragraphs to translate. The second reads:

> Ever since the upheaval in his own intestines that eventually forced him to cede power to his not-much-younger brother, Raúl, Fidel Castro has been seeking (and easily enough finding) an audience for his views in the Cuban press. Indeed, now that he can no longer mount the podium and deliver an off-the-cuff and uninterruptable six-hour speech, there are two state-run newspapers that don't have to compete for the right to carry his regular column. Pick up a copy of the Communist Party's daily *Granma* (once described by radical Argentine journalist Jacobo Timerman as 'a degradation of the act of reading') or of the Communist youth paper *Juventud Rebelde* (*Rebel Youth*), and in either organ you can read the moribund musings of the maximum leader.

His *own* intestines? In whose, one asks oneself, if not his own? My intestines have been behaving rather well recently. Likewise bladder and belly. I can't remember the last time I had any pains. I only go to the bathroom a couple of times a night. Since the second trip usually occurs between five and six, I repair to the sitting room to meditate. The house is very still at this hour. The day dawns. Mind and body renew their acquaintance in wordless quiet. Sometimes it seems the whole unhappy experience was just leading me to this. I feel grateful.

On the other hand, I'm evidently not free as yet from 'attachment through aversion'. Because here I am deliberately listening for irritating noises, constantly checking how unpleasantly hot it is and taking far too much pleasure in my ironic response to Hitchens. Moribund musings! Hitchens presents himself as wittily embattled on behalf of right and reason but the only thing this article leaves you with is an impression of the man's boundless self-regard. Castro's first and most important goal, Hitchens writes towards the end of the piece, was always 'his own enshrinement as an immortal icon'. Not an unusual ambition it turns out.

You envy him.

Paola's books clatter to the floor again. I get to my feet and start walking round the room. When I first started invigilating exams, twenty and more years ago, I used to resent the wasted time. I used to bring work with me and then be annoyed when my determination to stop the students cheating prevented me from getting on with my own reading or writing. A tussle in the mind. I hated the students for it and myself. But over the last few years I've come to accept these strange mornings. I even look forward to them. Well, a bit. I don't try to do my own work any more. I rather enjoy watching these young people as they give themselves to the task in hand. Having taught them for two years, I know them well. I find myself wishing them well, even the ones who've consistently irritated me during lessons. Why is Anna wearing a neck scarf on a day like today? And long tight trousers? Bruna's hair curls in damp ringlets on cheeks blushed with heat. She is biting a knuckle. I find myself hoping that she will get a good result, I hope they *all* get good results, I don't want them to be disappointed. At the same time I know very well that some of them are going to be very disappointed and that when I mark the papers I will be my usual severe self. No favours.

The achievement with Hitchens, I reflect, walking behind the students as they type, would be to arrive at a calm assessment of the man's prose without feeling any hostility, any resentment. Why is that so hard? Enrico has found a very smart solution for 'off the cuff and uninterruptable'. I feel quite proud of the boy, as if he were my son.

Maybe because Hitchens is so pugnacious. Either you agree with him or you fight back. But I *do* agree with him, on Castro at least, and I fight back anyway. The prose invites a fight. The words are jumping up and down, making rude gestures and waving fists. Perhaps this is the problem with so many invitations to get involved in the world: they are inviting you to join in a fight without its being important what you're fighting about. It occurs to me that guru Coleman must have shared his merits with Fidel Castro a thousand times, achieving no more, but then again no less, than Hitchens with his aggressive journalism. Causing less bother, no doubt. I have no idea myself what is the proper way to engage with the world. Or if there *is* a proper way. Should I be trying to change the world, or not? One of the Silvias, I see, leaning over the girl's perfumed shoulder, has run into a problem with that imperative 'Pick up a copy of the Communist Party's daily *Granma* ...' Her incomprehension helps me to see how fake it is. Hitchens knows his readers are not going to be picking up *Granma.* Silvia hasn't understood that it's just empty paperspeak.

Let's hope nobody translates *Granma* as *Nonna.*

Paola drops her books *again.* The heat, the tension and the unexpected problem of having to balance dictionaries on a suitcase, are getting to her. I walk swiftly to the front, pick up my plastic chair and carry it across the classroom. She can rest her dictionaries on that. I set it down beside her. A few years older than the others, Paola smiles. I would say 'my pleasure' if I didn't observe a complete ban on talking during exams.

Perhaps this is the sort of involvement I should be looking at. Giving up my chair.

Passing behind Monica I'm worried that she hasn't started writing. One of the intriguing things about teaching translation is how each student betrays his personality in the way he translates. Even the twins are different on paper. Assuming they don't copy. Monica insists on writing stylish Italian. To do that she must first digest the English until it dissolves into a wordless energy from which her Italian can emerge. But Hitchens is hard work. He won't break down. She is paralysed between the imperfectly understood English and her unwillingness to write anything imperfect in Italian. I'm anxious for her.

How can one be *in the world*, even doing something as simple as invigilating an exam, and stay tension free? Would it be more healthy if I felt no sympathy at all? Perhaps my sympathy for Monica, like my aversion to Hitchens, is a form of self-regard. The one situation is a mirror of the other. I like to feel generous to the student as I like to feel hostile to the journalist. How can one arrive at an opinion, an attitude, without getting heated about it?

It's really dreadfully hot in classroom 503. It's a scandal that the air conditioning breaks down so often. For a while I just stand in the corner and contemplate: twenty-three students working: the smart and the less smart, the pretty and the plain, the witty and the dull. Someone is drinking water from a bottle, someone is hitching up a bra strap. Emilio is scribbling on his photocopies. For a few minutes they merge into each other, they seem one. Over these two years the class has become a group, of course, a group with its unique collective character and atmosphere. I love knowing my students' names, calling each one by his or her name – it seems the most elementary courtesy – but sometimes it's nice to think of them as nameless too. A class. A community. I try to imagine the larger community of all the students I have taught over twenty and more years. There have been so many. All nameless. And myself too. I try to imagine myself nameless among my colleagues, among the students I have taught. Would Hitchens write as he does, if writers remained nameless, if books and newspaper articles were, as Robert Walser wished, anonymous, anonymous as butlers carrying a chair to where madam required it? Words seem less noxious when unattached to names. 'Where now, who now, when now. Unquestioning. I, say I. Unbelieving.'

I'm just beginning to think of the Beckett passage I've given them when my substitute arrives, Andrea. It's break time.

Of course, I haven't asked the students to translate anything so hard as the opening lines of *The Unnameable*. Over coffee in the thankfully air-conditioned cafeteria I look through the passage, trying to decide what to expect of them, how to mark their work. It's a piece from *Malone Dies*.

> Then Mrs Lambert was alone in the kitchen … She stood a moment irresolute, bowed forward with her hands on the table, before she sat down again. Her day of toil over, day dawned on other toils within her, on the crass tenacity of life and its diligent pains. Sitting, moving about, she bore them better than in bed. From the well of this unending weariness her sigh went up unendingly, for day when it was night, for night when it was day ... Often she stood up and moved about the room, or out and round the ruinous old house, five years now it had been going on, five or six, not more. She told herself she had a woman's disease, but half-heartedly. Night seemed less night in the kitchen pervaded with the everyday tribulations, day less dead. It helped her, when things were bad, to cling with her fingers to the worn table at which her family would soon be united, waiting for her to serve them, and to feel about her, ready for use, the lifelong pots and pans.

It's curious. My attention was first drawn to this passage a dozen years ago in an essay by the critic Christopher Ricks. He was embroiled in an argument with other critics who claimed that Beckett had buried realism once and for all. What could be more realistic than this? Ricks was demanding. Later, I remember re-reading the passage when I was ill and thinking how accurate Beckett was when he said 'the crass tenacity of life and its diligent pains'. And how right about the way pains keep you on the move, as if you could simply walk away from them. From kitchen to bathroom.

From bathroom to garden. Then back to the kitchen. How they invited you to live outside the present, to long for day at night and for night during the day, growing ever more attached meanwhile to the reassuring things that reinforce your old identity – the lifelong pots and pans. They were all reactions that Dr Wise and later guru Coleman taught me to abandon.

In his collected letters published only a few weeks before this exam and presently in my bag for reading on the train, Beckett describes how illness forced him to change his life:

> For years I had been unhappy, consciously & deliberately ... I isolated myself more & more, undertook less & less & lent myself to a crescendo of disparagement of others & myself. But in all that there was nothing that struck me as morbid. ... It was not until that way of living, or rather negation of living, developed such terrifying physical symptoms that it could no longer be pursued, that I became aware of anything morbid in myself.

Skin conditions, boils, panic attacks and a racing heart finally forced Beckett into analysis. Over some years and with great, as he recalls, reluctance, he recovered.

I wonder, spooning the last sugar from my cup, whether his Mrs Lambert is meant to recover. What does it mean when it says that she was half-hearted about its being a woman's disease? That she knew deep down it was a psychosomatic problem, or simply ageing? Or that any diagnosis was irrelevant? She was doomed. A few days ago an older friend had called me and told me he had prostate cancer. Giorgio. It was lunchtime. He had got the diagnosis a few minutes before. We talked it up and down. He's an immensely tense man, frequently in the throes of depression, an insomniac who makes regular use of tranquillisers and writes excellent aphorisms of exquisite pessimism.

'How long were you in pain before getting yourself checked?' I asked.

He'd had no pains at all, he told me. No nocturnal peeing. No warning. Nothing. 'Should I get myself operated on right away?' he asked anxiously. 'What do you think?' The doctor had told him this would mean the end of his sex life.

When I couldn't answer he added, 'Still, better than no life at all, I suppose.'

'Giorgio,' I eventually said, 'you should get the best advice you can.'

But it is foolish to speculate on Mrs Lambert's prognosis, and the question of Beckett's realism is more vexed than it might seem. The suffering woman is a casual invention of Beckett's narrator Malone who is telling himself stories to pass the time while he dies. She only interests him, it seems, in so far as he can project his own predicament onto her. A few lines after this, he breaks off and dismisses the whole story as 'Mortal tedium'. Mrs Lambert doesn't appear again. She was pure fantasy. Later we discover that Malone himself was only one of the many identities of someone called 'the unnameable'.

'The self is a fantasy,' guru Coleman had said in his hypnotic voice. 'It doesn't exist.'

Thomas Hardy once said the same thing, yet he was always recognisably Thomas Hardy.

'Let go. Just let go.'

It's time for me to hurry back to the exam. I don't trust anyone else with my students for more than a few minutes. Another instance of over-weaning self-importance, no doubt. The classroom, as I walk in, is suffocating. One or two students glance up, but there is urgency in the atmosphere now. They are pushed. There are clenched jaws and worried eyes. Dictionary pages slap back and forth. I tell Andrea to come back five minutes from the end and help collect the papers. He's a solemn, bearded, rather Victorian young man. A Ph.D. student. He'd be happy to stay, he says.

'No, one's enough.'

Then it occurs to me that I shouldn't have given this Malone passage as an exam since it was written first in French. Damn, The thought comes to me as I watch Teresa anxiously chewing her blonde hair. The girl is half German, tall with broad bare shoulders. Her T-shirt is stained with sweat. I would like to tell the students that although the exam matters enormously – actually their degree depends on it – from another perspective it really doesn't matter at all, it's pure fantasy. Either way, they would do well to stay calm.

Should I be giving my students a translation from English that is already translated from French? Isn't this methodologically flawed?

But can one really talk of translation with Beckett who was after all working back into his mother tongue from French?

Standing by the door, I think of Beckett moving back and forth from one language to another. Towards the end, it seems, he would write a sentence in French, translate it into English then immediately translate it back into French. And so on. Perhaps this too was a way of stepping back from involvement. First the sentiment, the lyricism, the intensity – as in Mrs Lambert's story – then the stepping back from it, denying it; she was just someone that someone I made up made up. Perhaps the translation was part of the denial, the distancing. *Moi, moi non.* Like Walser writing tiny script in pencil. Or Coetzee putting his autobiography in the third person. Except that since Beckett's first language was

English the 'translation' often turns out to be more intense than the original French. Beckett is definitely more inventive in English. He can't resist his genius for it. So then he has to ironise all the more heavily what he has translated, he has to bring in puns and asides. 'There is a choice of images,' he adds at one point in the English version of *Malone*. He hadn't felt the need for that disparaging flourish in the plainer French.

Monica is in serious trouble. She is just starting the second of three pieces and the exam is more than half over. Francesco has almost finished. Late to arrive he will be first to go. The students sweat behind their screens, treading the borders between English and Italian. Mrs Lambert was Madame Louis in the original French. Who cares? She never existed. But the pain Beckett describes is entirely convincing.

I haven't made much progress with my meditation since that retreat last summer. Perhaps you need more than an hour a day to break new ground with Vipassana. All the same there comes a point, where, entering fully into the moment, entirely focused and concentrated, you do indeed cross a border and leave all pain, physical and mental, behind; you move into a kind of bliss. Then, and this is the odd thing, you can go back and forth across that border, at will, with the tiniest mental shift. Bliss … pain … bliss … pain ... bliss … pain. The reflection that one has achieved bliss is the return to pain. The elimination of the reflection is the return to bliss. You cannot be there *and* congratulate yourself on having arrived.

The students soldier on, anxious, but entranced too. I've often noticed that translation has an anaesthetising effect that writing does not. Even during an exam. The text has already been written. You are not the author. Your identity is not at stake. All you have to do is follow, however difficult that may be. Text, text, not my text.

The third passage I've given them is vintage Woolf, something I've used a hundred times. They have to look at the original and the translation and use the differences between the two to say something about the passage. We've been doing a lot of exercises in class so it shouldn't be a problem. It's one of those little street sketches from *Mrs Dalloway*, a single paragraph, a single sentence, a character who appears this once and no more. More fleeting even than Mrs Lambert.

> Then, while a seedy-looking nondescript man carrying a leather bag stood on the steps of St. Paul's Cathedral, and hesitated, for within was what balm, how great a welcome, how many tombs with banners waving over them, tokens of victories not over armies, but over, he thought, that plaguy spirit of truth seeking which leaves me at present without a situation, and more than that, the cathedral offers company, he thought, invites you to membership of a society; great men belong to it; martyrs have died for it; why not enter in, he thought, put this leather bag stuffed with pamphlets before an altar, a cross, the symbol of something which has soared beyond seeking and questing and knocking of words together and has become all spirit, disembodied, ghostly—why not enter in? he thought and while he hesitated out flew the aeroplane over Ludgate Circus.

What I want them to notice is how the nondescript man's dilemma – shall I go into the cathedral or shan't I? – occurs as an extended temporal parenthesis inside what is really a simple statement whose main clause appears only in the very last words: Then, while … bla bla bla… out flew the aeroplane over Ludgate Circus. The syntax, with the long interpolation after 'while', creates the sort of suspension – mind off at a tangent before some event intervenes – which Woolf loved. The effect is completely absent in the Italian which gives, 'Meantime a man carrying a leather bag did this that and the other... then a plane flew towards Ludgate Circus.' Towards?

It's tough comparing translations with their originals because the student has to overcome the expectation that the professional translator is always going to be right. He has to think *against* something already thought, undo something done. It's not unlike the effort one has to make to resist received ideas. In this case the translator didn't understand 'without a situation', didn't realise that we're probably talking about some unemployed sectarian pamphlet-pusher now tempted to return to mother church. Above all, she didn't really understand that provocative reflection: 'tokens of victories not over armies, but over, he thought, that plaguy spirit of truth seeking which leaves me at present without a situation', translating instead, 'signs of victory not over armies, but over that pestilential spirit of truth which guides me in my search of what leaves me without resources', a sentence that doesn't really mean anything but which actually reads rather elegantly in the Italian. Translations are full of such stylishly incomprehensible moments but readers rarely notice them. So long as there are words to keep it turning, the mind rattles on, content to be centre stage.

Mariangela has underlined 'truth seeking' on her photocopy. She is biting her lip. I have high hopes for Mariangela who I think will make an excellent translator. Then it occurs to me that there's a parallel between these reflections from *Mrs Dalloway* and the Hitchens article. A contrast rather. The journalist writes off religion as a self-indulgence. Equally atheist, Woolf nevertheless sees the Church as an opportunity for surrendering self and divisive ideas in community. What the seedy man is contemplating is a surrender of his supposed truths – 'put this leather bag stuffed with pamphlets before an altar, a cross, the symbol of something which has soared beyond seeking and questing and knocking of words together and has become all spirit, disembodied'.

The man hesitates. He needs guru Coleman to tell him, 'Let go!' Or the cathedral's patron saint to remind him that even if he handed out a million pamphlets and hath not charity, yet he is nothing. Surprisingly, the translator has written 'pure spirit, *disenchanted*'.

I hope the students notice.

When I returned from my ten days' meditation, the first thing I did was to go to my office, turn on my computer and set about knocking a few words together.

Are you, by any chance, Tim Parks, the writer?

Well, I was and I wasn't. I have never felt so strange. Wordless for ten days, I didn't know who I was. Closing my eyes, I found I was floating with the current of some strong river, or I was the river. I was no one. This seemed stranger on my office chair than on a meditation mat. I was no one, but I was in Tim Parks's chair. A guy I knew.

I sat. I couldn't decide if I was immeasurably happy or

desperately sad. The computer hummed. Every time I tried to swim against the stream, to *do* something that is, I felt inadequate, not exactly paralysed but quite unable to move, unable to want to move. Never fight the water, kayak instructors always tell you. It went on a fair while, ten minutes, twenty, a half-hour. The nerves had been stripped from my body, and the sinews, and the tendons. I imagined them tied in a bundle floating downstream beside me. Opening my eyes at one point I saw that eighty-three emails had arrived during my absence. I closed them again. I was waiting. Finally, of their own accord, my fingers began to move. Over and over they typed:

> I am so tired

Every time I typed the 'I', I did so in lower case, 'i', but Word at once converted it into a proud and proper 'I'.

In the days that followed, as the props that shore up personality were pushed back into place – wife, children, lessons, canoe – I discovered, coming day by day to my desk, that my feelings about words had shifted a little. I was a little less negative. Setting down a few pages – the opening pages of this book, as it turned out – everything seemed reassuringly slow and careful and very clear in my mind, freed from the usual turmoil and compulsion.

I wonder.

I wonder if it's not just a question of pruning down the tangled wisteria of one's ego year by year, retreat after retreat, not I, not I, not I.

Or of entering the text like a Mormon entering St Paul's, ready to surrender his precious pamphlets.

Letting go the lifelong plots and plans.

Or of sharing words with the reader like a glass of clear water on a hot summer afternoon. My hands on the keyboard, yours on the page.

Taking time to breathe, too. Remembering we are both of us here in the flesh. Now.

In any event, forgetting immortal icons, moribund musings, swaggering self-assertion.

Forgetting the sounding brass of Grub Street, the tinkling cymbals of the Booker, the Nobel.

Envieth not. Vaunteth not.

Endureth all things.

In the classroom the printer beeps to life. The strimmer has stopped. How much time has passed? It was Francesco broke the trance. He has finished. He is printing. Pale in the glow of their computers and sticky with heat, the others redouble their efforts. The keyboards seem very loud.

'Shall I tell them they have five more minutes?' Andrea asks. He is at my side. Since when? Andrea is such a serious, peremptory young man. With such a literary beard! He wants to take control.

'It's OK, Andrea. They have their watches.'

Standing at the front, feet slightly apart, arms folded, I keep guard. In a few minutes my two years with this class will be over. Two difficult but also wonderful years. The sun is pressing hard against the window and in the room the air is stale and damp. I'm not suffering. My body is used to it, the way you get used to hot water, or to sitting cross-legged. The seconds tick by, Andrea frets. Why don't I blow the whistle? Time is up. It's the intensity of their presence that holds me: the urgent eyes, pursed lips, flushed cheeks, the quick capable hands, raven hair coiled round a pencil, grimaces, grins, flurries of labour, and the violent stillness of a chin thrust down on bent fingers.

'Nearly quarter past,' Andrea mutters.

I've grown attached. I don't want it to end.

Someone else sets the printer whining. Francesco has gone over to the machine to sign his papers.

Deep breath.

Monica has her face in her hands.

'OK, everybody, that's the end. Time's up now.'

My voice is very loud. Eyes lift, alarmed, relieved.

'Just a couple of minutes, Prof!'

'Finish the sentence you're on and that's it. The end. No more writing! OK? Pain of death!'

Afterword

But that is too dramatic an injunction to close on. After all, half of this book has been written since that summer exam, and I'm neither dead nor in pain.

Let me sign off then with a few words about this morning, Monday, 26 October 2009. After a moderately interrupted night, I rose before six and went down in the dark to the bedroom that used to be my son's. Since the days are growing chill, I pulled on a sweater and tracksuit trousers, then set the alarm on my mobile for seven. One can't always have a Tibetan gong.

There's not much space here. I keep a blanket folded on the floor, a cushion to sit on, a couple of beanbags to slip under the knees. One day the left leg tucks in first, the next day the right; for symmetry. Careful not to hurry, I wrap a shawl round my shoulders, switch off the lamp and sit.

The room is pitch dark now. The shutters are closed. The Iron Maiden poster beside the door is invisible. In the silence, I say no formulas; I do not take refuge in the dhamma or wish for all beings to experience sympathetic joy. I am not prayerful. But taking a deep breath, I am aware of the sleeping house around me: of Lucy in the next room, Rita under the quilt upstairs, the dog curled in his basket, of all of us up here on the hill, looking south across the Italian plain.

Morning thoughts rise like bubbles. I concentrate on the breath in my nostrils, on my lips. Only steady awareness of the body will still that mental fizz. I'm not concerned when I don't succeed. The aim is quiet, but I will not crave it. Now I catch myself composing an email: Dear Prof. Proietti, although … Now I'm replaying Torres' goal last night against Man U. Where was Rio? Stop. I take the mind back to the breath. Back and back, again and again, until eventually the two fuse in a whispery stream on the upper lip. A warm tide swells in the chest. My wrists are pulsing.

There is nothing mystical about this. If I think back to when I started, I see there was a desire for extraordinary experience, for waves of cosmic healing. One lived torn between a determination to be reasonable, pragmatic, scientific, true to one's culture, and a desire to transcend reason, to escape from pragmatism and science. The two attitudes called to each other, like old sparring partners. One was always on edge. So, at the Vipassana retreats, the first-time meditators are hungry for drama, for an encounter with their demons, submission to a guru. We all want to add another episode to the narrative of our selves, the yarn we are constantly spinning of our dealings with the world. This is why so many go to India, I suppose, to do no more than sit on a cushion, eyes closed. They hope the exotic location, the guru's robes and foreign voice will add intensity to the tale.

But as words and thought are eased out of the mind, so the self weakens. There is no narrative to feed it. When the words are gone, whether you are in Verona or Varanasi hardly matters. Whether it is morning or evening, whether you are young or old, man or woman, poor or rich isn't, in the silence, in the darkness, in the stillness, so important. Like ghosts, angels, gods, 'self', it turns out, is an idea we invented, a story we tell ourselves. It needs language to survive. The words create meaning, the meaning purpose, the purpose narrative. But here, for a little while, there is no story, no rhetoric, no deceit. Here is silence and acceptance; the pleasure of a space that need not be imbued with meaning. Intensely aware, of the flesh, the breath, the blood, consciousness allows the 'I' to slip away.

So if I can recount the first minutes, I can't tell the rest. There are deepenings. There is a liquefaction of some kind, the thighs flowing into the calves, the head into the breast. And there are resistances: stones, obstructions, pains. The mind goes back and back to them. An ankle. A shoulder. Maybe they will shift, and maybe not. I am absolutely awake. I hear Rita pad downstairs with the dog behind her. I hear a scooter straining up the hill. And I am not there. I am in the stream.

Then the alarm sounds and I must move. I'm up, dressed and getting Lucy into the car in just a few minutes. By ten past seven we are speeding down the hill, trying to beat the traffic light at San Felice. Lucy is anxious about some homework, a possible low grade. I repeat the parents' mantra: you do your best, then what happens happens.

We stop at a pasticceria for cappuccino and croissant. On the table newspaper headlines tell me that a bomb in Baghdad has killed 147, the Governor of Lazio has resigned after being filmed naked together with male prostitute and cocaine, AC Milan scored in the ninetieth minute to beat Chievo 2–1. I pay in a hurry and drive Lucy another mile to her bus stop. She disappears in the crowd.

Parking outside my office, I'm aware of those small everyday actions that stand between me and my work. The blue key for the gate. The yellow key for the front door. The stairs, the big key for the flat. Switch electricity on, switch computer on, raise the shutters. I have always resented these tedious actions, these dumb routines that are merely in my way. I try to take them slowly, with equanimity. This is life too, I tell myself. Now and now. But I can't, I'm so eager to get going, to write down this tale, to have it finished, to move on.

Acknowledgements

Extracts from Martha Dow Fehsenfeld, Lois More Overbeck, George Craig and Dan Gunn (eds), *The Letters of Samuel Beckett* © The Estate of Samuel Beckett 2009, published by Cambridge University Press

Extracts from Samuel Beckett's *Watt*, *Endgame* and *Malone Dies* by permission of the Estate of Samuel Beckett and Faber and Faber Ltd.

Lines from 'The Dry Savages' found in T.S. Eliot, *Four Quartets* by permission of the Estate of T.S. Eliot and Faber and Faber Ltd.

Extract from Virginia Woolf by permission from The Society of Authors as the Literary Representative of the Estate of Virginia Woolf

Permission to use part of an article by Christopher Hitchens by permission of Christopher Hitchens

The author is grateful for permission to reproduce the following images:

p13: TURP. National Institute of Diabetes and Digestive and Kidney Diseases, National Institutes of Health
p23: *The Waterseller of Seville*. Diego Rodriguez de Silva y Velázquez, Galleria degli Uffizi, Florence, Italy/The Bridgeman Art Library

p37: Painting of church facade and clergyman. John Parks, www.johnparks.com

p40: Diagram of body. Shuttershock

p42: Canoeist. Isaac Levinson, www.isaackayak.com

p47: Artwork for urine test graph. Lucia Parks

p51: Detail from *The Waterseller of Seville*. Diego Velázquez, Galleria degli Uffizi/Bridgeman

p80: Yamuna. Lian Chang

p83: Gandhi. Kanu Gandhi/GandhiServe

p90: Cystoscope. MedTec Applications, Inc., www.medtecapp.com

p100: Aneros anal massager. Aneros, www.highisland.com

p119: Bench in park. John Parks, www.johnparks.com

p122: *Il bell'Antonio* book cover. Mondadori, and Reporters Associati-Roma

p127: Tap in sky. www.funny-potato.com

p145: *A Headache in the Pelvis* book cover. David Wise, Ph.D. and Rodney U. Anderson, M.D., National Center for Pelvic Research, P.O. Box 54, Occidental, CA 95465, USA

p155: Lizard. Shuttershock

p157: Bonfires. Harriet Purkey

p164: Wave. Shuttershock

p168: Pouring tea into cup. Shuttershock

p177: Trigger point complex. Lucia Parks

p177: Anal massage. David Wise, Ph.D. and Rodney U. Anderson, M.D.

p183: Eisack. Andy Turton, www.andyturton.com

p194: The author kayaking. Andy Turton

p198: Scafell. Richard Adam, www.richardadam.pwp.blue-yonder.co.uk

p212: Shiatsu points on feet. Bastari Alessandro & Sinerbiotica, www.sinerbiotica.eu

p215: Shiatsu charts. Shiatsu Society (UK), www.shiatsusociety.org

p225: Wisteria. Cathy Smith
p226: Maroggia building. Edoardo Parisi, www.imcitalia.it
p229: Cushions. Lanfranco Brisighelli
p240: Valley. Massimo Dei Cas, www.paesidivaltellina.it and www.webalice.it/massimodeicas
p250: Vedic fire altar. Lucia Parks
p254: Crossed legs. Zen Center of Los Angeles, www.zcla.org
p258: Monastery. Il Convento di Sandetole, www.sandetole.it
p271: Garden. Il Convento di Sandetole
p281: Detail from *The Waterseller of Seville*. Diego Velázquez, Galleria degli Uffizi/Bridgeman
p283: Coals. Shuttershock
p292: *La mente tranquilla* book cover. IMC Italia, International, Meditation Center Italia, Via Borsieri, 14, Milano, www.imcitalia.it
p294: Monastery corridor. Il Convento di Sandetole
p301: Dark window. Susan Hayek
p307: Sculpture. Giles Penny, www.gilespenny.co.uk
p318: Pots and pans. Lucia Parks
p324: St Paul's. Shuttershock

www.vintage-books.co.uk